Notes from the Road

I've been a writer for 35 years, having finished my first novel in 1986, and I'm no stranger to the ups and downs that come with the business. Heck, even though my work won awards in the interim, I didn't truly break into publishing until 1995 when my first full-length work of nonfiction catapulted its way onto bestseller lists. That work was followed by a dozen other topsellers, nearly all of which were published by Macmillan and distributed to the world by Simon & Schuster, that is until the business turned and I found myself at a crossroads.

The year was 1998 and I turned away from full-time writing for a short while to work for a Seattle-based startup. Around the same time, I jumped ship from Macmillan and an opportunity to write for Microsoft arose. Microsoft was working on a new series of books called *Pocket Consultants*. They needed a writer

who could write fast, clearly, concisely, authoritatively and just as important meet crazy timelines not just once or a few times but always. Surprisingly, always hitting timelines isn't something many writers can do while delivering quality work.

I went over to Microsoft without any hesitation. They loved my writing so much that my style became the *Pocket Consultant* style and soon I had not just one contract with them but three, then four. I not only hit my timelines while writing clearly, concisely and authoritatively, I consistently walloped them.

Microsoft loved this. Soon the *Pocket Consultants* and I were synonymous. In the years that followed, I wrote dozens. Not only were the books read in print by millions (thank you, readers!), articles and extracts from the books were posted on Microsoft websites and read by millions more.

To all the readers out there who miss my *Pocket Consultants*, great things are still happening. In my *IT Pro Solutions* series. In my *Tech Artisans* series. In my *Administrator's Reference* series. Hang in there with me as I blaze new trails with *Stanek & Associates* and we'll get to visit new places together.

—William R. Stanek

Notes from the Road

I began my tech career as an intern at Stanek & Associates in 2007 and worked as a development and engineering lead for the company for a number of years. While most were out enjoying spring break and summer vacations, I was working as an assistant on the publishing side of the business, before moving over to the technical side of the business during my college years at University of Washington.

I'm thankful to my father for sharing his knowledge with me for the past fifteen years. I've learned so much and am now honing my advanced skills with SQL Server, Exchange Server, Windows Server, IIS, PowerShell and more. Although I made contributions to over a dozen other books I worked on with my father, this was the first book I had co-author credit for and I'm glad that I was able to produce this new edition for my father.

—William R. Stanek Jr.

PowerShell for Administration

Covers PowerShell versions 7, 6, 5, 4 and 3 for
Windows Server 2019 - 2012
Windows 10, 8.1, and 7
(Linux, macOS, ARM)

IT Pro Solutions

www.williamrstanek.com

William R. Stanek
Author & Series Editor

William R. Stanek, Jr.
Author

PowerShell for Administration

IT Pro Solutions

Published by Stanek & Associates

Stanek & Associates publishes in a variety of formats, including print, electronic and by print-on-demand. Some materials included with standard print editions may not be included in electronic or print-on-demand editions or vice versa.

Country of First Publication: United States of America.

Cover Design: Creative Designs Ltd.
Editorial Development: Andover Publishing Solutions
Technical Review: L & L Technical Content Services

You can provide feedback related to this book by emailing the author at williamstanek @ aol.com. Please use the name of the book as the subject line.

Version: 2.4.5.3b

> **Note** I may periodically update this text and the version number shown above will let you know which version you are working with. If there's a specific feature you'd like me to write about in an update, message me on Facebook (http://facebook.com/williamstanekauthor). Please keep in mind readership of this book determines how much time I can dedicate to it.

Thank you for buying this book...

Find out about special offers, free book giveaways, amazing deals, and exclusive content. Plus get updates on favorite books and more when you join William Stanek on Facebook at facebook.com/William.Stanek.Author. William's on twitter at twitter.com/williamstanek.

www.williamrstanek.com

Connect with Will by visiting him on LinkedIn @ linkedin.com/in/will-stanek/.

Table of Contents

How to Use This Guide

This book is designed to provide the tools and guidance you need to get the most out of PowerShell running on Windows and Windows Server. Generally, techniques learned in this book also can be applied to PowerShell running on Linux, macOS and ARM. The first chapter, *PowerShell Running Start,* takes you through the essentials for working with the technology. Following this are chapters that will take an in-depth look at specific tasks and aspects of PowerShell.

Not only has William Stanek been developing expert solutions and writing professionally about Windows and Windows Server for many years, he's also written a number of bestselling books on PowerShell and scripting. In this book, William shares his extensive knowledge, delivering ready answers for day-to-day usage while zeroing in on core commands and techniques.

As with all books in the IT Pro Solutions series, this book is written especially for IT professionals working with, supporting, and managing specific versions of Microsoft products. Here, the products written about include PowerShell versions 7, 6, 5, 4 and 3. Odds are, if you are using Windows or Windows Server, these are the versions of PowerShell available. That said, Microsoft can make higher versions of PowerShell available for download and installation. Don't worry, I'll let you know how you can determine the version available and how you can install new versions.

You can run PowerShell 7 or later on Linux, macOS, and ARM. Although running PowerShell on these operating systems is similar to running PowerShell on Windows and Windows Server, some modules and features discussed in this book are specific to Windows and Windows Server. Always check for module and feature availability.

All versions of PowerShell are backwards compatible with each other; you can hone your skills with any base version and use these skills with any higher version.

Print Readers

Print editions of this book include an index and some other elements not available in the digital edition. Updates to this book are available online. Visit http://www.williamrstanek.com/powershell/ to get any updates. This content is available to all readers.

Digital Book Readers

Digital editions of this book are available at all major retailers, at libraries upon request and with many subscription services. If you have a digital edition of this book that you downloaded elsewhere, such as a file sharing site, you should know that the author doesn't receive any royalties or income from such downloads.

Support Information

Every effort has been made to ensure the accuracy of the contents of this book. As corrections are received or changes are made, they will be added to the online page for the book available at:

http://www.williamrstanek.com/powershell/

If you have comments, questions, or ideas regarding the book, or questions that are not answered by visiting the site above, send them via e-mail to:

williamstanek@aol.com

It's important to keep in mind that Microsoft software product support is not offered. If you have questions about Microsoft software or need product support, please contact Microsoft.

Microsoft also offers software product support through the Microsoft Knowledge Base at:

http://support.microsoft.com/

Conventions & Features

This book uses a variety of elements to help keep the text clear and easy to follow. You'll find code terms and listings in `monospace`, except when you are told to actually enter or type a command. In that case, the command appears in **bold**. When new terms are introduced and defined, they are put it in *italics*.

The first letters of the names of menus, dialog boxes, user interface elements, and commands are capitalized. Example: the Add Roles And Features Wizard. This book also has notes, tips and other sidebar elements that provide additional details on points that need emphasis.

Keep in mind that throughout this book, where click, right-click or double-click is used, you also can use touch equivalents: tap, press and hold, or double tap. Also, when using a device without a physical keyboard, you are able to enter text by using the onscreen keyboard. If a device has no physical keyboard, simply touch an input area on the screen to display the onscreen keyboard.

Share & Stay in Touch

The marketplace for technology books has changed substantially over the past few years. In addition to becoming increasingly specialized and segmented, the market has been shrinking rapidly, making it extremely difficult for books to find success. To ensure the books you need for your career remain available, raise your voice and support this work.

Without support from you, the reader, future books will not be possible. Your voice matters. If you found the book to be useful, informative or otherwise helpful, please take the time to let others know by sharing about the book online.

To stay in touch, use Facebook or Twitter. Your messages and comments about the book, especially suggestions for improvements and additions, are always welcome. If there is a topic you think should be covered in the book, write to the email address provided.

IMPORTANT   The focus of this book is on putting PowerShell to work in the enterprise. If you need help learning the core features of PowerShell, you should refer to the companion book: *PowerShell: IT Pro Solutions*.

MORE INFO   The success and sales of this book determine how much time the authors can dedicate to updates, revisions and extras. Your suggestions are always welcome. If you have suggestions for additions or changes to this book, please write. Be sure to reference the full title and edition of the book in your initial correspondence.

Part I: Scripting Essentials

Chapter 1. PowerShell Running Start

Chances are good that if you are reading this book, you already know PowerShell essentials, such as those covered in the recommended companion book: *PowerShell: IT Pro Solutions*. You may even know the difference between entering commands at the prompt and entering commands in scripts. If so, this chapter will be a refresher for you. Otherwise, this chapter will give you a running start for administration with PowerShell.

Navigating PowerShell Versions

Microsoft has been developing and finetuning PowerShell ever since its initial release to the public. This is good news for IT professionals as it means new features and innovations are constantly being developed and introduced. But it's also bad news for IT professionals as it makes PowerShell, like the Windows operating systems, a moving target that you must try to keep current with.

Whether you are working with Windows or Windows Server, the PowerShell version available depends on the operating system version installed and whether updates have been applied. As Microsoft designed PowerShell versions to be backward compatible, the functional core of PowerShell is the same regardless of which version you are working with. Because of this, you typically can use skills and tools developed for an earlier PowerShell version with a current version, such as 7. However, when you are working across operating systems or versions, you should always test commands, options, and scripts before using them in live production environments.

> **NOTE** Prior to version 5, Microsoft had not released any dot releases (minor version updates) of PowerShell. This changed when version 5.1 was officially released with the first anniversary update of Windows 10 and Windows Server 2016. Because there are now dot release versions of PowerShell, I try to use general references to versions whenever possible, such as saying version 6 instead of version 6.0. This ensures any generally applicable references to version are accurate. As necessary, however, I will refer to specific dot release versions, such as referring to version 5.1 as opposed to version 5.0.

All versions of PowerShell prior to 7 have the same prerequisites. To use PowerShell, you need to:

- **Ensure a corresponding .NET framework is installed.** Currently, PowerShell 4-6 require Microsoft .NET Framework 4.5 or above.
- **Ensure a corresponding management framework is installed.** PowerShell 4 requires Windows Management Framework 4, PowerShell 5 requires Windows Management Framework 5, and so on.

The availability of these features depends on which version of Windows or Windows Server you are working with. With current releases, the default version of PowerShell and the necessary frameworks are made available as part of a standard installation. With older releases, you may need to download and install the necessary frameworks and then make PowerShell itself available by adding it as a feature.

PowerShell 7 uses .NET Core 3.1 as the runtime. Not only does PowerShell 7 run on Windows and Windows Server, it also runs on Linux, macOS and ARM. Although running PowerShell on these operating systems is similar to running PowerShell on Windows and Windows Server, some modules and features discussed in this book are specific to Windows and Windows Server. Always check for module and feature availability.

> **NOTE**   For years we've referred to Windows PowerShell as PowerShell and was scolded by Microsoft for doing so. How funny that they've now transitioned to calling this command environment just plain PowerShell. Did we finally wear them down we wonder? ;)

To use a version of PowerShell other than the one that ships with the operating system, you need to ensure the PowerShell version is supported on the operating system you are using and that this operating system has been appropriately updated. Afterward, you need to download and install, the required frameworks. The newer version of PowerShell will then be available when you restart the computer.

You can verify the PowerShell version as shown in the following example and sample output:

```
$PSVersionTable.PSVersion

Major  Minor  Build  Revision
-----  -----  -----  --------
5      1      19041  610
```

Here, the computer is running PowerShell 5.1.

Verifying and Recording Your Actions

When you are performing administration with PowerShell, you may want to, or be required to, verify commands prior to execution. You may also want to, or be required to, record your actions. PowerShell includes several features to help you do this, and you should take advantage of them whenever you are working with live production environments.

For command verification, you can use the –WhatIf parameter to show what would happen if a command runs. As any command that makes changes to the operating environment accepts this parameter, you can be sure –WhatIf is available whenever you need it. In the following example, you use –WhatIf to confirm that the command will stop the Task Scheduler service (and not some other service):

```
set-service -inputobject (get-service -name "schedule")
-status stopped -whatif
```

> **REAL WORLD**   Generally speaking, you should type a cmdlet and all its related parameters as a single line of text and then press Enter to execute. If you split the command text over multiple lines, you must end each line with the backward apostrophe key (`) to show that the line continues. In this book, I split lines out of necessity and only use the line continuation character when I am talking about it specifically. This is to avoid confusion, as I don't want you to get into the habit of unnecessarily breaking lines with the backward apostrophe key (`).

For recording your actions at the prompt, PowerShell includes a transcript feature. Commands you use with transcripts include:

- **Start-Transcript**   Initializes a transcript file and then creates a record of all subsequent actions in the PowerShell session

```
Start-Transcript [[-path] FilePath] [-force] [-noClobber]
[-append]
```

- **Stop-Transcript**   Stops recording actions in the session and finalizes the transcript

```
Stop-Transcript
```

You tell PowerShell to start recording your activities using the Start-Transcript cmdlet. This cmdlet creates a text transcript that includes all commands that you type at the prompt and all the output from these commands that appears on the console. The basic syntax for Start-Transcript is

```
Start-Transcript [[-path] FilePath]
```

where FilePath specifies an alternate save location for the transcript file, such as:

```
start-transcript -path c:\data\logs.txt
```

Although you cannot use wildcards when you set the path, you can use variables. If the directories in the path do not exist, PowerShell creates them.

> **NOTE**   If you do not specify a path, Start-Transcript uses the path in the value of the $Transcript global variable. If you have not created this variable, Start-Transcript stores the transcript in the $Home\Documents directory as a PowerShell_transcript.TimeStamp.txt file, where TimeStamp is a date-time stamp.

Use the –Force parameter to override restrictions that prevent the command from succeeding. For example, –Force will override the read-only attribute on an existing file. However, –Force will not modify security or change file permissions.

By default, if a transcript file exists in the specified path, Start-Transcript overwrites the file without warning. Use the –noClobber parameter to stop PowerShell from overwriting an existing file. Alternatively, use the –Append parameter to add the new transcript to the end of an existing file. Here are examples:

```
start-transcript -path c:\data\logs.txt -noclobber
start-transcript -path c:\data\logs.txt -append
```

When you start a transcript, PowerShell initializes the transcript file by inserting a header similar to the following:

```
* * * * * * * * * * * * * * * * * * * * *
PowerShell Transcript Start
Start time: 20211179105920
Username: IMAGINEDLANDS\williams
RunAs User: IMAGINEDLANDS\williams
Machine: CORPSERVER64 (Microsoft Windows NT 10.0.19041.0)
Host Application:
C:\Windows\System32\WindowsPowerShell\v1.0\powershell.exe
Process ID: 6872
PSVersion: 5.1.19041.610
PSEdition: Desktop
PSCompatibleVersions: 1.0, 2.0, 3.0, 4.0, 5.0, 5.1.19041.610
BuildVersion: 10.0.19041.610
CLRVersion: 4.0.30319.42000
WSManStackVersion: 3.0
PSRemotingProtocolVersion: 2.3
SerializationVersion: 1.1.0.1
* * * * * * * * * * * * * * * * * * * * *
```

This header specifies the time the transcript was started, the user who started the transcript, the computer for which the transcript was created, and the full path to the transcript file. Note that the user name is provided in DOMAIN\UserName or MachineName\UserName format and that the machine information includes the Windows version and build. This information is helpful when you are troubleshooting as it enables you to know if the script is running in the wrong user context or against a computer running an incompatible version of Windows.

To stop recording a transcript, you can either exit the console or type Stop-Transcript. The Stop-Transcript cmdlet requires no additional parameters.

When you stop a transcript, PowerShell inserts a footer into the transcript file similar to the following:

```
* * * * * * * * * * * * * * * * * * * *
PowerShell Transcript End
End time: 20211129110214
* * * * * * * * * * * * * * * * * * * *
```

This footer specifies the time the transcript was stopped. The difference between the start time and the stop time is the elapsed run time for a script or the total troubleshooting/work time when you are working at the prompt.

Scripting Essentials

You'll more often work with PowerShell directly at the PowerShell prompt. You can create some extensive one-liners that'll let you do just about anything, and if one line won't suffice, you can type multiple lines of commands. Additionally, if you want to copy examples from a document, the PowerShell console allows you to copy and paste a series of commands in the same way as you copy and paste a single command. The only difference is that with a series of commands, PowerShell executes each command separately.

When you want to do more with PowerShell than the prompt allows, you can use scripts. PowerShell scripts are text files containing a series of commands you want to execute. These are the same commands you normally type at the PowerShell prompt. However, rather than type the commands each time you want to use them, you create a script to store the commands for easy execution.

Because scripts contain standard text characters, you can create and edit scripts using any standard text editor, such as Notepad or Wordpad. You also can create scripts using the PowerShell Integrated Scripting Environment (ISE). When you enter commands in a script, be sure to place each command or group of commands that should be executed together on a new line or to separate commands with a semicolon. Both techniques ensure proper execution of the commands. When you have finished creating a PowerShell script, save the script file using the .ps1 extension. Keep in mind that in most cases, you'll only be able to save scripts to restricted areas of the file system when you start the PowerShell ISE or your text editor as an administrator.

When you save a script, you can execute it as if it were a cmdlet or external utility: simply type the path to the script, type the name of the script, and press Enter. When you do this, PowerShell reads the script file and executes its commands one by one. It stops executing the script when it reaches the end of the file. Any output from the script is written to the PowerShell console, unless you explicitly specify otherwise.

Consider the following example:

```
c:\scripts\test-system.ps1
```

Here, you run the Test-System.ps1 script which is stored in the c:\scripts directory. If a script is in the current working directory, you must reference the current working directory, type the name and the script and press Enter. You reference the current working directory by entering **.** as shown in this example:

```
.\test-system.ps1
```

> **MORE INFO**   Technically, you don't need to specify the .ps1 extension and could instead simply enter the name of the script. However, if there are other programs or files with this name, PowerShell might executive those programs or files instead. Thus, to be sure PowerShell only runs the test-system script, you would specify the script name along with the .ps1 extension.

As you set out to work with scripts, keep in mind that you shouldn't use command aliases in scripts because the practice can lead to unpredictable results. Aliases are associated with specific user profiles and can be overwritten and changed by other users. As you can't always be certain where scripts will run or who will run them, it is a best practice to avoid using aliases in scripts.

Before you can run scripts on a system, you must set execution policy to allow it. If execution policy requires remote scripts to be signed, you need to add a signature to the script before you can run it. Additionally, before PowerShell runs the script, you will likely see a security warning similar to the following:

```
Security Warning
Run only scripts that you trust. While scripts from the Internet can
be useful, this script can potentially harm your computer.

Do you want to run \\192.168.1.252\wrs\test.ps1?
[D] Do not run   [R] Run once   [S] Suspend   [?] Help (default is "D"):
```

To proceed and run the script, you need to type R and press Enter. For more information about execution policy and scripting signing, see Chapter 2, "Working with Cmdlets and Scripts," in *PowerShell: IT Pro Solutions*.

Chapter 2. Scripting with PowerShell

Now that you have a running start with PowerShell and we've covered scripting essentials, let's look at common elements you'll use in your scripts, including

- Comments
- Initializing statements
- Conditional statements

Using Comments in Scripts

Most scripts begin with comments that specify what a script is for and how it is used. PowerShell supports two types of comments:

- Single-line comments that begin with #. PowerShell interprets everything from the begin-comment mark to the end of the line as a comment. Here is an example:

```
$myVar = "$env:computername" #Get the computer name
```

> **NOTE** Because values in strings are interpreted differently and # is not interpreted as a special character in a string, you can use # in single-quoted and double-quoted strings, and # will not be handled as the beginning of a comment.

- Multiple-line comments that begin with the <# delimiter and end with the #> delimiter. If you have a begin-comment delimiter, you must have a matching end-comment delimiter. PowerShell interprets everything between the begin and end comment tags as a comment. Here is an example:

```
<# --------------------------

   ScriptName: EvaluateComp.ps1
   Description: This script checks the working environment
   of a computer to determine issues with drive space,
   network    connections, etc.

   ------------------------- #>
```

Every script you create should have comments that include the following details:

- When the script was created and last modified
- Who created the script
- What the script is used for
- How to contact the script creator
- Whether and where the script output is stored

Not only are the answers to the questions of who, what, how, where, and when important for ensuring that the scripts you create can be used by other administrators, they can also help you remember what a particular script does, especially if weeks or months have passed since you last worked with the script. An example of a script that uses comments to answer these questions follows:

```
<# -------------------------
   ScriptName: CheckIPConfig.ps1
   Creation Date: 12/18/2020
   Last Modified: 2/21/2021
   Author: William R. Stanek
   E-mail: williamstanek@aol.com
   ***********************
   Description: Checks IPv4 and IPv6 configuration.
   ***********************
   Files: Stores output in c:\data\checkip.txt.
------------------------- #>
```

Keep in mind that you can also use comments to:

- Insert explanatory text within scripts, such as documentation on how a function works.
- Prevent a command from executing. On the command line, add # before the command to comment it out.
- Hide part of a line from interpretation. Add # within a line to block interpretation of everything that follows the # character.

Using Initializing Statements

After you add a header to your script, you might want to initialize the console so that the working environment appears the same way every time. For example, you might want to use Clear-Host to clear the console window and reset the screen buffer, and use the Start-Transcript cmdlet to record all output to a transcript file. If you start a transcript, be sure to add a Stop-Transcript cmdlet at the end of your script to end the transcript session.

Initializing the Console Window

You also might want your script to initialize the PowerShell window by setting the window size, text color, and window title. Here is an example:

```
if ($host.name -eq "ConsoleHost") {
$size=New-Object System.Management.Automation.Host.Size(120,60);
$host.ui.rawui.WindowSize=$size }

$myHostWin = $host.ui.rawui
$myHostWin.ForegroundColor = "Blue"
$myHostWin.BackgroundColor = "Yellow"
$myHostWin.WindowTitle = "Working Script"
```

Here, you get an instance of the System.Management.Automation.Host object so that you can set the window size to 120 characters wide by 60 lines high if you are working with the PowerShell console. Then you use properties of the $host.ui.rawui object to specify that you want to use blue text on a yellow background and a window title of Working Script. For more information on these object instances, see Chapter 21, "Conquering Objects," in *PowerShell: IT Pro Solutions*.

NOTE When you dynamically reset the size of the PowerShell console, you must keep in mind the current display resolution and the console's configured dimensions. You shouldn't set the width and height of the console so that it is larger than the display size. Additionally, you'll get an error if you try to set the width of the console so that it is greater than the screen buffer size. Because resizing the window won't work with the PowerShell application, you may want to check the value of the $Host.Name property to ensure that you are working with the console and not the PowerShell ISE. $Host.Name is set to "PowerShell ISE Host" for the PowerShell application and "ConsoleHost" for the PowerShell console.

Adding Requires Statements

When you are initializing the script, you also want to ensure the following:

- The script will run on a computer with a compatible version of PowerShell.
- The host application is indeed PowerShell.
- Required PowerShell snap-ins, providers, and modules are available.

PowerShell includes a #Requires statement that you can use to validate the PowerShell version, the host application, and the availability of snap-ins. Using #Requires statements, you can do the following:

- Verify the PowerShell version, where N is the version number and n is the optional revision number. For example, to verify the PowerShell version is 5.0 or later, use 5 or 5.0.

```
#requires -Version N[.n]

#requires -version 5
#requires -version 5.0
```

- Verify the host application ID, where ShellID is the identifier for the host application. To verify the host application is the PowerShell console or PowerShell ISE, use a value of Microsoft.PowerShell.

```
#requires -ShellId ShellId

#requires -ShellId "Microsoft.PowerShell"
```

- Verify a specified snap-in—or, optionally, a specified version of the snap-in—is loaded in the current session, where PSSnapIn is the snap-in identifier and the optional N and .n values set the required version.

```
#requires -PsSnapIn PsSnapIn [-Version N[.n]]

#requires -PsSnapIn ADRMS.PS.Admin -Version 4

#requires -PsSnapIn ADRMS.PS.Admin -Version 5.1
```

Whenever you use #Requires statements, the script runs only if the computer meets the criteria set in the #Requires statements.

Passing Arguments to Scripts

As with most cmdlets and external utilities, you can pass arguments to scripts when you start them. You use arguments to set special parameters in a script or to pass along information needed by the script. Each argument should follow the script name and be separated by a space (and enclosed in quotation marks if necessary). In the following example, a script named Check-Computer in the current working directory is passed the arguments FileServer26 and Extended:

```
.\check-computer fileserver26 extended
```

Each value passed along to a script can be examined using the $args array. You reference the first argument using $args[0], the second using $args[1], and so on. The script name itself is represented by the $MyInvocation.MyCommand.Name property. The full file path to the script is represented by the $MyInvocation.MyCommand.Path property.

> **NOTE** Because PowerShell stores arguments in an array, there is no limit to the number of arguments you can pass to a script. Further, regardless of the number of arguments you use, the last argument is always represented by $args[$arg.length - 1], and the total number of arguments used is represented by $args.count. If no arguments are passed to a script, the argument count is zero.

Using Conditional Statements

Now that you know how to work with and initialize scripts, let's look at the selection statements used to control the flow of execution based upon conditions known only at run time. These statements include:

- If...Else, to execute a block of statements if a condition is matched (true or false) and to otherwise execute a second block of statements.
- If...ElseIf...Else, to execute a block of statements if a condition is matched (true or false). Otherwise, it's used to execute a second block of statements if a second condition is matched. Finally, it's used to execute a third block of statements if neither of the previous conditions is met.

- If Not, to execute a statement when a condition is false. Otherwise, the statement is bypassed.
- Switch, to perform a series of three or more conditional tests.

Executing Conditionally

If your background doesn't include programming, you probably will be surprised by the power and flexibility of conditional statements, of which there are several variations. The basic If statement is used for conditional branching. It can be used to route script execution through two different paths. Its standard syntax is

```
if (condition) {codeblock1} [else {codeblock2}]
```

Here, each code block can contain a single command or multiple commands. The condition is any expression that returns a Boolean value of True or False when evaluated. The Else clause is optional, meaning you can also use the following syntax:

```
if (condition1) {codeblock1}
```

The If statement works like this: If the condition is true, codeblock1 is executed. Otherwise, codeblock2, if defined by an Else clause, is executed. In no case will both the If and Else clauses be executed. Frequently, the expression used to control If statements involves a test for equality. In fact, the most basic type of string comparison is when you compare two strings using the equality operator (=), such as

```
if (stringA = stringB) {codeblock}
```

Here, you are performing a literal comparison of the strings; if they are exactly identical, the related code block is executed. This syntax works for literal strings but is not ideal for use in scripts. Parameters, property values, and arguments might contain spaces, or there might be no value at all for a variable. In this case, you might get an error if you perform literal comparisons. Instead, use the comparison operators to perform more advanced comparisons.

As discussed in Chapter 15, "Expressions and Operators," in *PowerShell: IT Pro Solutions,* −eq, −like, −match, −contains, −gt and −lt are all comparison operators, as are –le, –ge, –notlike, –notmatch, –notcontains and –replace. In the following example, the If clause is executed if the computer is running PowerShell version 5 or later and otherwise if the computer is running PowerShell version 4 or earlier, the else clause is executed:

```
if ($PSVersionTable.PSVersion.Major -ge 5)
{
    Write-Output "Version 5 or later"
}
else
{
    Write-Output "Version 4 or earlier"
}
```

Checking for Arguments

To learn about other techniques, consider the following example and sample output:

```
if ($args.count -eq 0) {throw "No arguments passed to script"}
else {write-host "You passed args to the script"}

No arguments passed to script
At C:\Users\Bubba\dat.ps1:1 char:25
+ if ($args.count) {throw "No arguments passed to script"}
    + CategoryInfo          : OperationStopped: (No arguments passed
to script:String) [], RuntimeException
    + FullyQualifiedErrorId : No arguments passed to script
```

Here, if you don't pass any arguments to the script, the script throws an error. Because the default error action for PowerShell is to halt execution, this is an effective way to stop processing a script when expected conditions are not met. The Else condition applies when you pass arguments to the script, and in this example, "You passed args to the script" is written to the output.

Alternatively, if a script requires an argument, such as a computer name, you could use the If...Else construct to catch the missing argument and prompt the user to enter it using the Read-Host cmdlet as shown in this example and sample output:

```
if ($args.count -eq 0) {
    $compName = read-host "Enter name of the computer to check"
} else {
    $compName = $args[0]
```

```
}
```

Here, if you don't type an argument, the Read-Host cmdlet prompts you and then stores the value you specify in the $compName variable. Otherwise, the $compName variable is set to the value of the first argument you pass to the script.

Checking Multiple Conditions

Using any of the logical operators, such as –and, –or, –is, or –isnot, you can check two conditions. In the following example, the If condition is met only when the conditions on either side of the logical AND are true:

```
if (($args.count -ge 1) -and ($args[0] -eq "Check")) {
   write-host "Performing system checks..."
 } else {
   write-host "Script will not perform system checks..."
}

.\check-sys.ps1 Check

Performing system checks...
```

PowerShell also allows you to check multiple conditions using If...ElseIf...Else constructs. Here, PowerShell:

1. Executes a block of statements if the first condition is met (and does not check any other conditions).
1. Should the first condition not be met, PowerShell checks the second condition and executes the second block of statements if the second condition is met.
2. If neither of the previous conditions is met, PowerShell executes a third block of statements.

The basic syntax is

```
if (condition1) {action1} elseif (condition2) {action2}
else {action3}
```

The following example uses the If...ElseIf...Else construct to perform actions depending on the value of the first argument passed to the script:

```
if (($args.count -ge 1) -and ($args[0] -eq "Check")) {
    write-host "Performing system checks..."

  } elseif (($args.count -ge 1) -and ($args[0] -eq "Test")) {
    write-host "Performing connectivity tests..."

} else {
    write-host "Script will not perform system checks or tests."
}

.\check-sys.ps1 Test

Performing connectivity tests...
```

The first block of statements is executed if the value passed to the script is Check. The second block of statements is executed if the value passed to the script is Test. The third block of statements is executed if neither value is passed to the script.

You can combine the multiple condition techniques as well, using both logical operators and the If... ElseIf... Else construct. Here is an example:

```
if (($PSVersionTable.PSVersion.Major -eq 5)  and
($PSVersionTable.PSVersion.Minor -eq 1))
{
    Write-Output "Version 5.1"
}
elseif ($PSVersionTable.PSVersion.Major -eq 6)
{
    Write-Output "Version 6 or later"

}
elseif ($PSVersionTable.PSVersion.Major -ge 7)
{
    Write-Output "Version 7 or later"

} else {

    Write-Output "Other version"

}
```

The first If statement tests for two conditions. If the computer is running PowerShell 5.1, the first block of statements is executed. The second block of statements is executed if the computer is running PowerShell 6. The third block of statements is executed if the computer is running PowerShell 6. The fina block of statements is executed if the computer isn't running PowerShell 5.1 or later.

Executing Only When False

When you want to execute a statement only if a condition is false, you can use If Not. The basic syntax is

```
if (!condition) {codeblock1} [else {codeblock2}]
```

or

```
if (-not (condition)) {codeblock1} [else {codeblock2}]
```

Here PowerShell evaluates the condition. If it is false, PowerShell executes the statements in codeblock1. Otherwise, codeblock1 doesn't execute, and PowerShell proceeds to codeblock2, if present. The Else clause is optional, meaning you can also use the following syntax:

```
if (!condition) {codeblock1}
```

Consider the following example:

```
if (!$args.count -ge 1) {
    read-host "Enter the name of the computer to check"
}
```

Here you execute the code block when the argument count is not greater than or equal to one (meaning the argument count is zero).

TIP A nested If is an If statement within an If statement. Nested Ifs are common in programming, and PowerShell scripting is no exception. When you nest If statements, you place the required If...Else or If...ElseIf...Else construct with its subconditions and subcodeblocks inside the code block of the original If...Else or If...ElseIf...Else construct.

Chapter 3. Digging Deeper into Scripting

PowerShell has many features to help you create powerful scripts for administration. In the previous chapter, you learned about comments, initializing statements and conditional statements. Although If...Else, If...ElseIf...Else and similar constructs are handy, you'll sometimes need more versatile options, such as being able to handle a number of conditions, not just a few. You also may need to control the flow of execution while, or until, certain conditions are met. To do this, you can use:

- Switch statements
- While loops
- Do While loops
- Do Until loops

Checking Conditions with Switch

Checking for multiple conditions using If...ElseIf...Else constructs is a lot of work for you and for PowerShell. An easier way to check three or more conditions is to use Switch constructs. Using Switch, you can check multiple conditions in a way that is clear and easy to understand. You can also add a default code block that is executed if none of the other conditions are met.

Getting Started with Switch

The basic syntax for a Switch construct is

```
switch (pipeline_expression) {

   value1 { codeblock1 }
   value2 { codeblock2 }
   value3 { codeblock3 }
 . . .
   valueN { codeblockN }
   default { default_codeblock}
}
```

The Switch construct is essentially an extended series of If statements that get the condition to test from a pipeline value you provide. If a value in the pipeline matches a specified value, the related code block is executed. To see how switch works, consider the following example:

```
switch ($PSVersionTable.PSVersion.Major) {
  7 { Write-Output "Version 7" }
  6 { Write-Output "Version 6" }
  5 { Write-Output "Version 5" }
  default { Write-Output "Earlier version" }
}
```

Here, the PowerShell version on the computer is evaluated. If the computer is running version 7, the version 7 block of statements is executed. If the computer is running version 6, the version 6 block of statements is executed, and so on.

Each Switch construct can have only one default. If there is more than one default clause, an error results. In the earlier example, if the computer isn't running PowerShell version 7, 6, or 5, the default block of statements is executed.

After a code block is executed, PowerShell exits the switch. If there are additional values in the pipeline to process, PowerShell evaluates those values, each in turn, in the same way.

Using Switch with Arrays

Switch constructs can be used with any valid data type. If the value to check is an array of numbers, strings, or objects, each element is evaluated in order against the switch conditions, starting with element 0. At least one element must be present that meets at least one condition, or PowerShell generates an error. In the following example and sample output, you define an array called $myValue, assign four values, and then process the values through a Switch construct:

```
$myValue = 4, 5, 6, 0

switch ($myValue) {
    0 { write-host "The value is zero."}
    1 { write-host "The value is one."}
    2 { write-host "The value is two."}
    3 { write-host "The value is three."}
    default { write-host "Value doesn't match."}
}
```

```
Value doesn't match.
Value doesn't match.
Value doesn't match.
The value is zero.
```

> **NOTE** With Switch, you also can use Continue and Break statements. A Continue statement says continue processing, while a Break statement says stop processing and exit the switch statement. Continue and break are best use when you want PowerShell to continue processing if one circumstance occurs and stop processing if another circumstance occurs.

Optimizing Switch

By default, when you use Switch, PowerShell does not consider the letter case and looks for exact matches only. To control what determines matches, you can add the following flags:

- **–regex** Matches string values against a regular expression. If the value you are testing is not a string, this option is ignored. Don't use this flag with the –wildcard and –exact flags.
- **–wildcard** Matches string values using wildcards. Indicates that the match clause, if a string, is treated as a wildcard string. If the value you are testing is not a string, this option is ignored. Don't use this flag with the –regex and –exact flags.
- **–exact** Performs an exact match of string values. If the value you are testing is not a string, this option is ignored. Don't use it with the –regex and –exact flags.
- **–casesensitive** Performs a case-sensitive match. If the value you are testing is not a string, this option is ignored.
- **–file** Takes input from a file rather than a statement. Each line of the file is read as a separate element and passed through the switch block, starting with the first line of the file. At least one element must be present that meets at least one condition, or PowerShell generates an error.

The following example switches based on the status of a service you specify by name in the first argument or when prompted:

```
if (!$args.count -ne 1) {
    $rh = read-host "Enter the name of the service to check"
    $myValue = get-service $rh
```

```
} else {
   $myValue = get-service $args[0]
}
$serName = $myValue.Name

switch -wildcard ($myValue.Status) {
   "S*" { write-host "The $serName service is stopped."}
   "R*" { write-host "The $serName service is running."}
   "P*" { write-host "The $serName service is paused."}
   default { write-host "Check the service."}
}
```

```
Enter the name of the service to check: w32time
The W32Time service is running.
```

Before moving on, let's put this technique to work in another example where we check the number of information, warning and error events in a specified event log. Here's the code:

```
clear-host
$i = 0; $w = 0; $e = 0;

if (!$args.count -ge 1) {
   $rh = read-host "Enter the name of the event log to check"
   $eventlog = get-eventlog $rh -newest 500
   $logName = $rh
} else {
   $eventlog = get-eventlong $args[0]
   $logName = $args[0]
}
$logName = $myValue.Name

Switch -Wildcard ($eventlog.entrytype) {
   "info*" {$i++}
   "warn*" {$w++}
   "err*" {$e++}
    default { }
}
write-host ""
write-host
"=========================================================="
write-host "Evaluating the 500 most recent events in the $rh log."
write-host
"=========================================================="
write-host "$i information events."
write-host "$w warning events."
```

```
write-host "$e error events."
write-host
"========================================================="
```

In this example, you set up the operating environment by clearing the console and setting working values for $i, $w and $e variables. You then determine whether any arguments were passed to the script. If no arguments were passed in, the script prompts for a log name. Otherwise, the script uses the first argument passed in as the name of the event log to check.

Next, the script uses a wildcard switch based on the event log entry type. If the entry type begins with info, the $i variable is incremented. If the entry type begins with warn, the $w variable is incremented. If the entry type begins with err, the $e variable is incremented.

Finally, you write output to the console that specifies which log was examined and the number of information, warning and error events found in the 500 most recent events:

```
Enter the name of the event log to check: application

=======================================================
Evaluating the 500 most recent events in the application log.
=======================================================
326 information events.
20 warning events.
136 error events.
=======================================================
```

Controlling the Flow of Execution

When you want to execute a command or a series of commands repeatedly, you use control loops. A loop is a method for controlling the logical flow and execution of commands. In PowerShell, you can perform controlled looping in several ways, including

- For looping
- ForEach looping
- While looping

- Do While looping
- Do Until looping

Using For Statements

The For statement allows you to control the flow of execution by specifying code you want to conditionally execute for a specific count. The structure of For loops is as follows:

```
for (countStartValue; condition; countNextValue) { CodeBlockToRepeat
}
```

where countStartValue is a statement that initializes the counter that controls the For loop, condition is a statement that specifies what value the counter must reach to stop looping, and countNextValue is a statement that sets the next value for the counter. Note that the elements in parentheses are separated with semicolons and that the next value for the counter is set after each iteration (and not before iteration begins).

You can set the next value for the counter using any assignment operator. In the following example and sample output, you initialize the counter to 1, loop as long as the counter is less than or equal to 10, and increment the counter by 1 after each iteration:

```
for ($c=1; $c -le 10; $c++){write-host $c}

1
2
3
4
5
6
7
8
9
10
```

In the following example and sample output, you initialize the counter to 10, loop as long as the counter is greater than or equal to 0, and decrement the counter by 1 after each iteration:

```
for ($c = 10; $c -ge 0; $c--) {Write-Host $c}

10
9
8
7
6
5
4
3
2
1
0
```

You can just as easily increment or decrement the counter by twos, threes, or more as shown in these examples:

```
for ($c=1; $c -le 100; $c += 2){write-host $c}
for ($c=1; $c -le 100; $c += 3){write-host $c}

for ($c = 20; $c -ge 0; $c -= 2) {Write-Host $c}
for ($c = 20; $c -ge 0; $c -= 3) {Write-Host $c}
```

Performing ForEach Iteration

Another type of controlled execution loop is a ForEach loop. With ForEach loops, you iterate through each element in a collection of items. Although you can work with other types of collections, you'll more typically work with collections of items in an array.

ForEach loops are similar to standard For loops. The key difference is that the number of elements in the collection determines the number of times you go through the loop. For example, if there are eight items in the collection, the loop is executed eight times.

The basic syntax of ForEach is

```
ForEach ( Item in Collection) { CodeBlockToRepeat }
```

where Item is a variable that PowerShell creates automatically when the ForEach loop runs, and Collection is the collection of items to iterate through. The collection can come directly from the pipeline. In the following example and sample output, you perform an action against each process in a collection of processes:

```
foreach ($p in get-process) {
    if ($p.handlecount -gt 500) {
        Write-Host $p.Name, $p.pm }
}

chrome 902361088
chrome 131362816
Creative Cloud 73117696
csrss 2154496
csrss 2617344
DeviceAgent 52842496
Dropbox 161198080
```

Here, every running process is examined. The If statement checks for processes with greater than 500 file handles and lists their name and private memory set. This technique can help you find processes that are using a lot of resources on the computer.

In the following example and sample output, you perform an action against each file in a collection of files:

```
if (!$args.count -ge 1) {
    $path = read-host "Enter the base directory path to check"
} else {
    $path = $args[0]
}

foreach ($file in Get-ChildItem -path $path -recurse) {
    if ($file.length -gt 100mb) {
        $size = [Math]::Round($file.length/1MB.ToString("F0"))
        Write-Host $file.lastaccesstime, $file, $size MB}
}

10/18/2021 9:54:52 PM Q2Report2020-working.xls 327 MB
10/18/2021 9:54:56 PM Q2Report2020-save.xls 381 MB
10/18/2021 9:55:00 PM Q2Report2020-final.xls 202 MB
```

Here, every file in a specified base directory and its subdirectories is examined. The If statement looks for files with a file size greater than 100 MB and lists their last access time, name, and size in MB. This technique can help you find large files that haven't been accessed in a long time.

> **TIP** With For and ForEach loops, you'll sometimes want to break out of the loop before iterating through all of the possible values. To break out of a loop ahead of schedule, you can use the Break statement. The best place for this statement is within the code blocks for If, If...Else, and If...ElseIf...Else constructs.

Using While Loops

Sometimes you'll want to execute a code segment while a condition is met. To do this, you use While looping. The structure of this loop is as follows:

```
while (condition) {CodeBlockToRepeat}
```

With the While statement, the loop is executed as long as the condition is met. To break out of the loop, you must change the condition at some point within the loop. Here is an example of a While loop that changes the status of the condition:

```
$x = 0
$continuetoggle = $true
while ($continuetoggle) {
    $x = $x + 1
    if ($x -lt 5) {write-host "x is less than 5."}
    elseif ($x -eq 5) {write-host "x equals 5."}
    else { write-host "exiting the loop."
      $continuetoggle = $false }
}

X is less than 5.
X is less than 5.
X is less than 5.
X is less than 5.
X equals 5.
Exiting the loop.
```

By placing the condition at the top of the loop, you ensure that the loop is executed only if the condition is met. In the previous example, this means the loop won't be executed at all if continueToggle is set to False beforehand.

Using Do While

While statements are handy but sometimes you want to execute the loop at least once before you check the condition. To do this, you can use the Do While construct, which places the condition test at the bottom of the loop, as in the following example:

```
do {CodeBlockToRepeat} while (condition)
```

In the following example, the code block is processed at least once before the condition is checked:

```
$x = 0
$continuetoggle = $true
do { $x = $x + 1
   if ($x -lt 5) {write-host "x is less than 5."}
   elseif ($x -eq 5) {write-host "x equals 5."}
   else { write-host "exiting the loop."
     $continuetoggle = $false }
}
while ($continuetoggle)

X is less than 5.
X is less than 5.
X is less than 5.
X is less than 5.
X equals 5.
Exiting the loop.
```

Using Do Until

The final type of control loop available in PowerShell is the Do Until loop. With Do Until, you execute a loop until a condition is met instead of while a condition is met. As with Do While, you place the condition test at the end of the loop. The basic syntax is

```
do {CodeBlockToRepeat} until (condition)
```

The following loop is executed one or more times until the condition is met:

```
do {
   $cont = read-host "Do you want to continue? [Y/N]"
```

```
} until ($cont -eq "N")
```

```
Do you want to continue? [Y/N]: y
Do you want to continue? [Y/N]: y
Do you want to continue? [Y/N]: n
```

Part II: Managing System Configuration

Chapter 4. Configuring Windows Clients

Things would be easier for IT professionals if Microsoft figured out how to make it possible to manage components for Windows clients and Windows servers using the same techniques. For now though, you need to use different techniques to manage the components of clients and servers and this is why we separate the related discussions into two chapters. In this chapter, we teach you how to manage the components of Window clients. In the next chapter, we discuss techniques for working with the components of Windows servers.

Navigating Client Component Options

The base configuration of Windows clients is managed with system images. An image is simply a saved configuration of the operating system. When you install a Windows client, the image stored on the installation media determines the basic configuration as well as what components are available.

As you also can mount images to manage their configuration, images have two basic configuration states: live or offline. A live image is one that is loaded and in-use, such as when you are working directly or remotely with a computer running Windows. An offline image is one that is mounted or otherwise accessible, such as a base image on a shared network drive.

Whether you are working with a live or offline image, you can work with optional components using the following commands:

- **Get-WindowsOptionalFeature**   Lists the state of optional features in a specified image.

```
Get-WindowsOptionalFeature -Online
Get-WindowsOptionalFeature -Path PathtoImage

AddtlParams=
[-FeatureName ComponentName] [-LogPath LogPathtoFile]
[-PackageName PackageName] [-PackagePath PathtoCabFile]
[-ScratchDirectory PathtoScratchDir] [-SystemDrive PathtoBootMgr]
[-WindowsDirectory PathtoWinDir]
```

- **Enable-WindowsOptionalFeature**   Enables the named feature. The –All parameter allows you to install all subordinate features of the named component.

```
Enable-WindowsOptionalFeature -FeatureName ComponentNames -Online

Enable-WindowsOptionalFeature -FeatureName ComponentNames
-Path PathtoImage

AddtlParams=
[-All] [-LimitAccess] [-PackageName PackageName]
[-LogPath LogPathtoFile] [-NoRestart] [-Source PathtoReqFiles]
[-ScratchDirectory PathtoScratchDir] [-SystemDrive PathtoBootMgr]
[-WindowsDirectory PathtoWinDir]
```

- **Disable-WindowsOptionalFeature**   Disables the named feature.

```
Disable-WindowsOptionalFeature -FeatureName ComponentNames -Online

Disable-WindowsOptionalFeature -FeatureName ComponentNames
-Path PathtoImage

AddtlParams=
[-Remove] [-NoRestart] [-PackageName PackageName]
[-LogPath LogPathtoFile] [-ScratchDirectory PathtoScratchDir]
[-SystemDrive PathtoBootMgr] [-WindowsDirectory PathtoWinDir]
```

When applicable, you can

- Use the –Online parameter to specify that you want to work with the live image.
- Use the –Path parameter to provide the path to an offline image.
- Use the –Source parameter to provide the path to required binary source files.
- Use the –LogPath parameter to log error details to a named log file as an alternative to the default logging used.
- Use the –NoRestart parameter to prevent automatic restart (if restarting is necessary to complete the operation).
- Use the –WhatIf parameter to display the operations that would be performed if the command were executed.

When you are enabling or disabling features, you can use the –FeatureName parameter to specify the components to manage. This parameter matches actual component names and not display names. With Get-WindowsOptionalFeature, you can use wildcard characters. With Enable-WindowsOptionalFeature and Disable-

WindowsOptionalFeature, you can use pipelining to get the required input names from another command, such as Get-WindowsFeature.

Not all components available on Windows clients are configured as optional features which can be enabled or disabled. Some components are configured by adding or removing packages. A package is set of related files and components that extend the operating system and are typically stored in a .cab or .msu file.

Most Windows clients have packages installed for language features, language packs, and more. When you add a package to a client, the related .cab or .msu file is added to the related image. When you remove a package to a client, the related .cab or .msu file is removed from the related image.

Although PowerShell provides a separate set of commands for working with packages, the good news is that they have a similar syntax to those for working with optional features and also can be added to or removed from either live or offline images.

The package commands include:

- **Get-WindowsPackage** Lists the state, release type and install time of packages in a specified image.

```
Get-WindowsPackage -Online
Get-WindowsPackage -Path PathtoImage

AddtlParams=
[-LogPath LogPathtoFile] [-PackageName PackageName]
[-PackagePath PathtoCabFile] [-ScratchDirectory PathtoScratchDir]
[-SystemDrive PathtoBootMgr] [-WindowsDirectory PathtoWinDir]
```

- **Add-WindowsPackage** Adds the named package.

```
Add-WindowsPackage -PackagePath PathtoPackage -Online

Add-WindowsPackage -PackagePath PathtoPackage -Path PathtoImage

AddtlParams=
[-LogPath LogPathtoFile] [-NoRestart] [-PreventPending]
[-ScratchDirectory PathtoScratchDir] [-SystemDrive PathtoBootMgr]
[-WindowsDirectory PathtoWinDir]
```

- **Remove-WindowsPackage**   Removes the named package.

```
Remove-WindowsPackage -PackagePath PathtoPackage -Online

Remove-WindowsPackage -PackagePath PathtoPackage -Path PathtoImage

AddtlParams=
[-LogPath LogPathtoFile] [-PackageName PackageName]
[-PackagePath PathtoCabFile] [-NoRestart]
[-ScratchDirectory PathtoScratchDir] [-SystemDrive PathtoBootMgr]
[-WindowsDirectory PathtoWinDir]
```

As you can see, the Windows Package cmdlets have options similar to those available for optional features. With Get-WindowsPackage, you can use wildcard characters. You can add packages to or remove packages from both live and offline images. You can use the –NoRestart parameter to prevent an automatic restart, if one is required. A restart will, however, still be necessary at some point to complete the installation.

Checking Installed Components on Clients

Before adding or removing components, you should check the client's current configuration. At an administrator PowerShell prompt, you can determine the installed components on a running client by typing **Get-WindowsOptionalFeature -Online**. Get-WindowsOptionalFeature then lists the configuration status of each available component by name and state as shown in the following example and sample output:

```
Get-WindowsOptionalFeature -online

FeatureName : Microsoft-Windows-Subsystem-Linux
State       : Disabled

FeatureName : LegacyComponents
State       : Disabled

...


FeatureName : DataCenterBridging
State       : Disabled
```

To work with components in an offline image, use the –Path parameter and specify the path to the mounted image instead, such as:

```
Get-WindowsOptionalFeature -path c:\mountdir
```

You can clean up the formatting of the output by adding **| format-table** to the command. Here is an example:

```
Get-WindowsOptionalFeature -online | ft
```

You then get a more neatly organized list, like the following:

```
FeatureName                                 State
-----------                                 -----
Microsoft-Windows-Subsystem-Linux           Disabled
LegacyComponents                            Disabled
...
DataCenterBridging                          Disabled
```

To check the status of a specific feature, use the –FeatureName parameter, as shown in this example:

```
Get-WindowsOptionalFeature -featurename smbdirect -online
```

If you don't know the exact name of the feature or want to check the status of a subset of related components, you can use wildcard characters. For example, if you want to check the status of only HyperV–related components, you could enter **Get-WindowsOptionalFeature -featurename *hyper-v***.

In addition to helping you determine at a glance what components are installed, Get-WindowsOptionalFeature can help you document a client's configuration. To do this, you can save the output in a file as standard text using the redirection symbol (>) as shown in this example:

```
Get-WindowsOptionalFeature -online > ServerConfig12-28-2017.txt
```

In this example, you save the output to a text file named EngPC73Config12-28-2017.txt.

Checking Installed Packages on Clients

In additional to optional components, Windows clients can be configured with support packages that add language packs, language features, foundation components and other important options. You can determine the installed packages on a running client by entering the following command:

```
Get-WindowsPackage -online | ft
```

To work with packages in an offline image, use the –Path parameter and specify the path to the mounted image instead, such as:

```
Get-WindowsPackage -path c:\mountdir | ft
```

Here, in both examples, I've added **| ft** to format the output for easier reading and reference. In the output, you'll find packages listed by name, state, release type and install time. The standard release types you will see include: foundation, language pack, update, security update and other.

```
PackageName               PackageState ReleaseType InstallTime
-----------               ------------ ----------- -----------
Package_for_KB3250513~    Installed     Update 11/23/2020 5:20:00 PM
Package_for_KB3276936~    Installed     Update 12/23/2020 6:43:00 PM
Package_for_KB3299209~    Installed     Update 11/18/2020 7:41:00 PM
Package_for_KB3299986~    Installed     Update 11/28/2020 4:37:00 PM
```

If you are looking for a specific type of package, such as a securityupdate, you could also pipe the output through where-object and check for this specific release type, as shown in the following example:

```
Get-WindowsPackage -online | where ReleaseType -like "securityupdate"
```

Adding Features to Clients

At an administrator PowerShell prompt, you can add optional features and packages on clients using Enable-WindowsOptionalFeature and Add-WindowsPackage. Whether you are working with features or packages, you must specify which image you want to work with. You can work with the live image on the running client by using the –Online parameter. The following example adds the Containers feature to the client:

```
Enable-WindowsOptionalFeature -FeatureName containers -online
```

You can work with an offline image by using the –Path parameter and then specifying the image path. Here, you add a named package to a mounted offline image:

```
Add-WindowsPackage -Path "c:\mountdir" -PackagePath
c:\packages\livestream.msu
```

With either command, the output tells you several things, including whether the change was successful and whether a restart is needed, such as:

```
Path           :
Online         : True
RestartNeeded  : False
```

Keep in mind that if you are trying to add components that are already installed, you won't see an error message. The command will simply proceed and the component will be re-installed.

Customizing the Client Changes

You can manage the way Enable-WindowsOptionalFeature and Add-WindowsPackage work in several ways. Because some components might require a restart, you may want to use –NoRestart to ensure the client doesn't automatically restart, which is handy when you are working remotely or if you have a series of changes to make and don't want the computer to possibly restart multiple times.

With Enable-WindowsOptionalFeature, you can add the –All parameter to ensure all required parent features and dependencies are also enabled. If you don't do this and there are parent features or dependencies, the installation will fail, as shown here:

```
enable-windowsoptionalfeature -featurename microsoft-hyper-v-services
-online

enable-windowsoptionalfeature : One or several parent features are
disabled so current feature can not be enabled.
```

When you are working with Enable-WindowsOptionalFeature, it's important to point out that the source for components can be removed from the operating system by administrators. Here, if you try to add a component that has its source removed, PowerShell uses Windows Update to get the source from the Windows Update website. You can prevent this in one of two ways. If you add the –LimitAccess parameter, PowerShell is prevented from using Windows Update if the required source isn't available and the install will fail. If you add the –Source parameter and specify a source path, PowerShell can use the specified source instead of Windows Update.

Because component names aren't always easy to type, you may want to specify names by getting the input from the output of another command. Consider the following example and sample output:

```
get-windowsoptionalfeature -featurename smb* -online | Enable-
WindowsOptionalFeature -online

Path           :
Online         : True
RestartNeeded  : False
```

Here, Enable-WindowsOptionalFeature gets the list of components to install from the Get-WindowsOptionalFeature cmdlet and then uses this information to install the SMBDirect feature.

Handling Add Errors

If an error occurs and Enable-WindowsOptionalFeature or Add-WindowsPackage is not able to perform the operation specified, you see an error. Generally, error text is shown in red and includes an error flag and error text as shown in the following example output:

```
Enable-WindowsOptionalFeature : One or several parent features are
disabled so current feature can not be enabled.

At line:1 char:59
+ ...  -featurename *direct -online | Enable-WindowsOptionalFeature
-online
+
~~~~~~~~~~~~~~~~~~~~~~~~~~~~~~~~~
```

```
    + CategoryInfo             : NotSpecified: (:) [Enable-
WindowsOptionalFeature], COMException
    + FullyQualifiedErrorId :
Microsoft.Dism.Commands.EnableWindowsOptionalFeatureCommand
```

This error indicates the component has required parent features or other dependencies. You can resolve this error by adding the –All parameter.

To test prior to enabling or adding components, you can use the –WhatIf parameter. Another common error you'll see occurs because elevated permissions are required to work with components and you are using a standard prompt instead:

```
Get-WindowsPackage : The requested operation requires elevation.
At line:1 char:1
+ Get-WindowsPackage -online
+ ~~~~~~~~~~~~~~~~~~~~~~~~~~~~
    + CategoryInfo             : NotSpecified: (:) [Get-WindowsPackage],
COMException
    + FullyQualifiedErrorId :
Microsoft.Dism.Commands.GetWindowsPackageCommand
```

To resolve this problem, open an administrator PowerShell prompt.

When you add components, you can write the detailed information to a log by including the –LogPath parameter. This logging information details every operation performed. In this example, you write the logging information to C:\logs\addwin-features.log:

```
enable-windowsoptionalfeature -featurename microsoft-hyper-v-services
-logpath c:\logs\addwin-features.log -all -online
```

Removing Features from Clients

At an administrator PowerShell prompt, you can remove optional features and packages using Disable-WindowsOptionalFeature and Remove-WindowsPackage. Whether you are working with features or packages, you must specify which image you want to work with. To work with the live image on the running client use the –Online parameter, as shown in the following example:

```
Disable-WindowsOptionalFeature -FeatureName smbdirect -online
```

To remove a feature from with an offline image use the –Path parameter and then specify the image path. Here, you remove a package from a mounted offline image:

```
Remove-WindowsPackage -Path "c:\mountdir" -PackagePath
c:\packages\livestream.msu
```

With either command, the output tells you several things, including whether the change was successful and whether a restart is needed, such as:

```
Path          :
Online        : True
RestartNeeded : False
```

If an error occurs and Disable-WindowsOptionalFeature or Remove-WindowsPackage is not able to perform the operation specified, you see an error. Generally, error text is shown in red and includes an error flag and error text, such as:

```
Disable-WindowsOptionalFeature : The requested operation requires
elevation.
At line:1 char:1
+ Disable-WindowsOptionalFeature -FeatureName iis-hostablewebcore
-online
+ ~~~~~~~~~~~~~~~~~~~~~~~~~~~~~~~~~~
    + CategoryInfo          : NotSpecified: (:) [Get-
WindowsOptionalFeature], COMException
    + FullyQualifiedErrorId :
Microsoft.Dism.Commands.DisableWindowsOptionalFeatureCommand
```

Here, you are using a standard prompt instead of an administrator prompt. Resolve the issue by opening an administrator prompt and running the command again.

If you enter an incorrect feature name, you'll see an error similar to the following:

```
disable-windowsoptionalfeature : Feature name iis-host* is unknown.
At line:1 char:1
+ disable-windowsoptionalfeature -featurename iis-host* -online
+ ~~~~~~~~~~~~~~~~~~~~~~~~~~~~~~~~~~~~~~~~~~~~~~~~~~~~~~~~~~~~~~~
    + CategoryInfo          : NotSpecified: (:) [Disable-
WindowsOptionalFeature], COMException
    + FullyQualifiedErrorId :
Microsoft.Dism.Commands.DisableWindowsOptionalFeatureCommand
```

This error occurred because the -FeatureName parameter doesn't accept wildcards. The correct way to use wildcards is to use them with Get-WindowsOptionalFeature and then pipe the output to Disable-WindowsOptionalFeature as shown in this example:

```
Get-WindowsOptionalFeature -FeatureName iis-host* -online | Disable-
WindowsOptionalFeature -online
```

Keep in mind that if you are trying to remove components that are already removed, you won't see an error message. The command will simply proceed. Additionally, sometimes when you remove a component, a restart is required to complete the process. Add the –NoRestart parameter if you don't want the client to restart automatically.

When you remove components, you can write the detailed information to a log by including the –LogPath parameter. This logging information details every operation performed so that you can review it.

Chapter 5. Configuring Windows Servers

When you are working with Windows Server, you have many more configuration options than when you are working with Windows desktops. After you've installed a Windows server, you can manage the server configuration by installing and configuring the following components:

- **Server roles**   These related sets of software components allow servers to perform specific functions for users and other computers on networks. A server can be dedicated to a single role, such as File Services, or a server can have multiple roles.
- **Role services**   These software components provide the functionality of server roles. While some server roles have a single function and installing the role installs this function, most server roles have multiple, related role services and you are able to choose which role services to install.
- **Features**   These software components provide additional functionality. Features are installed and removed separately from roles and role services. A computer can have multiple features installed or none, depending on its configuration.

You can manage roles, role services, and features by importing the ServerManager module into the PowerShell console.

Navigating Server Component Options

You use the ServerManager module to manage server configuration. Not only can you use this module's cmdlets to add or remove roles, role services, and features, but you can use this module's cmdlets to view the configuration details and status for these software components.

The ServerManager module as implemented in PowerShell allows concurrent instances to add or remove components at the same time. This allows you to run multiple Server Manager sessions simultaneously. For example, you can add roles in one Server Manager session while you are removing features in a different Server Manager session.

> **REAL WORLD**   Installed modules generally are imported automatically the first time you use a command in a module. Because of this, you generally don't need to explicitly import modules. However, for modules to be imported automatically, they must be stored in the location specified by $env:PSModulePath and delivered as folders. Modules that consist of a file, such as a .DLL or .PSM1 file, are not imported automatically. Additionally, commands that use providers may not cause the related module to be imported. If so, the provider won't be available.
>
> You can explicitly import an available module into the current session by using the Import-Module cmdlet. Remember, the $PSModuleAutoloadingPreference variable can be used to enable or disable module importing. If automatic importing of modules is disabled, you must always explicitly import modules.
>
> If the server on which you want to install Windows components doesn't have all the required binary source files, the server gets the files from Windows Update by default or from a location specified in Group Policy. You also can specify an alternate path for the source files. For network shares, enter the Universal Naming Convention (UNC) path to the share, such as \\CorpServer41\WS12\. For mounted Windows images, enter the WIM path prefixed with WIM: and include the index of the image to use, such as WIM:\\CorpServer41\WS12\install.wim:4. For a locally mounted image, enter the alternate path for the mounted WIM file, such as c:\mountdir\windows\winsxs.

You can manage roles, role services, and features using the following cmdlets:

- **Get-WindowsFeature**   Lists the server's current state with regard to roles, role services, and features.

```
Get-WindowsFeature [[-Name] ComponentNames]
[-LogPath LogFile.txt]
```

- **Install-WindowsFeature**   Installs the named role, role service, or feature. The –IncludeAllSubFeature parameter allows you to install all subordinate role services and features of the named component.

```
Install-WindowsFeature [-Name] ComponentNames
[-IncludeAllSubFeature] [-IncludeManagementTools]
[-LogPath LogFile.txt] [-Restart] [-Source Path]
```

```
AddtlParams=
 [-Credential Credential] [-ComputerName ComputerName1,
ComputerName2, ...]
```

- **Uninstall-WindowsFeature**   Removes the named role, role service, or feature.

```
Uninstall-WindowsFeature [-Name] ComponentNames [-LogPath
LogFile.txt] [-Restart] [-IncludeManagementTools]
```

```
AddtlParams=
 [-Credential Credential] [-ComputerName ComputerName1,
ComputerName2, ...]
```

When applicable, you can

- Use the –ComputerName parameter to specify the remote computer or computers on which to perform the modifications.
- Use the –Source parameter to provide the path to required binary source files.
- Use the –LogPath parameter to log error details to a named log file as an alternative to the default logging used.
- Use the –Restart parameter to restart the computer automatically (if restarting is necessary to complete the operation).
- Use the –WhatIf parameter to display the operations that would be performed if the command were executed.

By default, management tools are not installed or uninstalled. Because of this, use the –IncludeManagementTools with Install-WindowsFeature to install related management tools and with Uninstall-WindowsFeature to uninstall related management tools. The parameter values that you can use with these commands include:

- **ComponentNames**   Identifies the roles, role services, or features to work with by their name (not their display name). The –Name parameter matches actual component names and not display names. With Get-WindowsFeature, you can use wildcard characters. With Install-WindowsFeature and Uninstall-WindowsFeature, you can use pipelining to get the required input names from another command, such as Get-WindowsFeature.
- **LogFile.txt**   Sets the path and name of the text file to which log error details should be written.

Most installable roles, role services, and features have a corresponding component name that identifies the component so that you can manipulate it from the PowerShell prompt. This also is true for supplemental components you've made available by downloading and installing their installer packages from the Microsoft Web site.

Checking Installed Server Components

Before modifying a server's configuration, you check its current configuration and carefully plan how adding or removing a role, role service, or feature will affect a server's overall performance. Although you typically want to combine complementary roles, doing so increases the workload on the server, so you need to optimize the server hardware accordingly.

At a standard or administrator PowerShell prompt, you can determine the roles, role services, and features that are installed on a server by typing **Get-WindowsFeature**. Get-WindowsFeature then lists the configuration status of each available role, role service, and feature. Installed roles, role services, and features are highlighted and marked as being installed. In the output, roles and role services are listed before features as shown in the following example and sample output:

```
get-windowsfeature

Display Name                                    Name
------------                                    ----
[X] Active Directory Domain Services            AD-Domain-Services
[ ] Active Directory Federation Services        ADFS-Federation
[ ] Active Directory Lightweight Directory Services   ADLDS
[ ] Active Directory Rights Management Services       ADRMS
[ ] Active Directory Rights Management Server   ADRMS-Server
[ ] Identity Federation Support                 ADRMS-Identity

. . .

[ ] DHCP Server                                 DHCP
[X] DNS Server                                  DNS
[ ] Fax Server                                  Fax
[X] File and Storage Services                   FileAndStorage-Services
[X] File and iSCSI Services                     File-Services
```

You can use wildcard characters to review the status for a subset of components by name. For example, if you want to check the status of only Active Directory–related components, you can enter **Get-WindowsFeature -name ad*** or **Get-WindowsFeature ad***.

In addition to helping you determine at a glance what components are installed, Get-WindowsFeature can help you document a server's configuration. To do this, you can save the output in a file as standard text using the redirection symbol (>) as shown in this example:

```
Get-WindowsFeature > ServerConfig12-02-2021.txt
```

In this example, you save the output to a text file named ServerConfig03-21-2021.txt.

Installing Server Components

The ServerManager module is the PowerShell component you use to install roles, role services, and features. Roles, role services, and features can be dependent on other roles, role services, and features. When you install roles, role services, and features, Server Manager prompts you to install any additional roles, role services, or features that are required.

Adding Server Features

At an administrator PowerShell prompt, you can install roles, role services, and features by typing **Install-WindowsFeature** *ComponentName*, where *ComponentName* is the name of the component to install. As related management tools aren't installed by default, you should use the –IncludeManagementTools option when installing features. You can install subordinate components by including the –IncludeAllSubFeature parameter as shown in the following example and sample output:

```
Install-WindowsFeature adrms -IncludeAllSubFeature

Success Restart Needed Exit Code Feature Result
------- -------------- --------- --------------
True    No             Success   {ADRMS-Server, ADRMS-Identity}
```

Here, you install the Active Directory Rights Management Services role service as well as the subordinate Server and Support role services. As PowerShell works, you see a Start Installation progress bar. When the installation is complete, you see the result. The output for a successful installation should look similar to the example.

As you can see, the output specifies whether the installation was successful, whether a restart is needed, an exit code, and a list of the exact changes made. The exit code can be different from the Success status. For example, if the components you specify are already installed, the exit code is NoChangeNeeded, as shown in this example and sample output:

```
Install-WindowsFeature -name net-framework-features
-includemanagementtools

Success    Restart Needed    Exit Code      Feature Result
-------    --------------    ---------      --------------
True       No                NoChangeNeeded {}
```

Here, you see that Install-WindowsFeature was successful but didn't actually make any changes. The Feature Result shows no changes as well.

Install-WindowsFeature allows you to specify component names by getting the input from the output of another command. Consider the following example and sample output:

```
get-windowsfeature bits* | Install-WindowsFeature

Success Restart Needed Exit Code      Feature Result
------- -------------- ---------      --------------
True    No             Success        {Background Intelligent
Transfer Service (...
```

Here, Install-WindowsFeature gets the list of components to install from the Get-WindowsFeature cmdlet. You install the Background Intelligent Transfer Service (BITS) role service as well as the subordinate Compact Server and IIS Server Extension role services.

If a restart is required to complete an installation, you can have the Install-WindowsFeature cmdlet restart the computer by including the –Restart parameter.

Also note that a pending restart could prevent you from adding or removing other components. If so, you'll see a related error message as well as the standard output:

```
Install-WindowsFeature: Please restart the computer before trying to
install more roles/features.

Success    Restart Needed   Exit Code             Feature Result
-------    --------------   ---------             --------------
False      Yes              FailedRestartRequired { }
```

Handling Errors and Other Issues

Some components cannot be installed from the command line. If you try to install one of these components, you'll see a warning such as:

```
WARNING: Installation of 'XYZ' is not supported on the command line.
Skipping . . .

Success    Restart Needed   Exit Code            Feature Result
-------    --------------   ---------            --------------
True       No               NoChangeNeeded       { }
```

You can use the –WhatIf parameter to test the installation prior to performing the actual operation. If you are trying to install components that are already installed, you see a message in the output stating no changes were made, such as

```
get-windowsfeature ad-d* | Install-WindowsFeature –whatif

What if: Checking if running in 'WhatIf' Mode.
Success    Restart Needed   Exit Code            Feature Result
-------    --------------   ---------            --------------
True       No               NoChangeNeeded       {}
```

If an error occurs and Install-WindowsFeature is not able to perform the operation specified, you see an error. Generally, error text is shown in red and includes an error flag and error text as shown in the following example output:

```
The term 'Install-WindowsFeature' is not recognized as a cmdlet,
function, operable program, or script file. Verify the term and try
again.
At line:1 char:19
+ Install-WindowsFeature <<<<  fs-dfs-replication
```

```
    + CategoryInfo          : ObjectNotFound: (Install-
WindowsFeature:String)
[], CommandNotFoundException
    + FullyQualifiedErrorId : CommandNotFoundException
```

This error indicates that PowerShell doesn't recognize the Install-WindowsFeature cmdlet. You see this error if automatic importing is disabled and you forget to import the ServerManager module using the command import-module servermanager.

Another common error you'll see occurs when elevated permissions are required and you don't use an administrator PowerShell prompt:

```
Uninstall-WindowsFeature: Because of security restrictions imposed by
User Account Control you must run Uninstall-WindowsFeature in a
PowerShell session opened with elevated rights.
```

To resolve this problem, open an administrator PowerShell prompt.

When you install components, you can write the detailed information to a log by including the –LogPath parameter. This logging information details every operation performed by Install-WindowsFeature. In this example, you write the logging information to C:\logs\install.log:

```
Install-WindowsFeature BITS -IncludeAllSubFeature -LogPath
c:\logs\install.log
```

Finally, because PowerShell returns the output as an object, you can pass the output object along the pipeline as necessary. You also can apply alternative formatting to the output, such as list formatting, as shown in this example and sample output:

```
get-windowsfeature net-* | Install-WindowsFeature | format-list *

Success       : True
RestartNeeded : No
FeatureResult : { }
ExitCode      : NoChangeNeeded
```

Uninstalling Server Components

The ServerManager module is the PowerShell component you use to uninstall roles, role services, and features. Roles, role services, and features can be dependent on other roles, role services, and features. If you try to remove a required component of an installed role, role service, or feature, Server Manager warns that you cannot remove the component unless you also remove the other role, role service, or feature.

Removing Server Features

At an administrator PowerShell prompt, you can uninstall roles, role services, and features by typing **Uninstall-WindowsFeature** *ComponentName*, where *ComponentName* is the name of the component to uninstall. When you uninstall a top-level component, subordinate components are automatically uninstalled as well. Consider the following example and sample output:

```
Uninstall-WindowsFeature net-framework-features

Success Restart Needed Exit Code      Feature Result
------- -------------- ---------      --------------
True    No             Success        {.NET Framework 3.5 (includes
.NET 2.0 and...
```

Here, you uninstall the .NET Framework 3.5 Features as well as the subordinate .NET Framework 3.5. As PowerShell works, you see a Start Removal progress bar. When the removal is complete, you see the result. The output for a successful removal should look similar to the example. If you must restart the server to complete a removal you see a warning message as well as results. The warning states a restart is required to complete the removal. You can have the Uninstall-WindowsFeature cmdlet restart the computer by including the –Restart parameter.

As with installation, you can test the removal prior to performing the actual operation using the –WhatIf parameter. If you are trying to remove components that aren't installed, you see a note stating no changes were made, such as

```
Uninstall-WindowsFeature net-framework-features -whatif

What if: Checking if running in 'WhatIf' Mode.
```

```
Success      Restart Needed      Exit Code          Feature Result
-------      --------------      ---------          --------------
True         No                  NoChangeNeeded     {}
```

Uninstall-WindowsFeature allows you to specify component names by getting the input from the output of another command. Consider the following example and sample output:

```
get-windowsfeature web-ftp* | Uninstall-WindowsFeature

Success      Restart Needed      Exit Code          Feature Result
-------      --------------      ---------          --------------
True         No                  Success            {FTP Service, FTP
Extensibility}
```

Here, Uninstall-WindowsFeature gets the list of components to remove from the Get-WindowsFeature cmdlet. You uninstall the FTP Service as well as FTP Extensibility.

Handling Errors and Other Issues

If an error occurs and Uninstall-WindowsFeature is not able to perform the operation specified, you see an error. The errors you see are similar to those for adding components.

In some cases, you might not be able to uninstall a component. Typically, this occurs because a component is required by or depended on by another role, role service, or feature. Consider the following example and sample output:

```
get-windowsfeature FileAndStorage* | Uninstall-WindowsFeature

Success Restart Needed Exit Code      Feature Result
------- -------------- ---------      --------------
False   Maybe          Failed         {}

uninstall-windowsfeature : A prerequisite check for the
FileAndStorage-Services feature failed.
1. Storage Services cannot be removed.
At line:1 char:38
+ get-windowsfeature fileandstorage* | uninstall-windowsfeature
+                                      ~~~~~~~~~~~~~~~~~~~~~~~~~~
    + CategoryInfo          : InvalidOperation: (File and
```

```
Storage Services:ServerComponentWrapper) [Uninstall-
WindowsFeature], Exception    + FullyQualifiedErrorId :
Alteration_PrerequisiteCheck_Failed,Microsoft.Windows.
ServerManager.Commands.RemoveWindowsFeatureCommand
```

Here, you try to uninstall the File and Storage role service. However, you are unable to remove this role because it is a required role for servers.

When you uninstall components, you can write the detailed information to a log by including the –LogPath parameter. This logging information details every operation performed by Uninstall-WindowsFeature. In this example, you write the logging information to C:\logs\install.log:

As with the installation process, you can write the detailed information to a log by including the –logPath parameter. Here is an example:

```
Uninstall-WindowsFeature BITS -IncludeAllSubFeature -LogPath
c:\logs\uninstall.log
```

Chapter 6. Managing Computer Accounts

Computers have attributes that you can manage, including names and group memberships. You can add computer accounts to any container or organizational unit (OU) in Active Directory. However, the best containers to use are Computers, Domain Controllers, and any OUs that you've created. The standard Windows tool for working with computer accounts is Active Directory Users And Computers. In PowerShell, you have many commands, each with a specific use. Whether you are logged on to a Windows desktop or Windows Server, you can use the techniques discussed in this chapter to manage computers.

Commands for Managing Computers

Commands you'll use to manage computers in PowerShell include:

- **Add-Computer**   Adds computers to a domain or workgroup. You can specify computers by their NetBIOS name, IP address, or fully qualified domain name. To join a domain, you must specify the name of the domain to join. In domains, if a computer doesn't have a domain account, this command also creates the domain account for the computer. A restart is required to complete the join operation. To get the results of the command, use the –Verbose and –PassThru parameters.

```
Add-Computer [-OUPath ADPath] [-Server Domain\ComputerName]
[[-ComputerName] ComputerNames] [-DomainName] DomainName
[-Unsecure] [-PassThru] [-Reboot] [[-Credential] CredentialObject]

Add-Computer [[-ComputerName] ComputerNames] [-WorkGroupName]
 Name [-PassThru] [-Reboot] [[-Credential] CredentialObject]
```

- **Remove-Computer**   Removes local and remote computers from their current workgroup or domain. When you remove a computer from a domain, Remove-Computer also disables the computer's domain account. A restart is required to complete the unjoin operation. For domain computers, you must provide authentication credentials.

```
Remove-Computer [[-ComputerName] ComputerNames]
[-PassThru] [-Reboot] [[-Credential] CredentialObject]
```

- **Rename-Computer**   Renames computers in workgroups and domains. When you rename a computer in a domain, Rename-Computer also changes the name in the computer's domain account. You cannot use Rename-Computer to rename domain controllers. For remote computers, you must provide authentication credentials.

```
Rename-Computer [[-ComputerName] ComputerName]
[-NewComputerName] NewComputerName [-Credential
CredentialObject] [-Reboot]
```

- **Restart-Computer**   Restarts the operating system on local and remote computers. Use the –Force parameter to force an immediate restart of the computers.

```
Restart-Computer [[-ComputerName] ComputerNames] [-AsJob]
[-Authentication AuthType] [[-Credential] CredentialObject]
[-Force] [-Impersonation ImpType] [-ThrottleLimit Limit]
```

- **Stop-Computer**   Shuts down local or remote computers. The –AsJob parameter runs the command as a background job, providing the computers are configured for remoting.

```
Stop-Computer [[-ComputerName] ComputerNames] [-AsJob]
[-Authentication AuthType] [[-Credential] CredentialObject]
[-Force] [-Impersonation ImpType] [-ThrottleLimit Limit]
```

- **Test-ComputerSecureChannel**   Checks the secure channel between a Windows client and its domain and optionally resets the computer account password to re-enable the trust between the client and the domain.

```
Test-ComputerSecureChannel [-Server] ServerName [-Repair]
[-Credential CredentialObject]
```

- **Test-Connection**   Sends Internet Control Message Protocol (ICMP) echo request packets (pings) to one or more remote computers, and returns the responses. As long as ICMP is not blocked by a firewall, this can help you determine whether a computer can be contacted across an IP network. You can specify both the sending and receiving computers. You also can set a time-out and the number of pings.

```
Test-Connection [-Count NumPings] [-Delay DelayBetweenPings]
[-TimeToLive MaxTime] [[-Source] SourceComputers]
[-Destination] DestinationComputers
```

```
[-AsJob] [-Authentication AuthType] [-BufferSize Size]
[-Credential CredentialObject] [-Impersonation ImpType]
[-ThrottleLimit Limit]
```

You'll usually want to run these commands at an administrator PowerShell prompt. Regardless, you also might need to provide the appropriate credentials, and you can do this as shown in the following example:

```
$cred = get-credential
add-computer -domainname imaginedlands -credential $cred
```

When you use Get-Credential, PowerShell prompts you for a user name and password and then stores the credentials provided in the $cred variable. These credentials are then used for authentication.

When you test a connection to a computer, restart a computer, or stop a computer, note the following:

- The –Authentication parameter sets the authentication level for the WMI connection to the computer. The default value is Packet. Valid values are Unchanged (the authentication level is the same as the previous command), Default (Windows Authentication), None (no COM authentication), Connect (Connect-level COM authentication), Call (Call-level COM authentication), Packet (Packet-level COM authentication), PacketIntegrity (Packet Integrity–level COM authentication), and PacketPrivacy (Packet Privacy–level COM authentication).
- The –Impersonation parameter sets the impersonation level to use when establishing the WMI connection. The default value is Impersonate. Valid values are Default (default impersonation), Anonymous (hides the identity of the caller), Identify (allows objects to query the credentials of the caller), and Impersonate (allows objects to use the credentials of the caller).

As you can see, the default authentication technique is to use Packet-level COM authentication, and the default impersonation technique is to use the credentials of the caller. Most of the time, these are what you'll want to use. Occasionally, you might want to use Windows Authentication rather than COM authentication. To do this, set the –Authentication parameter to Default.

Test-Connection is the same as Ping. With Test-Connection, you can determine whether you can connect to a computer by its name or IP address. To test the IPv4 address 192.168.10.55, you use the following command:

```
test-connection 192.168.10.55
```

To test the IPv6 address FEC0::02BC:FF:BECB:FE4F:961D, you use the following command:

```
test-connection FEC0::02BC:FF:BECB:FE4F:961D
```

If you receive a successful reply from Test-Connection, Test-Connection was able to connect to the computer. If you receive a time-out or "Unable to Connect" error, Test-Connection was unable to connect to the computer either because the computer was disconnected from the network, the computer was shut down, or the connection was blocked by a firewall.

Much like user accounts, computer accounts have passwords. Unlike user accounts, however, computer accounts have two associated passwords. One is a standard account password and the other is a secure-channel password for connecting to the domain. These passwords are maintained automatically and changed every 30 days. As both passwords must be synchronized with the domain, a problem can occur if synchronization is lost, such as when a Windows client has been offline for more than 30 days due to a user taking an extended leave of absence.

Should the secure channel password and the computer account password get out of sync, the Windows client won't be allowed to log on to the domain, and a domain authentication error message will be logged for the Netlogon service with an event ID of 3210 or 5722. To resolve this, you need to reset the passwords stored on the client. You also may need to remove the Windows client from the domain and then rejoin the client to the domain.

If you suspect there is a trust problem between a Windows client and the domain, you can test the trust using Test-ComputerSecureChannel. This cmdlet returns $true if the secure channel is working correctly and $false otherwise. To correct a trust problem and reset the passwords, enter the following command:

```
Test-ComputerSecureChannel -Repair
```

> **NOTE** Test-ComputerSecureChannel is meant for Windows clients, and not Windows servers. If you run Test-ComputerSecureChannel on a domain controller, you will get an error stating the operation failed.

Renaming Computer Accounts

Using Rename-Computer, you can easily rename workstations and member servers. If the workstation or member server is joined to a domain, the computer's account is renamed as well. You should not, however, use Rename-Computer to rename domain controllers, servers running Certificate Services, or servers running any other services that require a specific, fixed server name.

You can rename a workstation or member server using the following command syntax:

```
rename-computer -ComputerName ComputerName -NewComputerName NewName -reboot
```

where *ComputerName* is the current name of the computer, and *NewName* is the new name for the computer. If you are renaming the local computer, you omit the –ComputerName parameter as shown in the following example:

```
rename-computer -NewComputerName TechPC12 -reboot
```

Here, you rename the local computer TechPC12. Because a reboot is required to complete the renaming, you specify that you want to reboot the computer after renaming it. If you need to specify credentials to rename a computer, you can do so as shown in the following example:

```
$cred = get-credential
rename-computer -NewComputerName TechPC12 -credential $cred
-reboot
```

Joining Computers to a Domain

Any authenticated user can join a computer to a domain using Add-Computer. If the related computer account hasn't been created, running Add-Computer also creates the computer account. When a computer joins a domain, the computer establishes a trust relationship with the domain. The computer's security identifier is changed to match that of the related computer account in Active Directory, and the computer is made a member of the appropriate groups in Active Directory. Typically, this means the computer is made a member of the Domain Computers group. If the computer is later made a domain controller, the computer will be made a member of the Domain Controllers group instead.

> **REAL WORLD** Before trying to join a computer to a domain, you should verify the computer's network configuration. If the network configuration is not correct, you will need to modify the settings before attempting to join the computer to the domain. Additionally, if the computer account was created previously, only a user specifically delegated permission or an administrator can join the computer to a domain. Users must also have local administrator permissions on the local computer.

When logged on to the computer you want to join to a domain, you can use Add-Computer to simultaneously join a computer to a domain and create a computer account in the domain with the following command syntax:

```
add-computer -DomainName DomainName -reboot
```

where *DomainName* is the name of the Active Directory domain to join. Because you must reboot the computer to complete the join operation, you typically will want to include the –Reboot parameter. This isn't required, however. If you don't specify the organizational unit to use, the default organizational unit is used. Consider the following example:

```
$cred = get-credential
add-computer -domainname imaginedlands -credential $cred -reboot
```

Here, you join the local computer to the imaginedlands.com domain and create the related computer account in the default Computers container. If the computer's name is TechPC85, the full path to this computer object is CN=TechPC85,CN=Computers,DC=imaginedlands,DC=com.

> **TIP** Add the –PassThru and –Verbose parameters to get detailed results. Additionally, when you join a computer to a domain, you can specify the domain controller to use with the –Server parameter. Specify the server name in *Domain\ComputerName* format, such as imaginedlands\DcServer14. If you

don't specify the domain controller to use, any available domain controller is used.

Additionally, you can use the –OUPath parameter to specify the distinguished name of the OU into which the computer account should be placed. Consider the following example:

```
$cred = get-credential
add-computer –domainname imagined –outpath
ou=engineering,dc=imaginedlands,dc=com
–credential $cred -reboot
```

Here, you join the local computer to the imaginedlands.com domain and create the related computer account in the Engineering OU. If the computer's name is TechPC85, the full path to this computer object is CN=TechPC85,OU=Engineering,DC=imaginedlands,DC=com.

When running Add-Computer from another computer and connecting to the computer you want to join to a domain, you use the following command syntax:

```
add-computer –DomainName DomainName –computername ComputerNames
-reboot
```

where *DomainName* is the name of the Active Directory domain to join and *ComputerNames* is a comma-separated list of computers joining the domain. As before, this command creates the related computer account if necessary and you optionally can use the –OUPath parameter to specify the distinguished name of the OU into which the computer account should be placed.

Consider the following example:

```
$cred = get-credential
add-computer –domainname imaginedlands –computername EngPC14, EngPC17
–outpath ou=engineering,dc=imaginedlands,dc=com
–credential $cred -reboot
```

Here, you join EngPC14 and EngPC15 to the imaginedlands.com domain and create the related computer account in the Engineering OU.

You can read the list of computers to join to a domain from a file as well. Here is an example:

```
add-computer -domainname imaginedlands -computername
(get-content c:\data\clist.txt)
```

Here, you add the computers listed in the C:\Data\CList.txt file to the imaginedlands.com domain. If you are renaming the local computer as well as other computers, you can type **"."** or **"localhost"** as the computer name.

Adding Computers to a Workgroup

In addition to using Add-Computer to add computers to domains, you can use Add-Computer to add computers to workgroups. To add the local computer to a specified workgroup, use the following syntax:

```
add-computer -WorkgroupName WorkgroupName -reboot
```

where *WorkgroupName* is the name of the workgroup to join. Because you must reboot the computer to complete the join operation, you typically will want to include the –Reboot parameter. This isn't required, however.

Consider the following example:

```
$cred = get-credential
add-computer -workgroupname testing -credential $cred -reboot
```

Here, you join the local computer to the Testing workgroup. Add the –PassThru and –Verbose parameters to get detailed results.

When running Add-Computer from another computer and connecting to the computer you want to join to a workgroup, you use the following command syntax:

```
add-computer -WorkgroupName WorkgroupName -computername
ComputerNames -reboot
```

where *WorkgroupName* is the name of the workgroup to join, and *ComputerNames* is a comma-separated list of computers joining the domain.

Consider the following example:

```
$cred = get-credential
add-computer -workgroupname testing -computername TestPC11,
TestPC12 -credential $cred -reboot
```

Here, you join TestPC11 and TestPC12 to the Testing workgroup.

You can read the list of computers to join to a workgroup from a file as well. Here is an example:

```
add-computer -workgroupname testing -computername
(get-content c:\data\clist.txt)
```

Here, you add the computers listed in the C:\Data\CList.txt file to the Testing workgroup. If you are renaming the local computer as well as other computers, you can type "." or **"localhost"** as the computer name.

Removing Computers from Domains and Workgroups

Only authorized users can remove a computer from a domain or workgroup. Removing a computer from a domain disables the computer account in the domain and breaks the trust relationship between the computer and the domain. The computer's security identifier is changed to match that of a computer in a workgroup. The computer then joins the default workgroup, called Workgroup.

You remove computers from a domain or workgroup using Remove-Computer. Consider the following example:

```
$cred = get-credential
remove-computer -credential $cred -reboot
```

Here, you remove the local computer from its current domain or workgroup and make it a member of the default workgroup, Workgroup.

When running Add-Computer from another computer and connecting to the computer you want to manage, you use the following command syntax:

```
remove-computer -computername ComputerNames -reboot
```

where *ComputerNames* is a comma-separated list of computers to remove from domains or workgroups.

Consider the following example:

```
$cred = get-credential
remove-computer –computername TestPC11, TestPC12 –credential
$cred -reboot
```

Here, you remove TestPC11 and TestPC12 from their current domain or workgroup and make them members of the default workgroup, Workgroup.

Managing the Restart and Shutdown of Computers

You'll often find that you need to shut down or restart systems. One way to do this is to run Shutdown-Computer or Restart-Computer at the PowerShell prompt, which you can use to work with both local and remote systems. Another way to manage system shutdown or restart is to schedule a shutdown. Here, you can use the Schtasks utility to specify when shutdown should be run, or you can create a script with a list of shutdown commands for individual systems.

Although Windows systems usually start up and shut down without problems, they can occasionally stop responding during these processes. If this happens, try to determine the cause. Some of the reasons systems might stop responding include the following:

- The system is attempting to execute or is running a startup or shutdown script that has not completed or is itself not responding (and in this case, the system might be waiting for the script to time out).
- A startup initialization file or service might be the cause of the problem and, if so, you might need to troubleshoot startup items using the System Configuration (Msconfig) utility. Disabling a service, startup item, or entry in a startup initialization file might also solve the problem.
- The system might have an antivirus program that is causing the problem. In some cases, the antivirus program might try to scan the floppy disk drive when you try to shut down the system. To resolve this, configure the antivirus software so that it doesn't scan the floppy drive or other drives with removable media on shutdown. You can also try temporarily disabling or turning off the antivirus program.

- Improperly configured sound devices can cause startup and shutdown problems. To determine what the possible source is, examine each of these devices in turn. Turn off sound devices and then restart the computer. If the problem clears up, you have to install new drivers for the sound devices you are using, or you might have a corrupted Start Windows or Exit Windows sound file.
- Improperly configured network cards can cause startup and shutdown problems. Try turning off the network adapter and restarting. If that works, you might need to remove and then reinstall the adapter's driver or obtain a new driver from the manufacturer.
- Improperly configured video adapter drivers can cause startup and shutdown problems. From another computer, remotely log on and try to roll back the current video drivers to a previous version. If that's not possible, try uninstalling and then reinstalling the video drivers.

When logged on to the computer you want to restart or shut down, you can type **restart-computer** or **stop-computer** to restart or shut down the computer, respectively. To force an immediate restart or shutdown, add the –Force parameter.

When running Restart-Computer or Stop-Computer from another computer and connecting to the computer you want to restart or stop, you use the following command syntax:

```
restart-computer -computername ComputerNames
```

or

```
stop-computer -computername ComputerNames
```

where *ComputerNames* is a comma-separated list of computers to restart or stop. As before, you can use the –Force parameter to force a restart or shutdown. You also might need to specify credentials. You can do that as shown in this example:

```
$cred = get-credential
stop-computer -computername TestPC11, TestPC12 -credential $cred
```

Here, you shut down TestPC11 and TestPC12 using specific credentials.

You can read the list of computers to restart or shut down from a file as well. Here is an example:

```
$cred = get-credential
restart-computer -computername (get-content c:\data\clist.txt)
-credential $cred -force
```

Here, you restart the computers listed in the C:\Data\CList.txt file using specific credentials.

Chapter 7. Working with System Services

Services provide much of the core functionality to clients and servers. Every service has a primary executable, and can be managed. Some services have dependencies, which can be components the service depends on, components that depend on the service, or both.

As part of a standard configuration of the operating system, some services are configured to started automatically with the operating system, while others start automatically with a delay or manually. Some manually started services can be triggered to start by the startup of other services.

Commands for Managing Services

To manage system services on local and remote systems, you use the following commands:

- **Get-Service** Gets information about the services on a local or remote computer, including running and stopped services. You can specify services by their service names or display names, or you can pass in references to service objects to work with.

```
Get-Service [[-Name] ServiceNames] [AddlParams]
Get-Service -DisplayName ServiceNames [AddlParams]
Get-Service [-InputObject ServiceObjects] [AddlParams]

{AddlParams}
[-ComputerName ComputerNames] [-DependentServices] [-Exclude
ServiceNames] [-Include ServiceNames] [-ServicesDependedOn]
```

- **Stop-Service** Stops one or more running services. You can specify services by their service names or display names, or you can pass in references to service objects to work with. Services that can be stopped indicate this because the CanStop property is set to True. Further, you can stop only a service that is in a state where stopping is permitted.

```
Stop-Service [-Name] ServiceNames [AddlParams]
Stop-Service -DisplayName ServiceNames [AddlParams]
Stop-Service [-InputObject ServiceObjects] [AddlParams]
```

```
{AddlParams}
[-Include ServiceNames] [-Exclude ServiceNames] [-Force]
[-PassThru]
```

- **Start-Service**   Starts one or more stopped services. You can specify services by their service names or display names, or you can pass in references to service objects to work with.

```
Start-Service [-Name] ServiceNames [AddlParams]
Start-Service -DisplayName ServiceNames [AddlParams]
Start-Service [-InputObject ServiceObjects] [AddlParams]
```

```
{AddlParams}
[-Include ServiceNames] [-Exclude ServiceNames] [-Force]
[-PassThru]
```

- **Suspend-Service**   Suspends (pauses) one or more running services. While paused, a service is still running, but its execution is halted until it is resumed. You can specify services by their service names or display names, or you can pass in references to service objects to work with. Services that can be suspended indicate this because the CanPauseAndContinue property is set to True. Further, you can pause only a service that is in a state where pausing is permitted.

```
Suspend-Service [-Name] ServiceNames [AddlParams]
Suspend-Service -DisplayName ServiceNames [AddlParams]
Suspend-Service [-InputObject ServiceObjects] [AddlParams]
```

```
{AddlParams}
[-Exclude ServiceNames] [-Include ServiceNames] [-PassThru]
```

- **Resume-Service**   Resumes one or more suspended (paused) services. If you reference a service that is not paused, the control change is ignored. You can specify services by their service names or display names, or you can pass in references to service objects to work with.

```
Resume-Service [-Name] ServiceNames [AddlParams]
Resume-Service -DisplayName ServiceNames [AddlParams]
Resume-Service [-InputObject ServiceObjects] [AddlParams]
```

```
{AddlParams}
[-Exclude ServiceNames] [-Include ServiceNames] [-PassThru]
```

- **Restart-Service** Stops and then starts one or more services. If a service is already stopped, it is started. You can specify services by their service names or display names, or you can pass in references to service objects to work with.

```
Restart-Service [-Name] ServiceNames [AddlParams]
Restart-Service -DisplayName ServiceNames [AddlParams]
Restart-Service [-InputObject ServiceObjects] [AddlParams]

{AddlParams}
[-Include ServiceNames] [-Exclude ServiceNames] [-Force]
[-PassThru]
```

- **Set-Service** Changes the properties or status of a service on a local or remote computer. Use the status to change the state of the service.

```
Set-Service [-Name] ServiceName [ | -InputObject ServiceObjects]
[-DisplayName DisplayName] [-Description Description]
[-StartupType {Automatic | Manual | Disabled}]
[-Status {Running | Stopped | Paused}] [-PassThru]
[-ComputerName ComputerNames]
```

- **New-Service** Creates a new Windows service in the registry and in the services database. Pass in a credential if required to create the service.

```
New-Service [-Credential CredentialObject] [-DependsOn
ServiceNames] [-Description Description] [-DisplayName
DisplayName] [-StartupType {Automatic | Manual | Disabled}]
[-Name] Name [-BinaryPathName] PathtoExeFile
```

With some of these commands, you can specify the name of the remote computer whose services you want to work with. To do this, use the –ComputerName parameter and then specify the NetBIOS name, IP address, or fully qualified domain name (FQDN) of the remote computer or computers that you want to work with. In some cases, you might want to specify the local computer as well as a remote computer. To reference the local computer, type the computer name, a dot (.), or "localhost".

Viewing Configured Services

To get a list of all services configured on a system, type **get-service** at the command prompt. Using the –ComputerName parameter, you can specify a remote computer to work with, as shown in the following example and sample output:

```
get-service -computername server92

Status    Name                DisplayName
------    ----                -----------
Running   ADWS                Active Directory Web Services
Stopped   AeLookupSvc         Application Experience
Stopped   ALG                 Application Layer Gateway Service
Running   AppHostSvc          Application Host Helper Service
Stopped   AppIDSvc            Application Identity
Running   Appinfo             Application Information
```

The –ComputerName parameter accepts multiple name values. You can check the status of services on multiple computers simply by entering the names of the computers to check in a comma-separated list as shown in the following example:

```
get-service –computername fileserver86, dcserver22, printserver31
```

Rather than type computer names each time, you can enter computer names on separate lines in a text file and then get the list of computer names from the text file, as shown in the following example:

```
get-service -computername (get-content c:\data\clist.txt)
```

Here, you get the list of remote computers to check from a file called CList.txt in the C:\Data directory.

When you are looking for a specific service, you can reference the service by its service name or display name. To match partial names, you can use wildcard characters as shown in the following example and sample output:

```
get-service –displayname *browser* –computername fileserver86

Status    Name                DisplayName
------    ----                -----------
Running   Browser             Computer Browser
```

Here, you look for all services where the display name includes the word *browser*.

Get-Service returns objects representing each service matching the criteria you specify. From previous examples and sample output, you can see that the standard output includes the Status, Name, and DisplayName properties. To view all of the available properties, you need to format the output as a list, as shown in the following example and sample output:

```
get-service -displayname *browser* -computername server12 | format-
list *

Name                 : Browser
RequiredServices     : {LanmanServer, LanmanWorkstation}
CanPauseAndContinue  : False
CanShutdown          : False
CanStop              : False
DisplayName          : Computer Browser
DependentServices    : {}
MachineName          : .
ServiceName          : Browser
ServicesDependedOn   : {LanmanServer, LanmanWorkstation}
ServiceHandle        : SafeServiceHandle
Status               : Stopped
ServiceType          : Win32ShareProcess
Site                 :
Container            :
```

The output shows the exact configuration of the service. As an administrator, you will work with the following properties most often:

- **Name/ServiceName**   The abbreviated name of the service. Only services installed on the system are listed here. If a service you need isn't listed, you'll need to install it.
- **DisplayName**   The descriptive name of the service.
- **Status**   The state of the service as Running, Paused, or Stopped.
- **DependentServices**   Services that cannot run unless the specified service is running.
- **ServicesDependedOn**   The services this service relies on to operate.
- **Type**   The type of service and whether it is a shared process.
- **MachineName**   The name of the computer the service is configured on. This property is available only when you use the –ComputerName property.

> **TIP**   When you are configuring services, it is sometimes important to know whether a process runs in its own context or is shared. Shared processes are listed as WIN32SHAREPROCESS. Processes that run in their own context are listed as WIN32OWNPROCESS.

By default, Get-Service looks at all services regardless of their status. With the Status property, you can work with services in a specific state, such as Stopped or Paused. Consider the following examples:

```
get-service | where-object {$_.status -eq "Running"}
get-service | where-object {$_.status -eq "Stopped"}
```

In the first example, you list all services that are running. In the second example, you list all services that are stopped.

Starting, Stopping, and Pausing Services

As an administrator, you'll often have to start, stop, or pause Windows services. When you are working with an administrator PowerShell prompt, you can do this using the service-related cmdlets or the methods of the Win32_Service class. Examples using the service cmdlets follow:

Start a service:
```
start-service ServiceName
start-service -displayname DisplayName
get-service ServiceName | start-service
```

Pause a service:
```
suspend-service ServiceName
suspend-service -displayname DisplayName
get-service ServiceName | suspend-service
```

Resume a paused service:
```
resume-service ServiceName
resume-service -displayname DisplayName
get-service ServiceName | resume-service
```

Stop a service:
```
stop-service ServiceName
stop-service -displayname DisplayName
get-service ServiceName | stop-service
```

In this example, *ServiceName* in each case is the abbreviated name of a service, and *DisplayName* is the descriptive name of a service, such as

```
stop-service -displayname "DNS Client"
```

Although Start-Service, Suspend-Service, Resume-Service, and Stop-Service don't support the –ComputerName parameter, you can use the following technique to manage the state of services on remote computers:

```
get-service dnscache -computername engpc18 | stop-service
get-service dnscache -computername engpc18 | start-service

invoke-command -computername engpc18 –scriptblock
{get-service dnscache | stop-service }

invoke-command -computername engpc18 –scriptblock
{get-service dnscache | start-service }
```

Here, you use Get-Service to get a Service object on a remote computer, and then you manage the service using Start-Service, Suspend-Service, Resume-Service, or Stop-Service as appropriate. Note that these commands report only failure. They won't tell you that the service was already started, stopped, paused, or resumed.

Before you stop or pause a service, you should check to see if the service can be stopped or paused. With Service objects, the properties you can check are CanPauseAndContinue and CanStop. An example and sample output follow:

```
$sname = read-host "Enter service name to stop"
$cname = read-host "Enter computer to work with"

$s = get-service $sname -computername $cname
if ($s.CanStop -eq $True) { $s | stop-service }

Enter service name to stop : dnscache
Enter computer to work with : engpc85
```

Here, you get the name of the service and computer to work with by prompting the user, and then you get the related Service object. If the service can be stopped, you stop the service. As shown in the following example and sample output, you can easily extend this basic functionality to perform other actions on services:

```
$cname = read-host "Enter computer to work with"
$sname = read-host "Enter service name to work with"

$s = get-service $sname -computername $cname
write-host "Service is:" $s.status -foregroundcolor green
```

```
$action = read-host "Specify action [Start|Stop|Pause|Resume]"

switch ($action) {

"start" { $s | start-service }
"stop" { if ($s.CanStop -eq $True) { $s | stop-service } }
"pause" { if ($s.CanPauseAndContinue -eq $True) { $s | pause-service
} }
"resume" { $s | resume-service }

}

$su = get-service $sname -computername $cname
write-host "Service is:" $su.status -foregroundcolor green

Enter computer to work with: techpc12
Enter service name to work with: dnscache
Service is: Running
Specify action [Start|Stop|Pause|Resume]: stop
Service is:  Stopped
```

Here, you get the name of the service and computer to work with by prompting the user, and then you get the related Service object. Next, you display the current status of the service and then get the action to perform on the service. After performing CanStop and CanPauseAndContinue tests if appropriate and taking the appropriate action on the service, you display the updated status of the service.

REAL WORLD   Want to manage services any time you are working with PowerShell? Wrap this code in a function, and add it to your profile. Then you can manage services simply by calling the function. Here is an example:

function ms {

 #Insert code here

}

Now any time your profile is loaded and you type **ms** at the PowerShell prompt, you'll be able to manage services on any computer in the enterprise.

Configuring Service Startup

You can set Windows services to start manually or automatically. You also can turn services off permanently by disabling them. You configure service startup using

```
set-service ServiceName -StartupType Type [-ComputerName
ComputerNames]
```

or

```
set-service -displayname DisplayName -StartupType Type
[-ComputerName ComputerNames]
```

where *ServiceName* or *DisplayName* identifies the service to modify, *Type* is the startup type to use, and *ComputerNames* are the names of the computers to work with. The valid startup types are:

- **Automatic** Starts a service at system startup. If the service requires a delayed start, the subtype Automatic (Delayed Start) is assigned automatically.
- **Manual** Allows the service to be started manually by the service control manager when a process invokes the service.
- **Disable** Disables the service to prevent it from being started the next time the computer is started. If the service is running, it will continue to run until the computer is shut down. You can stop the service if necessary.

Following this, you can configure a service to start automatically by using

```
set-service dnscache –startuptype automatic
```

or

```
set-service dnscache –startuptype automatic –computername techpc85
```

Instead of typing a comma-separated list of computer names, you can enter computer names on separate lines in a text file and then get the list of computer names from the text file as shown in the following example:

```
set-service dnscache –startuptype automatic –computername
(get-content c:\data\clist.txt)
```

Here, you get the list of remote computers to work with from a file called CList.txt in the C:\Data directory.

Set-Service also lets you start, stop, and pause services. If you are enabling a service on multiple computers, you also might want to start the service. You can enable and start a service as shown in the following example:

```
set-service w3svc -startuptype automatic -status running
```

If you are disabling a service on multiple computers, you also might want to stop the service. You can disable and stop a service as shown in the following example:

```
set-service w3svc -startuptype disabled -status stopped
```

Managing Service Logon and Recovery Modes

Occasionally, you might need to manage service logon and recovery options. The easiest way to do this is to use the Services Configuration utility. This utility has several subcommands that allow you to work with Windows services. The executable for this utility is sc.exe. Although you normally can type **sc** at the prompt and run this utility, *sc* is a default alias for Set-Content in PowerShell. For this reason, you must type **sc.exe** whenever you work with this utility at the PowerShell prompt.

Configuring Service Logon

Using the SC config command, you can configure Windows services to log on as a system account or as a specific user. To ensure a service logs on as the LocalSystem account, use

```
sc.exe ComputerName config ServiceName obj= LocalSystem
```

where *ComputerName* is the Universal Naming Convention (UNC) name of the computer to work with, and *ServiceName* is the name of the service you are configuring to use the LocalSystem account. If the service provides a user interface that can be manipulated, add the flags **type= interact type= own**, as shown in the following example:

```
sc.exe config vss obj= LocalSystem type= interact type= own
```

or

```
sc.exe \\techpc85 config vss obj= LocalSystem type= interact type=
own
```

> **NOTE** You must include a space after the equal sign (=) as shown. If you
> don't use a space, the command will fail. Note also these commands report
> only SUCCESS or FAILURE. They won't tell you that the service was already
> configured in a specified way.

The *type= interact* flag specifies that the service is allowed to interact with the
Windows desktop. The type= own flag specifies that the service runs in its own
process. In the case of a service that shares its executable files with other services,
you use the type= share flag, as shown in this example:

```
sc.exe config dnscache obj= LocalSystem type= interact type= share
```

> **TIP** If you don't know whether a service runs as a shared process or in its
> own context, you should determine the service's start type using Get-Service.

Services can also log on using named accounts. To do this, use

```
sc.exe config ServiceName obj= [Domain\]User password= Password
```

where *Domain* is the optional domain name in which the user account is located,
User is the name of the user account whose permissions you want to use, and
Password is the password of that account. Consider the following example:

```
sc.exe config vss obj= adatum\backers password= TenMen55!
```

Here, you configure Microsoft Visual SourceSafe (VSS) to use the Backers account in
the Adatum domain. The output of the command should state SUCCESS or FAILED.
The change will fail if the account name is invalid or doesn't exist, or if the password
for the account is invalid.

> **NOTE** If a service has been previously configured to interact with the
> desktop under the LocalSystem account, you cannot change the service to run
> under a domain account without using the *type= own* flag. The syntax
> therefore becomes *sc config ServiceName obj= [Domain\]User password=
> Password type= own.*

Although SC is designed to work with individual computers, you can use the built-in features of PowerShell to modify the way SC works, as shown in the following example:

```
$c = "\\techpc85"
sc.exe $c query dnscache
```

Here, rather than specifying the computer name explicitly, you pass in the computer name as a variable.

You can extend this basic technique to get a list of remote computers to work with from a file. Here is an example:

```
$computers = (get-content c:\data\unclist.txt)
foreach ($c in $computers) { sc.exe $c query dnscache }
```

Here, you get the list of computers to work with from a file called UncList.txt in the C:\Data directory and then execute an SC query for each computer name.

> **TIP**   Don't forget that SC requires computer names to be specified using Universal Naming Convention. This means you must type **\\techpc85** rather than **techpc85** in the text file from which computer names are obtained.

Configuring Service Recovery

Using the SC Qfailure and Failure commands, you can view and configure actions taken when a service fails. For example, you can configure a service so that the service control manager attempts to restart it or to run an application that can resolve the problem.

You can configure recovery options for the first, second, and subsequent recovery attempts. The current failure count is incremented each time a failure occurs. You can also set a parameter that specifies the time that must elapse before the failure counter is reset. For example, you can specify that if 24 hours have passed since the last failure, the failure counter should be reset.

Before you try to configure service recovery, check the current recovery settings using SC Qfailure. The syntax is

```
sc.exe ComputerName qfailure ServiceName
```

where *ComputerName* is the UNC name of the computer to work with, and *ServiceName* is the name of the service you want to work with, such as

```
sc.exe qfailure adws
```

or

```
sc.exe \\techpc85 qfailure adws
```

In the output, the failure actions are listed in the order they are performed. In the following example output, ADWS is configured to attempt to restart the service the first and second times the service fails:

```
[SC] QueryServiceConfig2 SUCCESS

SERVICE_NAME: adws
    RESET_PERIOD (in seconds)    : 900
    REBOOT_MESSAGE               :
    COMMAND_LINE                 :
    FAILURE_ACTIONS  : RESTART -- Delay = 120000 milliseconds.
                       RESTART -- Delay = 300000 milliseconds.
```

> **NOTE** Windows automatically configures recovery for some critical system services during installation. Typically, these services are configured so that they attempt to restart the service. A few are configured to restart the server if they fail. Services also can be configured so that they run programs or scripts upon failure.

The command you use to configure service recovery is SC Failure, and its basic syntax is

```
sc.exe failure ServiceName reset= FailureResetPeriod actions=
RecoveryActions
```

where *ServiceName* is the name of the service you are configuring; *FailureResetPeriod* specifies the time, in seconds, that must elapse without failure in order to reset the failure counter; and *RecoveryActions* are the actions to take when failure occurs plus the delay time (in milliseconds) before that action is initiated. The available recovery actions are:

- **Take No Action (indicated by an empty string "")**   The operating system won't attempt recovery for this failure but might still attempt recovery of previous or subsequent failures.
- **Restart The Service**   Stops and then starts the service after a brief pause.
- **Run A Program**   Allows you to run a program or a script in case of failure. The script can be a batch program or a Windows script. If you select this option, set the full file path to the program you want to run, and then set any necessary command-line parameters to pass in to the program when it starts.
- **Reboot The Computer**   Shuts down and then restarts the computer after the specified delay time has elapsed.

> **NOTE**   When you configure recovery options for critical services, you might want to try to restart the service on the first and second attempts and then reboot the server on the third attempt.

When you work with SC Failure, keep the following in mind:

- The reset period is set in seconds.

Reset periods are commonly set in multiples of hours or days. An hour is 3,600 seconds, and a day is 86,400 seconds. For a two-hour reset period, for example, you'd use the value 7,200.

- Each recovery action must be followed by the time to wait (in milliseconds) before performing the action.

For a service restart, you'll probably want to use a short delay, such as 1 millisecond (no delay), 1 second (1,000 milliseconds), or 5 seconds (5,000 milliseconds). For a restart of the computer, you'll probably want to use a longer delay, such as 15 seconds (15,000 milliseconds) or 30 seconds (30,000 milliseconds).

- Enter the actions and their delay times as a single text entry, with each value separated by a forward slash (/).

For example, you could use the following value: restart/1000/restart/1000/reboot/15000. Here, on the first and second attempts the service is restarted after a 1-second delay, and on the third attempt the computer is rebooted after a 15-second delay.

Consider the following examples:

```
sc.exe failure w3svc reset= 86400 actions=
restart/1/restart/1/reboot/30000
```

Here, on the first and second attempts the service is restarted almost immediately, and on the third attempt the computer is rebooted after a 30-second delay. In addition, the failure counter is reset if no failures occur in a 24-hour period (86,400 seconds). You can also specify a remote computer by inserting the UNC name or IP address as shown in previous examples.

If you use the Run action, you specify the command or program to run using the Command= parameter. Follow the Command= parameter with the full file path to the command to run and any arguments to pass to the command. Be sure to enclose the command path and text in double quotation marks, as in the following example:

```
sc.exe failure w3svc reset= 86400 actions=
restart/1/restart/1/run/30000 command= "c:\restart_w3svc.exe 15"
```

Digging Deeper into Service Management

Although the Get-Service cmdlet provides sufficient details to help you perform many administrative tasks, it doesn't provide the detailed information you might need to know to manage the configuration of services. At a minimum, to manage service configuration, you need to know a service's current start mode and start name. The start mode specifies the startup mode of the service, and the start name specifies the account name under which the service will run. A service's start mode can be set to any of the following:

- **Automatic**   Indicates the service is started automatically by the service control manager during startup of the operating system.
- **Manual**   Indicates the service is started manually by the service control manager when a process calls the StartService method.
- **Disabled**   Indicates the service is disabled and cannot be started.

Most services run under one of the following accounts:

- **NT Authority\LocalSystem**   LocalSystem is a pseudo account for running system processes and handling system-level tasks. This account is part of the Administrators group on a computer and has all user rights on the computer. If services use this account, the related processes have full access to the computer. Many services run under the LocalSystem account. In some cases, these services have the privilege to interact with the desktop as well. Services that need alternative privileges or logon rights run under the LocalService or NetworkService accounts.

- **NT Authority\LocalService**   LocalService is a pseudo account with limited privileges. This account grants access to the local system only. The account is part of the Users group on the computer and has the same rights as the NetworkService account, except that it is limited to the local computer. If services use this account, the related processes don't have access to other computers.

- **NT Authority\NetworkService**   NetworkService is a pseudo account for running services that need additional privileges and logon rights on a local system and the network. This account is part of the Users group on the computer and provides fewer permissions and privileges than the LocalSystem account (but more than the LocalService account). Specifically, processes running under this account can interact throughout a network using the credentials of the computer account.

You can obtain the start mode, start name, and other configuration information for services using Windows Management Instrumentation (WMI) and the Win32_Service class. You use the Win32_Service class to create instances of service objects as they are represented in WMI.

By typing **get-wmiobject -class win32_service** you can list all services configured on a computer, as shown in the following example and sample output:

```
get-wmiobject -class win32_service | format-table name, startmode,
state, status
```

name	startmode	state	status
ADWS	Auto	Running	OK
AeLookupSvc	Manual	Stopped	OK
ALG	Manual	Stopped	OK
AppHostSvc	Auto	Running	OK
AppIDSvc	Manual	Stopped	OK
Appinfo	Manual	Running	OK
AppMgmt	Manual	Stopped	OK
AppReadiness	Manual	Stopped	OK

```
AppXSvc           Manual        Stopped        OK
aspnet_state      Manual        Stopped        OK
Audiosrv          Manual        Stopped        OK
AxInstSV          Manual        Stopped        OK
BFE               Auto          Running        OK
BITS              Manual        Stopped        OK
Browser           Disabled       Stopped        OK
CertPropSvc       Manual        Running        OK
COMSysApp         Manual        Stopped        OK
CryptSvc          Auto          Running        OK
CscService        Disabled       Stopped        OK
```

If you want to work with a specific service or examine services with a specific property value, you can add the –Filter parameter. In the following example and sample output, you check the configuration details of the Browser service:

```
get-wmiobject -class win32_service -filter "name='browser'"
```

```
ExitCode  : 1077
Name      : Browser
ProcessId : 0
StartMode : Disabled
State     : Stopped
Status    : OK
```

If you format the output as a list, you'll see additional configuration information including PathName, which specifies the executable that starts the service and any parameters passed to this executable, and StartName, which specifies the account under which the service runs. In the following example and partial output, you examine the properties of the DNS Client service:

```
$s = get-wmiobject -class win32_service -filter "name='dnscache'"
$s | format-list *
```

```
Name              : Dnscache
Status            : OK
ExitCode          : 0
DesktopInteract   : False
ErrorControl      : Normal
PathName          : C:\Windows\system32\svchost.exe -k
                    NetworkService
ServiceType       : Share Process
StartMode         : Auto
AcceptPause       : False
```

```
AcceptStop                : True
Caption                   : DNS Client
CheckPoint                : 0
CreationClassName         : Win32_Service
Description               : The DNS Client service (dnscache)
                            caches Domain Name System (DNS) names
DisplayName               : DNS Client
InstallDate               :
ProcessId                 : 332
ServiceSpecificExitCode   : 0
Started                   : True
StartName                 : NT AUTHORITY\NetworkService
State                     : Running
SystemCreationClassName   : Win32_ComputerSystem
SystemName                : CORPSERVER64
```

Get-WmiObject supports a –ComputerName parameter that lets you specify the remote computer or computers to work with, as shown in these examples:

```
get-wmiobject -class win32_service –computername fileserver86,
dcserver22, printserver31
```

```
get-wmiobject -class win32_service -computername (get-content
c:\data\clist.txt)
```

> **NOTE** When you are working with multiple computers, you can use the SystemName property to help you determine the name of the computer the service is configured on.

You can work with the properties of Win32_Service objects in much the same way as you work with properties of Service objects. To see a list of all services configured to start automatically, you can type the following command:

```
get-wmiobject -class win32_service -filter "startmode='auto'" |
format-table name, startmode, state, status
```

To view all running services, you can type

```
get-wmiobject -class win32_service -filter "state='running'" |
format-table name, startmode, state, status
```

The Win32_Service class provides a number of methods for managing system services. These methods include:

- **Change()** Changes the configuration of a user-configurable service. This method accepts the following parameters in the following order: DisplayName, PathName, ServiceTypeByte, ErrorControlByte, StartMode, DesktopInteractBoolean, StartName, StartPassword, LoadOrderGroup, LoadOrderGroupDependenciesArray, and ServiceDependenciesArray.

> **CAUTION** Not all services can be reconfigured. Modifying services at the PowerShell prompt is not something you should do without careful forethought. PowerShell will let you make changes that could put your computer in an unstable state. Before you make any changes to services, you should create a system restore point as discussed in Chapter 13, "Enabling Recovery."

- **ChangeStartMode()** Changes the start mode of a user-configurable service. This method accepts a single parameter, which is the start mode to use. Valid values are Manual, Automatic, or Disabled.

> **NOTE** Some services are configured by default to use delayed-start automatic mode. When you are working with Win32_Service, any time you set these services to Automatic, they use delayed-start automatic mode. Additionally, note that disabling a service doesn't stop a running service. It only prevents the service from being started the next time the computer is booted. To ensure that the service is disabled and stopped, disable and then stop the service.
>
> **CAUTION** Before you change the start mode of a service, you should check dependencies and ensure any changes you make won't affect other services.

- **Delete()** Deletes a user-configurable service (if the service is in a state that allows this). Rather than delete a service, you should consider disabling it. Disabled services no longer run and can easily be enabled if needed in the future. Deleted services, however, must be reinstalled to be used in the future.

> **CAUTION** Exercise extreme caution if you plan to delete services using PowerShell. PowerShell will not warn you if you are making harmful changes to your computer.

- **InterrogateService()** Connects to the service using the service control manager. If the return value is zero, the service control manager was able to connect to and interrogate the service using its configured parameters. If the return value wasn't zero, the service control manager encountered a problem while trying to communicate with the service using the configured parameters. If the service is stopped or paused, this method will always return an error status.

- **PauseService()**   Pauses the service, which might be necessary during troubleshooting or when performing diagnostics. Services that can be paused indicate this by setting the AcceptPause property to True for their services. Further, you can pause only a service that is in a state where pausing is permitted.
- **ResumeService()**   Resumes the service after it has been paused.
- **StopService()**   Stops the service, which might be necessary during troubleshooting or when performing diagnostics. Services that can be stopped indicate this by setting the AcceptStop property to True for their services. Further, you can stop only a service that is in a state where stopping is permitted.
- **StartService()**   Starts a stopped service, including services that are configured for manual startup.

When you are working with an administrator PowerShell prompt, you can use these methods to manage system services. For example, you can set Windows services to start manually or automatically. You can also turn them off permanently by disabling them. You configure service startup using the ChangeStartMode() method to specify the desired start mode. The basic syntax is

```
$serviceObject.ChangeStartMode(StartMode)
```

where *$serviceObject* is a reference to a Win32_Service object, and *StartMode* is the desired start mode entered as a string value, as shown in this example and sample output:

```
$s = get-wmiobject -class win32_service -filter "name='dnscache'"

$s.changestartmode("automatic")

__GENUS          : 2
__CLASS          : __PARAMETERS
__SUPERCLASS     :
__DYNASTY        : __PARAMETERS
__RELPATH        :
__PROPERTY_COUNT : 1
__DERIVATION     : {}
__SERVER         :
__NAMESPACE      :
```

```
__PATH              :
ReturnValue         : 0
```

Here, you set the start mode to Automatic. The return value in the output is what you want to focus on. A return value of 0 indicates success. Any other return value indicates an error. Typically, errors occur because you aren't using an administrator PowerShell prompt, you haven't accessed the correct service, or the service isn't in a state in which it can be configured. Keep in mind that if you alter the configuration of required services, the computer might not work as expected. Because of this, don't make any changes to services without careful planning and forethought.

> **NOTE** These commands report only SUCCESS or FAILURE. They won't tell you that the service was already started, stopped, or configured in the startup mode you've specified.

A technique for invoking methods of WMI objects we haven't discussed previously is using a direct invocation using the Invoke-WMIMethod cmdlet. This cmdlet provides a one-line alternative to the two-line technique that requires you to get a WMI object and then invoke its method. For example, instead of using

```
$s = get-wmiobject -class win32_service
-filter "name='dnscache'"

$s.stopservice()
```

you can use

```
invoke-wmimethod -path "win32_service.name='dnscache'"
-name stopservice
```

Syntax options for Invoke-WmiMethod include the following:

```
Invoke-WmiMethod [-ComputerName [ComputerNames]] [-Credential
[CredentialObject]] [-Name] [MethodName] [-ThrottleLimit
[LimitValue]] [-AsJob]

Invoke-WmiMethod [-InputObject [WMIObject]] [-Name] [MethodName]
[-ThrottleLimit [LimitValue]] [-AsJob]

Invoke-WmiMethod [-Namespace [WMINamespace]] -Path [WMIPath]
[-ArgumentList [Objects]] [-Name] [MethodName] [-ThrottleLimit
[LimitValue]] [-AsJob]
```

```
Invoke-WmiMethod [-EnableAllPrivileges] [-Authority [Authority]]
[-Name] [MethodName] [-ThrottleLimit [LimitValue]] [-AsJob]

Invoke-WmiMethod [-Locale [Locale]] [-Name] [MethodName]
[-ThrottleLimit [LimitValue]] [-AsJob]
```

You can use the methods of the Win32_Service class and Invoke-WmiMethod to manage services as shown in the following examples:

Start a service:
```
invoke-wmimethod -path "win32_service.name='ServiceName'"
-name startservice

invoke-wmimethod -path "win32_service.displayname='DisplayName'"
-name startservice

get-wmiobject -class win32_service -filter "name='ServiceName'" |
invoke-wmimethod -name startservice
```

Pause a service:
```
invoke-wmimethod -path "win32_service.name='ServiceName'"
-name pauseservice

invoke-wmimethod -path "win32_service.displayname='DisplayName'"
-name pauseservice

get-wmiobject -class win32_service -filter "name='ServiceName'" |
invoke-wmimethod -name pauseservice
```

Resume a paused service:
```
invoke-wmimethod -path "win32_service.name='ServiceName'"
-name resumeservice

invoke-wmimethod -path "win32_service.displayname='DisplayName'"
-name resumeservice

get-wmiobject -class win32_service -filter "name='ServiceName'"
 | invoke-wmimethod -name resumeservice
```

Stop a service:
```
invoke-wmimethod -path "win32_service.name='ServiceName'"
-name stopservice

invoke-wmimethod -path "win32_service.displayname='DisplayName'"
-name stopservice
```

```
get-wmiobject -class win32_service -filter "name='ServiceName'"
 | invoke-wmimethod -name stopservice
```

Before you stop or pause a service, you should check to see if the service can be stopped or paused. With Win32_Service objects, the properties you can check are AcceptPause and AcceptStop.

You can use the techniques discussed previously to work with services when Get-WmiObject returns a single matching Win32_Service object. However, these techniques won't work as expected when Get-WmiObject returns multiple Win32_Service objects. The reason for this is that the objects are stored in an array, and you must specify the instance within the array to work with. One technique for doing so is shown in the following example and partial output:

```
$servs = get-wmiobject -class win32_service |
where-object {$_.name -match "client"}

foreach ($s in $servs) { $s.changestartmode("automatic") }

ReturnValue        : 0
ReturnValue        : 0
ReturnValue        : 0
```

Here, three Win32_Service objects were returned, and each was set to start automatically. This technique will work when there is only one matching service as well.

Chapter 8. Inventorying and Evaluating Windows Systems

Often when you are working with a user's computer or a remote server, you'll want to examine the working environment and computer configuration details. For example, you might want to know who is logged on, the current system time, or what accounts are available locally. You might also want to know what processor and how much RAM are installed. To do this and much more, you can take an inventory of your computers.

While you are inventorying your computers, you also might want to evaluate the hardware configuration and determine whether there are issues that need your attention. For example, if a computer's primary disk is getting low in free space or a computer has little available memory, you'll want to note this at the least and possibly take preventative measures.

Getting System Information

Sometimes when you are working with a computer, you won't know basic information, such as the name of the computer, the logon domain, or the current user. This can happen when you get called to support a computer in another department within your organization and when you are working remotely. Items that help you quickly gather basic user and system information include the following:

- **$env:computername**   Displays the name of the computer

```
$env:computername
```

- **$env:username**   Displays the name of the user currently logged on to the system, such as wrstanek

```
$env:username
```

- **$env:userdomain**   Displays the logon domain of the current user, such as IMAGINEDLANDS

```
$env:userdomain
```

- **Get-Date**   Displays the current system date or current system time

```
Get-Date [-Date] DateTime
```

```
Get-Date -DisplayHint [Date | Time]
```

- **Set-Date** Sets the current system date or current system time

```
Set-Date [-Date] DateTime
Set-Date [-Adjust] TimeChange
```

- **Get-Credential** Gets a credential needed for authentication

```
Get-Credential [-Credential] Credential
```

Checking Naming Information

Often, you can obtain the basic information you need about the working environment from environment variables. The most common details you might need to know include the name of the computer, the identity of the current user, and the logon domain.

You can obtain the user, domain, and computer name information by using $env:username, $env:userdomain, and $env:computername, respectively. In the following example and sample output, you write this information to the console:

```
write-host "Domain: $env:userdomain `nUser: $env:username `nComputer:
$env:computername"

Domain: IMAGINEDLANDS
User: wrstanek
Computer: TECHPC76
```

Here, the user is wrstanek, the computer is TechPC76, and the user's logon domain is IMAGINEDLANDS.

> **NOTE** The grave-accent character (`) is an escape character in PowerShell. Following the escape character with n, instructs PowerShell to display the output on a new line. Other useful escape sequences are `a which plays an audible beep and `t which insert a horizontal tab.
>
> **TIP** When used at the end of a line, the escape character is a line continuation marker, allowing command text to continue on the next line. The escape character can also be used to display otherwise unprintable characters. For example, if you wanted to write a single quote or double quote in the

> output and not have either be interpreted as a string delimiter, you'd insert the escape character and then the quote character.

A faster alternative that provides even more information about the working environment is to list all available environment variables and their values as shown in this example and sample output:

```
get-childitem env:

Name                          Value
----                          -----
ALLUSERSPROFILE               C:\ProgramData
APPDATA          C:\Users\williams.IMAGINEDLANDS\AppData\Roaming
CLIENTNAME                    ROOM4-PC
CommonProgramFiles            C:\Program Files\Common Files
CommonProgramFiles(x86)       C:\Program Files (x86)\Common Files
CommonProgramW6432            C:\Program Files\Common Files
COMPUTERNAME                  CORPPC38
ComSpec                       C:\Windows\system32\cmd.exe
FP_NO_HOST_CHECK              NO
HOMEDRIVE                     C:
HOMEPATH                      \Users\williams.IMAGINEDLANDS
LOCALAPPDATA     C:\Users\williams.IMAGINEDLANDS\AppData\Local
LOGONSERVER                   \\CORPSERVER64
NUMBER_OF_PROCESSORS          4
OS                            Windows_NT
Path  C:\Windows\system32;C:\Windows;C:\Windows\System32\Wbem...
PATHEXT                       .COM;.EXE;.BAT;.CMD;.VBS;.VBE;.JS;
                              .JSE;.WSF;.WSH;.MSC;.CPL
PROCESSOR_ARCHITECTURE        AMD64
PROCESSOR_IDENTIFIER          Intel64 Family 6 Model 58
PROCESSOR_LEVEL               6
PROCESSOR_REVISION            3a09
ProgramData                   C:\ProgramData
ProgramFiles                  C:\Program Files
ProgramFiles(x86)             C:\Program Files (x86)
ProgramW6432                  C:\Program Files
PSModulePath     C:\Users\williams.IMAGINEDLANDS\Documents\...
PUBLIC                        C:\Users\Public
SESSIONNAME                   RDP-Tcp#9
SystemDrive                   C:
SystemRoot                    C:\Windows
TEMP                 C:\Users\WILLIA~1.IMA\AppData\Local\Temp
TMP                  C:\Users\WILLIA~1.IMA\AppData\Local\Temp
USERDNSDOMAIN                 IMAGINEDLANDS.LOCAL
```

```
USERDOMAIN                    IMAGINEDLANDS
USERDOMAIN_ROAMINGPROFILE     IMAGINEDLANDS
USERNAME                       williams
USERPROFILE                   C:\Users\williams.IMAGINEDLANDS
windir                        C:\Windows
```

Managing Date and Time

You can get the current date and time using Get-Date. To use Get-Date, simply type
the cmdlet name at the PowerShell prompt and press Enter. The output of Get-Date
is the current date and time as shown in the following example and sample output:

```
get-date

Friday, December 15, 2021 11:12:58 PM
```

If you want only the current date or current time, use the –DisplayHint parameter.
While the output of Get-Date –DisplayHint Date is the current date—such as Friday,
December 15, 2017—the output of Get-Date –DisplayHint Time is the current time,
such as 11:12:58 PM. Here is an example and sample output:

```
get-date -displayhint time

11:18:33 AM
```

To set the date, time, or both, you must use an administrator PowerShell prompt.
Simply follow Set-Date with the desired date and time enclosed in quotation marks.

You enter the current date in MM-DD-YY format, where *MM* is for the two-digit
month, *DD* is for the two-digit day, and *YY* is for the two-digit year, such as typing
12-20-21 for December 20, 2021, as shown in the following example:

```
set-date "12-20-21"
```

You enter the current time in HH:MM or HH:MM:SS format, where *HH* is for the two-
digit hour, *MM* is for the two-digit minute, and *SS* is for the two-digit second. If you
enter the time without designating AM for A.M. or PM for P.M., the time command
assumes you are using a 24-hour clock, where hours from 00 to 11 indicate A.M. and
hours from 12 to 23 indicate P.M. The following example sets the time to 3:30 P.M.:

```
set-date "3:30 PM"
```

You can set the date and time at the same time. All of the following examples set the date and time to December 20, 2021, 5:15 P.M.:

```
set-date "12-20-21 5:15 PM"
set-date "12-20-21 05:15:00 PM"
set-date "12-20-21 17:15:00"
```

You also can adjust the time forward or backward using the –Adjust parameter. Type **Set-Date -Adjust** followed by the time adjustment. Specify the time change in HH:MM:SS format. The following example sets the time ahead 30 minutes:

```
set-date -adjust 00:30:00
```

To adjust the time backward, use a minus sign (–) to indicate that you want to subtract time. The following example sets the time back one hour:

```
set-date -adjust -01:00:00
```

> **TIP** The Get-Date cmdlet returns a DateTime object. Before you experiment with setting the date and time, store the current date and time in a variable by typing **$date = get-date**. When you are done testing, restore the date and time by typing **set-date $date**. Then adjust the time as necessary to get the current time exactly.

Specifying Credentials

When you are working with some cmdlets and objects in PowerShell that modify system information, you might need to specify a credential for authentication. Whether in a script or at the prompt, the easiest way to do this is to use Get-Credential to obtain a Credential object and save the result in a variable for later use. Consider the following example:

```
$cred = get-credential
```

When PowerShell reads this command, PowerShell prompts you for a user name and password and then stores the credentials provided in the $cred variable. It is important to point out that the credentials prompt is displayed simply because you typed **Get-Credential**.

You also can specify that you want the credentials for a specific user in a specific domain. In the following example, you request the credentials for the TestUser account in the DevD domain:

```
$cred = get-credential -credential devd\testuser
```

A Credential object has UserName and Password properties that you can work with. Although the user name is stored as a regular string, the password is stored as a secure, encrypted string. Knowing this, you can reference the user name and password stored in $cred as follows:

```
$user = $cred.username
$password = $cred.password
```

Examining the Working Environment

Sometimes when you are working with a computer, you'll want to obtain detailed information on the system configuration or the operating system. With mission-critical systems, you might want to save or print this information for easy reference. Items that help you gather detailed system information include the following:

- **Get-HotFix** Gets information about service packs and updates applied to the local computer or specified computers. Use –Id to look for a specific hotfix by its identifier. Use –Description to get hotfixes by type.

```
Get-HotFix [[-Id | -Description] HotFixes] {AddtlParams}

AddtlParams=
 [-Credential Credential] [-ComputerName ComputerName1,
ComputerName2, ...]
```

- **Win32_ComputerSystem** Lists detailed information about the local computer or a specified computer.

```
Get-Wmiobject -Class Win32_ComputerSystem [-ComputerName
ComputerName1, ComputerName2, ...] [-Credential Credential] | fl *
```

- **Win32_OperatingSystem** Lists detailed information about the operating system installed on the local computer or a specified computer.

```
Get-Wmiobject -Class Win32_OperatingSystem [-ComputerName
```

```
ComputerName1, ComputerName2, ...] [-Credential Credential] | fl *
```

- **Win32_UserAccount** Lists the user accounts created or available on a computer, which can include local user accounts and domain user accounts.

```
Get-Wmiobject -Class Win32_UserAccount [-ComputerName
ComputerName1, ComputerName2, ...] [-Credential Credential] | format-
list Caption, Name, Domain, FullName, SID
```

- **Win32_Group** Lists the groups created or available on a computer, which can include local user accounts and domain user accounts.

```
Get-Wmiobject -Class Win32_Group [-ComputerName ComputerName1,
ComputerName2, ...] [-Credential Credential] | format-list Caption,
Name, Domain, SID
```

To use these commands on a local computer, simply type the commands on a single line using the syntax shown.

Checking Updates and Service Packs

With Get-HotFix, you can use the –ComputerName parameter to specify computers to examine in a comma-separated list as shown in this example:

```
get-hotfix -ComputerName fileserver84, dcserver32, dbserver11
```

However, to access remote computers, you'll often need to provide credentials, and you can do this using the –Credential parameter. Note that although you can provide credentials for remote connections, you typically won't be able to provide credentials for working with the local computer (and this is why you need to start with an elevated, administrator prompt if required). The following example shows how you can prompt directly for a required credential:

```
get-hotfix -Credential (get-credential) -ComputerName fileserver84,
dcserver32, dbserver11
```

You also can use a stored credential as shown in this example:

```
$cred = get-credential
get-hotfix -Credential $cred -ComputerName fileserver84, dcserver32,
dbserver11
```

Because you'll often work with the same remote computers, you might want to get the names of the remote computers from a file. To do this, enter each computer name on a separate line in a text file and save this text file to a location where you can always access it, such as a network share. Then get the content from the file as your input to the –ComputerName parameter as shown in this example:

```
get-hotfix –Credential (get-credential) –ComputerName (get-content
c:\data\servers.txt)
```

Or get it as shown in this example and sample output:

```
$comp = get-content c:\data\servers.txt
$cred = get-credential
get-hotfix –Credential $cred –ComputerName $comp

Source      Description        HotFixID   InstalledBy   InstalledOn
------      -----------        --------   -----------   -----------
CORPPC38    Update             KB3048778  NT AUTHORITY\SYSTEM
                                                        12/19/2020 12:00:00 AM
CORPPC38    Update             KB3049508  NT AUTHORITY\SYSTEM
                                                        11/29/2020 12:00:00 AM
CORPPC38    Security Update    KB3049563  NT AUTHORITY\SYSTEM
                                                        12/19/2020 12:00:00 AM
CORPPC38    Security Update    KB3050514  NT AUTHORITY\SYSTEM
                                                        12/19/2020 12:00:00 AM
CORPPC38    Hotfix             KB3046737  NT AUTHORITY\SYSTEM
                                                        12/19/2020 12:00:00 AM
```

Here, you are getting a list of hotfixes on a specified set of remote computers using credentials you entered when prompted. Each hotfix is listed by

- **Source**   Shows the name of the source computer.
- **Description**   Shows the type of hotfix. Types of hotfixes include software update, security update, and service pack. Hotfixes also can be listed simply as *update* or *hotfix*.
- **HotFixID**   Shows the identifier for the hotfix, which can be a globally unique identifier (GUID), an update identification number, or a knowledge base identification number.
- **InstalledBy**   Shows the name of the user who installed the update. If a specific user name is listed, this user installed the update or the update was installed on

behalf of the user when the user was logged on. If the user is listed as NT AUTHORITY\SYSTEM, the update was automatically installed by Windows Update.

▪ **InstalledOn**   Shows the date and time the update was installed.

Using the –Id and –Description parameters, you can look for hotfixes with a specific identifier or a specific descriptive type. In the following example and sample output, you look for security updates installed on the local computer:

```
get-hotfix -description "Security Update"

Source      Description        HotFixID  InstalledBy   InstalledOn
------      -----------        --------  -----------   -----------
CORPPC38    Security Update    KB3008923 NT AUTHORITY\SYSTEM
                                                   12/28/2020 12:00:00 AM
CORPPC38    Security Update    KB3010788 NT AUTHORITY\SYSTEM
                                                   12/13/2016 12:00:00 AM
CORPPC38    Security Update    KB3011780 NT AUTHORITY\SYSTEM
                                                   12/21/2016 12:00:00 AM
CORPPC38    Security Update    KB3013126 NT AUTHORITY\SYSTEM
                                                   12/28/2020 12:00:00 AM
```

When you are trying to determine the update status of computers throughout the enterprise, you can take this idea a step further by logging the output or by tracking computers that don't have a particular update installed. For example, if KB3013126 is an important security update that you want to ensure is installed on specific computers, you can type the name of each computer to check on a separate line in a text file and store this list in a file named computers.txt. Next, you can use Get-HotFix to check each of these computers and log your findings. One approach is shown in the following example:

```
$comp = get-content c:\data\computers.txt
$comp | foreach { if (!(get-hotfix -id KB3013126 –computername $_))
{ add-content $_ -path log.txt }}
```

Here, you retrieve a list of computer names and store each computer name as an item in an array called $comp, and then you use a ForEach loop to take an action on each item (computer name) in the array. That action is an If Not test that executes Get-HotFix for each computer. As a result, if a computer does not have the required hotfix, you write the computer's name to a file called log.txt in the current working directory. When you use $_ in this way, it refers to the current item in a specified array, which in this case is the name of a computer.

Obtaining Detailed System Information

When inventorying computers in the enterprise, you'll also want to use the Win32_OperatingSystem and Win32_ComputerSystem classes. You use the Win32_OperatingSystem object and its properties to obtain summary information regarding the operating system configuration, as shown in the following example and partial output:

```
Get-WmiObject -Class Win32_OperatingSystem |`Format-List *

Status             : OK
Name               : Microsoft Windows 10 Pro
|C:\Windows|\Device\Harddisk0\Partition3
FreePhysicalMemory                      : 6665648
FreeSpaceInPagingFiles                  : 804536
FreeVirtualMemory                       : 7100676
BootDevice                              : \Device\HarddiskVolume2
BuildNumber                             : 9600
BuildType                               : Multiprocessor Free
Caption                                 : Microsoft Windows 10 Pro
CodeSet                                 : 1252
CountryCode                             : 1
```

When you are working with Win32_OperatingSystem, some of the most important information includes the following:

- The amount of free physical memory and free virtual memory, which are tracked in the TotalVisibleMemorySize and TotalVirtualMemorySize properties, respectively.
- The boot device, system directory, build number, build type, and operating system type, which are tracked in the BootDevice, SystemDirectory, BuildNumber, BuildType, and Caption properties, respectively.
- The encryption level and operating system architecture, which are tracked in the EncryptionLevel and OSArchitecture properties, respectively.
- The last boot-up time, which is tracked in the LastBootUp time property.

The TotalVisibleMemorySize and TotalVirtualMemorySize are shown in kilobytes. To quickly convert the values provided to megabytes, copy each value separately, paste it at the PowerShell prompt, and then type **/1kb**. For example, if the TotalVisibleMemorySize is 3403604, you type **3403604/1kb** and the answer is 3323.832 MB.

> **NOTE**   Are you wondering why I didn't use **/1mb** to get a value in megabytes? The value of the kb constant is 1024. The value of the mb constant is 1048576. If a value is in bytes, you can type **/1mb** to convert the value to megabytes. However, if the value is in kilobytes already, you must divide by 1024 to convert the value to megabytes.

Knowing this, you can obtain and store the memory values in megabytes using the following technique:

```
$os = get-wmiobject -class win32_operatingsystem
$AvailMemInMB = $os.totalvisiblememorysize/1kb
$VirtualMemInMB = $os.totalvirtualmemorysize/1kb
```

Whether you are at the PowerShell prompt or working in a script, the $AvailMemInMB and $VirtualMemInMB variables are then available for your use.

The boot device, system device, system directory, and build information provide essential information about the configuration of the operating system. You can use this information to determine the physical disk device on which Windows is installed, the actual directory in the file system, the type of build as either single or multiprocessor, and the exact operating system version installed.

Knowing this, you can obtain and store the related information using the following technique:

```
$os = get-wmiobject -class win32_operatingsystem
$BootDevice = $os.bootdevice
$SystemDevice = $os.systemdevice
$SystemDirectory = $os.systemdirectory
$BuildType = $os.buildtype
$OSType = $os.caption
```

You can then work with these values as necessary. For example, if you want to perform an action only when Windows 10 is installed, you can use the following technique:

```
$os = get-wmiobject -class win32_operatingsystem
$OSType = $os.caption

if ($OSType -match "Windows 10") {
   #Windows 10 is installed; run the commands in this code block
} else {
   #Windows 10 is not installed; run these commands instead
}
```

Using the LastBootUpTime property of the Win32_OperatingSystem object, you can determine how long a computer has been running since it was last started. To do this, you perform a comparison of the current date and time with the date and time stored in the LastBootUpTime property. However, because the value stored in this property is a string rather than a DateTime object, you must first convert the string value to a DateTime object using the ConvertToDateTime() method. An example and sample output follows:

```
$date = get-date
$os = get-wmiobject -class win32_operatingsystem
$uptime = $os.ConvertToDateTime($os.lastbootuptime)
write-host ($date - $uptime)

09:20:57.2639083
```

Here, you store the current date and time in the $date variable; then you use Get-WmiObject to get the Win32_OperatingSystem object. Next, you use the ConvertToDateTime() method to convert the string value in the LastBootUpTime property to a DateTime object. Finally, you perform a comparison of the current date and the boot date and display the difference. In this example, the computer has been running about 9 hours and 20 minutes.

You use the Win32_ComputerSystem object and its properties to obtain summary information regarding the computer configuration as shown in the following example and partial output:

```
Get-WmiObject -Class Win32_ComputerSystem | Format-List *
```

```
AdminPasswordStatus          : 1
BootupState                  : Normal boot
ChassisBootupState           : 3
KeyboardPasswordStatus       : 2
PowerOnPasswordStatus        : 1
PowerSupplyState             : 3
PowerState                   : 0
FrontPanelResetStatus        : 2
ThermalState                 : 3
Status                       : OK
Name                         : CORPSERVER84
```

With the Win32_ComputerSystem object, there is a great deal of useful information about the computer and its configuration. Some of the most important information includes the following:

- The boot-up state and status of the computer, which are tracked in the BootUpState and Status properties, respectively.
- The name, DNS host name, domain, and domain role, which are tracked in the Name, DNSHostName, Domain, and DomainRole properties, respectively.
- The system type and total physical memory, which are tracked in the properties SystemType and TotalPhysicalMemory, respectively. Note that the total memory available is shown in bytes, not kilobytes.

The boot-up state and status can help you decide whether you want to modify the configuration of a computer, which is helpful when you are working with a remote computer and you don't know its current status. In the following example, you perform one block of commands if the computer is in a normal state and another block of commands if the computer is in a different state:

```
$cs = get-wmiobject -class win32_computersystem
$BootUpState = $cs.bootupstate

if ($BootUpState -match "Normal") {
   "Computer is in a normal state, so run these commands."
} else {
   "Computer not in a normal state, so run these commands."
}
```

A computer's name and domain information also can help you decide whether you want to work with the computer. For example, although you might want to reconfigure desktops and laptops, you might not want to reconfigure servers and domain controllers. To help you avoid modifying computers of a specific type inadvertently, you can perform actions based on a computer's role as shown in this example:

```
$cs = get-wmiobject -class win32_computersystem
$DomainRole = $cs.domainrole

switch -regex ($DomainRole) {
  [0-1] { "This computer is a workstation." }
  [2-3] { "This computer is a server but not a dc."}
  [4-5] { "This computer is a domain controller."}
  default { "Unknown value."}
}
```

In the shift to 64-bit computing, you might want to track which computers in the enterprise support 64-bit operating systems, which computers are already running 64-bit operating systems, or both. To determine whether a computer has a 64-bit operating system installed already, you can use the OSArchitecture property of the Win32_OperatingSystem object. To determine whether a computer supports a 64-bit operating system, you can use the Name and Description properties of the Win32_Processor object.

You can type the name of each computer to check on a separate line in a text file and store this list in a file called computers.txt.

Next, you can use Get-WmiObject to check each of these computers and log your findings. One approach is shown in the following example:

```
$comp = get-content computers.txt

#Get list of computers that don't have 64-bit OS installed
$comp | foreach {
 $os = get-wmiobject -class win32_operatingsystem -computername $_
 $OSArch = $os.osarchitecture
 if (!($OSArch -match "32-bit")) { add-content $_ -path next.txt
 }
}

#Determine which computers without 64-bit OS can have 64-bit OS
$comp2 = get-content next.txt
$comp2 | foreach {
```

```
$ps = get-wmiobject -class win32_processor -computername $_
$SystemType = $ps.description
if ($SystemType -like "*x64*") { add-content $_ -path final.txt
}
}
```

Here, you retrieve a list of computer names from a file called computers.txt in the current working directory and store each computer name as an item in an array called $comp. Then you use a ForEach loop to take an action on each item (computer name) in the array. As a result, if a computer has a 32-bit operating system installed, you write the computer's name to a file called next.txt in the current working directory. When you use $_ in this way, it refers to the current item in a specified array, which in this case is the name of a computer.

In the final series of commands, you retrieve the list of computers that don't have 64-bit operating systems installed and store each computer name as an item in an array called $comp2. Then you use a ForEach loop to take an action on each item (computer name) in the array. As a result, if a computer is capable of having a 64-bit operating system installed, you write the computer's name to a file called final.txt in the current working directory. The result is a quick but clean approach to inventorying your computers. Any computer listed in final.txt is capable of having a 64-bit operating system but currently has a 32-bit operating system.

Determining Available Users and Groups

As part of your inventory of computers in the enterprise, you'll often want to know what users and groups have been created and are available. One way to examine users and groups is to use the Win32_UserAccount and Win32_Group classes. As shown in the following example and sample output, Win32_UserAccount lists user accounts by name, domain, and more:

```
Get-Wmiobject -Class Win32_UserAccount | format-list
Caption,Name,Domain

Caption : TECHPC76\Administrator
Name : Administrator
Domain : TECHPC76

Caption : TECHPC76\Barney
```

```
Name : Barney
Domain : TECHPC76
```

Here, you are working with the local computer. If the user or group was created on the local computer, the computer name is set as the domain. Otherwise, the Active Directory domain name is set as the domain.

You can use the –ComputerName parameter to specify the remote computer or computers that you want to work with and –Credential to specify credentials required for authentication. To see how these could be used, consider the following example:

```
$cred = get-credential
$comp = get-content c:\data\computers.txt

$comp | foreach { Get-Wmiobject -Class Win32_UserAccount
-ComputerName $_ -Credential $cred }
```

Here, you prompt the user for a credential and store the credential in the $cred variable. Then you retrieve a list of computer names and store each computer name as an item in an array called $comp. Afterward, you use a ForEach loop to take an action on each item (computer name) in the array. That action is to list the user accounts available on the computer.

Because some scheduled jobs and backup processes require a computer to have a specific local user or group available, you might want to determine whether computers have this user or group. One way to do this is shown in the following example:

```
$comp = get-content computers.txt

#Get list of computers that don't have the BackUpUser account
$comp | foreach {

 $Global:currentc = $_
 $ua = get-wmiobject -class win32_useraccount -computername $_

 $ua | foreach {
  $user = $_.name
  if ($user -eq "sqldb") {add-content $currentc -path valid.txt}
  }
}
```

Here, you retrieve a list of computer names from a file called computers.txt in the current working directory and store each computer name as an item in an array called $comp. Then you use a ForEach loop to take an action on each item (computer name) in the $comp array. First, you store the current computer name in a global variable so that you can access it later. Then you retrieve objects representing all the user accounts on the computer and store these in an array called $ua. Next, you use a second ForEach loop to take action on each item (group object) in the $ua array. As a result, if a computer has a group called SqlDb, you write the computer's name to a file called valid.txt in the current working directory.

Because we are using direct matching, you can use the –Filter parameter of the Get-WmiObject to get only the user account you are looking for in the first place. The –Filter parameter works like a Where clause in a WMI query. Here is an example of the revised code:

```
$comp = get-content computers.txt

#Get list of computers that don't have the BackUpUser account
$comp | foreach {
if (get-wmiobject -class win32_useraccount -computername `
 $_ -filter "Name='sqldb'") { add-content $_ -path valid.txt }
}
```

> **NOTE** For clarity, we added the line continuation character.

The syntax for the Where clause in the string passed to the –Filter parameter is important. Because you use double quotes to enclose the string, you must use single quotes to match a specific property value.

You can work with Win32_Group in much the same way. Although this is a quick and easy way to inventory users and groups, you'll want to use the Active Directory cmdlets to work with and manage users and groups. Other useful Win32 classes for inventorying computers include Win32_BIOS, Win32_NetworkAdapterConfiguration, Win32_PhysicalMemory, Win32_Processor, and Win32_LogicalDisk.

Evaluating System Hardware

When you are working with computers in the enterprise, you'll often need to obtain detailed configuration information for hardware components. This configuration information will help you evaluate hardware to ensure it is functioning properly and help you diagnose and resolve difficult issues, such as hardware malfunctions and improper configurations.

Checking Firmware Versions and Status

A computer's firmware can be the source of many hardware problems. The firmware must be configured properly and should be kept current with the latest revision.

You can use Win32_BIOS to examine the status, version, language, and manufacturer of a computer's BIOS firmware. When you are trying to determine whether a computer's BIOS is up to date, look at the SMBIOSBIOSVersion information. An example and sample output using WIN32_BIOS follow:

```
get-wmiobject win32_bios | format-list * |
Out-File -append -filepath save.txt


PSComputerName          : CORPPC38
Status                  : OK
Name                    : BIOS Date: 11/30/20 18:51:30 Ver: A05.00
Caption                 : BIOS Date: 11/30/20 18:51:30 Ver: A05.00
SMBIOSPresent           : True
__PATH                  :
\\CORPPC38\root\cimv2:Win32_BIOS.Name="BIOS Date: 11/30/20
18:51:30 Ver: A05.00 ",SoftwareElementID="BIOS Date: 11/30/20
BiosCharacteristics     : {7, 9, 11, 12...}
BIOSVersion             : {DELL   - 1072009, BIOS Date: 11/30/20
                          18:51:30 Ver: A05.00 }
CurrentLanguage         : en|US|iso8859-1
Description             : BIOS Date: 11/30/20 18:51:30 Ver: A05.00
ListOfLanguages         : {en|US|iso8859-1}
Manufacturer            : Dell Inc.
OtherTargetOS           :
PrimaryBIOS             : True
ReleaseDate             : 20170330000000.000000+000
SMBIOSBIOSVersion       : A05
SMBIOSMajorVersion      : 2
SMBIOSMinorVersion      : 7
```

```
SoftwareElementID      : BIOS Date: 11/30/20 18:51:30 Ver: A05.00
SoftwareElementState   : 3
TargetOperatingSystem  : 0
Version                : DELL   - 1072009
```

To help keep your computers current, you might want to inventory the firmware versions that are installed and determine whether computers need a firmware update. The SMBIOSBIOSVersion property provides the value you can use to do this. In the following example, you retrieve the BIOS version for a group of computers and store the computer name and BIOS version in a file called bioscheck.txt:

```
$comp = get-content computers.txt

#Store BIOS version for each computer
$comp | foreach {
 $bios = get-wmiobject -class win32_bios -computername $_
 $BiosVersion = $bios.SMBIOSBIOSVersion
 add-content ("$_ $BiosVersion") -path bioscheck.txt
}
```

If your organization has standardized its computers, you might want to determine whether the BIOS version for a group of computers is up to date. One way to do this is to check to see if the current BIOS version is installed and log information about computers that have a different BIOS version, as shown in this example:

```
 $comp = get-content computers.txt

$comp | foreach {
 $bios = get-wmiobject -class win32_bios -computername $_
 $BiosVersion = $bios.SMBIOSBIOSVersion
 if (!($BiosVersion -match "A05")) {
   add-content ("$_ $BiosVersion") -path checkfailed.txt }
}
```

Checking Physical Memory and Processors

Few things affect a computer's performance more than the physical memory and processors that are installed. You'll want to ensure computers have adequate memory and processors to support their daily tasks.

You can use Win32_PhysicalMemory to get detailed information for each individual DIMM of memory on a computer as well as status indicators that could indicate problems. A DIMM is a group of memory chips on a card handled as a single unit.

Many computers have an even number of memory card banks, such as two or four. A computer's memory cards should all have the same data width and speed. An example and sample output using Win32_PhysicalMemory follow:

```
get-wmiobject Win32_PhysicalMemory | format-list *  |
Out-File -append -filepath save.txt

__PATH                 : \\CORPPC38\root\cimv2:
                         Win32_PhysicalMemory.Tag="Physical Memory 1"
BankLabel              : BANK 1
Capacity               : 4294967296
Caption                : Physical Memory
DataWidth              : 64
Description            : Physical Memory
DeviceLocator          : ChannelA-DIMM1
FormFactor             : 8
HotSwappable           :
InstallDate            :
InterleaveDataDepth    : 2
InterleavePosition     : 1
Manufacturer           : Samsung
MemoryType             : 0
Model                  :
Name                   : Physical Memory
Speed                  : 1600
Status                 :
Tag                    : Physical Memory 1
TotalWidth             : 64
TypeDetail             : 128
Version                :
```

Depending on the type of computer and operating system, either the BankLabel entry or the DeviceLocation entry will show the channel and DIMM number, such as CHAN A DIMM 0 or ChannelA-DIMM1. Capacity is shown in bytes. To quickly convert the value provided to megabytes, copy the value and paste it at the PowerShell prompt and then type **/1mb**, such as **4294967296/1mb**.

The Status entry tells you the current error status. The error status can help you identify a malfunctioning DIMM. The error status also can help you identify a DIMM that is not valid for the computer.

REAL WORLD Windows and Windows Server have built-in features to help you identify and diagnose problems with memory. If you suspect a computer has a memory problem that isn't being automatically detected, you can run the Windows Memory Diagnostics utility by completing the following steps:

1. Run mdsched.exe. As an example, in the Start screen, type **mdsched.exe** in the Everywhere Search box, and then press Enter.

2. Choose whether to restart the computer and run the tool immediately or schedule the tool to run at the next restart.

3. Windows Memory Diagnostics runs automatically after the computer restarts and performs a standard memory test automatically. If you want to perform fewer or more tests, press F1, use the Up and Down arrow keys to set the Test Mix as Basic, Standard, or Extended, and then press F10 to apply the desired settings and resume testing.

4. When testing is completed, the computer restarts automatically. You'll see the test results when you log on.

Note also that if a computer crashes because of failing memory, and Windows Memory Diagnostics detects this, you are prompted to schedule a memory test the next time the computer is restarted.

The total memory capacity is the sum of the capacity of all memory banks on the computer. The Win32_PhysicalMemoryArray class has a MaxCapacity property that tracks the total physical memory in kilobytes as well as a MemoryDevices property that tracks the number of memory banks.

You can use Win32_Processor to get detailed information about each processor on a computer. When you are working with processors, note the clock speed, data width, deviceID, and cache details as well as the number of cores and number of logical processor. A single processor might have multiple processor cores, and each of those processor cores might have a logical representation. Processor cache usually is shown in kilobytes. Most computers have both L2 and L3 cache. An example and sample output using Win32_Processor follow:

```
get-wmiobject Win32_Processor | format-list * |
Out-File -append -filepath save.txt
```

```
PSComputerName                        : CORPPC38
Availability                          : 3
CpuStatus                             : 1
CurrentVoltage                        :
DeviceID                              : CPU0
ErrorCleared                          :
ErrorDescription                      :
LastErrorCode                         :
LoadPercentage                        : 2
Status                                : OK
StatusInfo                            : 3
AddressWidth                          : 64
DataWidth                             : 64
ExtClock                              : 100
L2CacheSize                           : 1024
L2CacheSpeed                          :
MaxClockSpeed                         : 3201
PowerManagementSupported              : False
ProcessorType                         : 3
Revision                              : 14857
SocketDesignation                     : CPU 1
Version                               :
VoltageCaps                           : 4
__PATH                                :
\\CORPPC38\root\cimv2:Win32_Processor.DeviceID="CPU0"
Architecture                          : 9
Caption                               : Intel64 Family 6 Model 58
Stepping 9
ConfigManagerErrorCode                :
ConfigManagerUserConfig               :
CreationClassName                     : Win32_Processor
CurrentClockSpeed                     : 3200
Description                           : Intel64 Family 6 Model 58
Stepping 9
Family                                : 205
InstallDate                           :
L3CacheSize                           : 6144
L3CacheSpeed                          : 0
Level                                 : 6
Manufacturer                          : GenuineIntel
Name                                  : Intel(R) Core(TM) i5-3470
CPU @ 3.20GHz
NumberOfCores                         : 4
NumberOfLogicalProcessors             : 4
```

```
OtherFamilyDescription                       :
PNPDeviceID                                  :
PowerManagementCapabilities                  :
ProcessorId                                  : BFEBFBFF000306A9
Role                                         : CPU
SecondLevelAddressTranslationExtensions :     True
Stepping                                     :
SystemCreationClassName                      : Win32_ComputerSystem
SystemName                                   : CORPPC38
UniqueId                                     :
UpgradeMethod                                : 36
VirtualizationFirmwareEnabled                : True
VMMonitorModeExtensions                      : True
```

In the output, note the ErrorCleared, ErrorDescription, and Status properties. These properties can help you identify a malfunctioning processor. Note error details or error conditions that are shown, and take corrective action as appropriate. For example, if a processor has an error status that restarting the computer doesn't resolve, you might need to service the motherboard, the processor, or both. In some cases, updating the motherboard firmware can resolve intermittent errors.

Checking Hard Disks and Partitions

Hard disks are used to store data. Computers need enough disk space to accommodate the operating system files, the working environment, and user data. To ensure proper performance, hard disks need ample free space as well because this ensures housekeeping tasks and disk cleanup activities can be performed automatically as necessary.

WMI provides several Win32 classes for working with disk drives. Using Win32_DiskDrive, you can work with physical drives, including both fixed hard drives and USB reader devices. If you want to see only a computer's fixed hard disks, you can filter on the media type as shown in the following example and sample output:

```
get-wmiobject -class win32_diskdrive -filter
"MediaType='Fixed hard disk media'"

Partitions : 2
DeviceID    : \\.\PHYSICALDRIVE0
Model       : ST3500630AS
Size        : 500105249280
```

```
Caption     : ST3500630AS
Partitions : 1
DeviceID    : \\.\PHYSICALDRIVE1
Model       : ST3500630AS
Size        : 500105249280
Caption     : ST3500630AS
Partitions : 4
DeviceID    : \\.\PHYSICALDRIVE2
Model       : ST500DM002-1BD142
Size        : 500105249280
Caption     : ST500DM002-1BD142
```

The computer in this example has two fixed hard drives. PhysicalDrive0 has two disk partitions. PhysicalDrive1 has one disk partition.

If you filter the output by the device ID or caption, you can get information that is more detailed for individual fixed hard drives. In the following example and sample output, you examine a fixed hard drive by its caption:

```
get-wmiobject -class win32_diskdrive -filter
"Caption='ST500DM002-1BD142'" | format-list *
```

```
ConfigManagerErrorCode    : 0
LastErrorCode             :
NeedsCleaning             :
Status                    : OK
DeviceID                  : \\.\PHYSICALDRIVE0
StatusInfo                :
Partitions                : 2
BytesPerSector            : 512
ConfigManagerUserConfig   : False
DefaultBlockSize          :
Index                     : 0
InstallDate               :
InterfaceType             : SCSI
SectorsPerTrack           : 63
Size                      : 500105249280
TotalCylinders            : 60801
TotalHeads                : 255
TotalSectors              : 976768065
TotalTracks               : 15504255
TracksPerCylinder         : 255
Caption                   : ST3500630AS
CompressionMethod         :
ErrorCleared              :
```

```
ErrorDescription          :
ErrorMethodology          :
FirmwareRevision          : 3.AA
Manufacturer              : (Standard disk drives)
MediaLoaded               : True
MediaType                 : Fixed hard disk media
Model                     : ST3500630AS
Name                      : \\.\PHYSICALDRIVE0
SCSIBus                   : 0
SCSILogicalUnit           : 0
SCSIPort                  : 0
SCSITargetId              : 0
```

As you can see, the detailed information tells you the exact configuration of the physical device, including:

- The number of bytes per sector, sectors per track, and tracks per cylinder.
- The interface type, such as SCSI or IDE.
- The size in bytes. Divide the value by 1gb to get the size in gigabytes.
- The total number of cylinders, heads, sectors, and tracks.
- The bus, logical unit, port, and target ID.

In the output, note the ErrorCleared, ErrorDescription, ErrorMethodology, and Status properties. These properties can help you identify a malfunctioning disk. Note error details or error conditions that are shown, and take corrective action as appropriate. For example, if a processor has an error status that restarting the computer doesn't resolve, you might need to service the hardware controller, the hard disk, or both. In some cases, updating the controller firmware can resolve intermittent errors.

You can use Win32_DiskPartition to obtain partitioning details for each fixed hard disk on the computer. The partitions correspond exactly to how you've partitioned fixed hard disks using Disk Management. As shown in the following example and sample output, each partition of each fixed hard disk is accessible:

```
get-wmiobject -class win32_diskpartition

NumberOfBlocks    : 18603207
BootPartition     : False
Name              : Disk #0, Partition #0
PrimaryPartition  : True
Size              : 9524841984
```

```
Index            : 0

NumberOfBlocks   : 958164795
BootPartition    : True
Name             : Disk #0, Partition #1
PrimaryPartition : True
Size             : 490580375040
Index            : 1

NumberOfBlocks   : 976768002
BootPartition    : False
Name             : Disk #1, Partition #0
PrimaryPartition : True
Size             : 500105217024
Index            : 0
```

The key information you need to know is listed as part of the standard output, so you might not need to view the extended properties. In this example, the computer has two fixed hard disks: Disk 0 and Disk 1. Disk 0 has two partitions: Partition 0 and Partition 1. Disk 1 has one partition: Partition 0. Because partition size is shown in bytes, you can divide the value listed by 1gb to get the size of the partition in gigabytes.

Windows represents formatted disk partitions as logical disks. The WMI object you can use to work with logical disks is Win32_LogicalDisk, which you can use to get detailed information for each logical disk on a computer. However, note that removable disks, CD/DVD drives, and paths assigned drive letters are also represented as logical disks. You can distinguish among these elements using the Description property. Values you'll see include:

- CD-ROM Disc, for CD/DVD drives
- Removable Disk, for removable disks
- Local Fixed Disk, for fixed hard drives

When you are working with the logical representation of partitions on fixed hard disks, note the device ID, compression status, file system type, free space, size, and supported options. DeviceID shows the drive designator, such as C:. An example and sample output using Win32_LogicalDisk follow:

```
get-wmiobject -class win32_logicaldisk -filter "name='c:'" |
format-list * | Out-File -append -filepath save.txt
```

```
Status                         :
Availability                   :
DeviceID                       : C:
StatusInfo                     :
Access                         : 0
BlockSize                      :
Caption                        : C:
Compressed                     : False
ConfigManagerErrorCode         :
ConfigManagerUserConfig        :
CreationClassName              : Win32_LogicalDisk
Description                    : Local Fixed Disk
DriveType                      : 3
FileSystem                     : NTFS
FreeSpace                      : 298870042624
InstallDate                    :
LastErrorCode                  :
MaximumComponentLength         : 255
MediaType                      : 12
Name                           : C:
NumberOfBlocks                 :
QuotasDisabled                 : True
QuotasIncomplete               : False
QuotasRebuilding               : False
Size                           : 490580373504
SupportsDiskQuotas             : True
SupportsFileBasedCompression   : True
SystemCreationClassName        : Win32_ComputerSystem
SystemName                     : ENGPC42
VolumeDirty                    : False
VolumeName                     :
VolumeSerialNumber             : 008EA097
```

The FreeSpace and Size properties are shown in bytes. To quickly convert the value provided to gigabytes, copy the value, paste it at the PowerShell prompt, and then type **/1gb**, such as **302779912192/1gb**. Here is an example and sample output:

```
$dr = get-wmiobject -class win32_logicaldisk -filter "name='c:'"
$free = [Math]::Round($dr.freespace/1gb)
$capacity = [Math]::Round($dr.size/1gb)

write-host $dr.name "on" $dr.systemname
write-host "Disk Capacity: $capacity"
write-host "Free Space: $free"
```

```
C: on ENGPC42
Disk Capacity: 457
Free Space: 278
```

Checking and Managing Device Drivers

Computers can have all sorts of hardware devices installed on and connected to them. Because all of these devices require device drivers to operate properly, you'll often want to know detailed information about a particular device's driver. For example, you might want to know whether the device driver is:

- Enabled or disabled.
- Running or stopped.
- Configured to start automatically.

The Win32 class for working with device drivers is Win32_SystemDriver. Using Win32_SystemDriver, you can obtain detailed configuration and status information on any device driver configured for use on a computer. You can examine device drivers by device display name using the DisplayName property, by state using the State property, or by start mode using the StartMode property. The display name for a device and its driver is the same as the one shown in Device Manager.

In the following example, you use the DisplayName property to check the RAID controller on a computer:

```
get-wmiobject -class win32_systemdriver | where-object
{$_.displayname -like "*raid c*"} | format-list *

Status                   : OK
Name                     : iaStor
State                    : Running
ExitCode                 : 0
Started                  : True
ServiceSpecificExitCode  : 0
AcceptPause              : False
AcceptStop               : True
Caption                  : Intel RAID Controller
CreationClassName        : Win32_SystemDriver
Description              : Intel RAID Controller
DesktopInteract          : False
DisplayName              : Intel RAID Controller
```

```
ErrorControl          : Normal
InstallDate           :
PathName              : C:\Windows\system32\drivers\iastor.sys
ServiceType           : Kernel Driver
StartMode             : Boot
StartName             :
SystemCreationClassName : Win32_ComputerSystem
SystemName            : ENGPC42
TagId                 : 25
Site                  :
Container             :
```

Generally, State is shown as either Running or Stopped. Knowing this, you can check for device drivers in either state as shown in the following example and sample output:

```
get-wmiobject -class win32_systemdriver -filter "state='Running'"

DisplayName : Microsoft ACPI Driver
Name        : ACPI
State       : Running
Status      : OK
Started     : True

DisplayName : Ancillary Function Driver for Winsock
Name        : AFD
State       : Running
Status      : OK
Started     : True
```

The start mode can be set as:

- **Boot**   Used for boot device drivers
- **Manual**   Used for device drivers that are started manually
- **Auto**   Used for device drivers that are started automatically
- **System**   Used for system device drivers

Using StartMode for your filter, you can list boot device drivers as shown in the following example:

```
get-wmiobject -class win32_systemdriver -filter "startmode='Boot'"
```

The Win32_SystemDriver class provides a number of methods for managing system drivers. These methods include:

- **Change()** Changes the device driver configuration. It accepts the following parameters in the following order: DisplayName, PathName, ServiceTypeByte, ErrorControlByte, StartMode, DesktopInteractBoolean, StartName, StartPassword, LoadOrderGroup, LoadOrderGroupDependenciesArray, and ServiceDependenciesArray.

> **CAUTION** Modifying devices at the PowerShell prompt is not something you should do without careful forethought. PowerShell lets you make changes that will make your computer unbootable. Before you make any changes to devices, you should create a system restore point as discussed in Chapter 13, "Enabling Recovery." You also might want to consider performing a full backup of the computer.

- **ChangeStartMode()** Changes the start mode of the device driver. It accepts a single parameter, which is the start mode to use. Valid values are boot, manual, auto, or system.

> **CAUTION** Before you change the start mode of a device driver, ensure the driver supports this start mode. You also should ensure that the start mode won't affect the computer's ability to start.

- **Delete()** Deletes the device driver (if the device is in a state that allows this). Deleting the device driver doesn't prevent the device from being used. To prevent the device from being used, you should disable it instead. If you delete a device driver without disabling a device, Windows will, in most cases, detect and reinstall the device the next time the computer is started. As part of troubleshooting, you can sometimes delete a device's driver to force Windows to reinstall the device.

> **CAUTION** Exercise extreme caution if you plan to delete device drivers using PowerShell. PowerShell will not warn you if you are making harmful changes to your computer.

- **InterrogateService()** Connects to the device using the device driver. If the return value is zero, WMI was able to connect to and interrogate the device using the device driver. If the return value isn't zero, WMI encountered a problem while trying to communicate with the device using the device driver. If the device is stopped or paused, this method always returns an error status.

- **PauseService()** Pauses the device, which might be necessary during troubleshooting or diagnostics. Devices that can be paused indicate this when the AcceptPause property is set to True for their device drivers. Further, you can pause only a device that is in a state where pausing is permitted.

- **ResumeService()** Resumes the device after it has been paused.

- **StopService()** Stops the device, which might be necessary during troubleshooting or diagnostics. Devices that can be stopped indicate this when the AcceptStop property is set to True for their device drivers. Further, you can stop only a device that is in a state where stopping is permitted.

- **StartService()** Starts a stopped device, including devices that are configured for manual start up.

If you want to change the start mode for a device driver, you can use the ChangeStartMode() method to specify the desired start mode. The basic syntax is

```
$driverObject.ChangeStartMode(StartMode)
```

where $driverObject is a reference to a Win32_SystemDriver object, and StartMode is the desired start mode entered as a string value, as shown in this example and sample output:

```
$d = get-wmiobject -class win32_systemdriver | where-object
{$_.displayname -like "creative audio*"}
```

```
$d.changestartmode("auto")
```

```
__GENUS          : 2
__CLASS          : __PARAMETERS
__SUPERCLASS     :
__DYNASTY        : __PARAMETERS
__RELPATH        :
__PROPERTY_COUNT : 1
__DERIVATION     : {}
__SERVER         :
__NAMESPACE      :
__PATH           :
ReturnValue      : 0
```

Here, you set the start mode to Auto for a Creative Audio device. The return value in the output is what you want to focus on. A return value of 0 (zero) indicates success. Any other return value indicates an error. Typically, errors occur because you aren't using an administrator PowerShell prompt, you haven't accessed the correct device driver, or the device isn't in a state in which it can be configured. Keep in mind that if you alter the configuration of required device drivers, you might not be able to start the computer. Because of this, don't make any changes to device drivers without careful planning and forethought.

Digging In Even More

Want to really dig in and explore what's available on a computer? Enter the following command as a single line to list every available .NET type:

```
[System.AppDomain]::CurrentDomain.GetAssemblies() |
Foreach-Object { $_.GetTypes() }
```

You can expand on this idea by creating a function and then calling this function with various filters to find specific .NET types. The code for a ListType function follows:

```
function ListType() {
  [System.AppDomain]::CurrentDomain.GetAssemblies() |
  Foreach-Object { $_.GetTypes() }
}
```

To list all .NET types, you can call the ListType function without any filters, as shown in this example:

```
ListType
```

You can view specific .NET types if you check for names that are like a specified value. For example, to list all .NET types with "parser" as part of the name, you could enter

```
ListType | ? { $_.Name -like "*parser*" }
```

To learn more about a .NET type, you can look at the constructors for the type. The following example lists the constructors for all .NET types with "parser" as part of the name:

```
ListType | ? { $_.Name -like "*parser*" } |
 % { $_.GetConstructors() }
```

Pretty cool. However, not every .NET type is loaded for use. Therefore, to use a .NET type you find, you might need to load it before you use it.

Another cool trick is to examine the available COM objects on a computer. COM objects are registered in the registry, and by exploring the appropriate registry branches, you can find COM objects that are registered for use on the computer. A function for checking the registry follows:

```
function ListProgID {
  param()
  $paths = @("REGISTRY::HKEY_CLASSES_ROOT\CLSID")
  if ($env:Processor_Architecture -eq "amd64") {
    $paths+="REGISTRY::HKEY_CLASSES_ROOT\Wow6432Node\CLSID" }

  Get-ChildItem $paths -include VersionIndependentPROGID `
 -recurse | Select-Object @{
    Name='ProgID'
    Expression={$_.GetValue("")}
  }, @{
    Name='Type'
    Expression={
      if ($env:Processor_Architecture -eq "amd64") { "Wow6432" }
      else { "32-bit" }
    }
  }
}
```

> **NOTE** For clarity, we added the line continuation character.

Here, you check the processor architecture on the computer. If the computer is running a 32-bit operating system, you look under HKEY_CLASSES_ROOT\CLSID for 32-bit COM objects. If the computer is running a 64-bit operating system, you look under HKEY_CLASSES_ROOT\CLSID for 32-bit COM objects and under HKEY_CLASSES_ROOT\Wow6432Node\CLSID for additional COM objects. You then list the registered COM objects by their progID and type.

To use this function to list all COM objects by their ProgID and type, you could enter the following command:

```
ListProgID
```

You can view specific COM objects if you check for names that are like a specified value. For example, to list all COM objects with "Microsoft" as part of the name, you could enter

```
ListProgID | Where-Object { $_.ProgID -like "*Microsoft*" }
```

Have fun; there's a lot here to explore. For more information on objects, .NET types, and COM objects, see Chapter 22, "COM and .NET," in *PowerShell: IT Pro Solutions*.

Part III: Managing File Systems and the Registry

Chapter 9. Managing File Systems

In this chapter, you'll learn techniques for managing file systems and security—and there's a lot more flexibility to this than most people realize. You can create, copy, move, and delete individual directories and files. You can read and write files, and you also can append data to files and clear the contents of files. You can examine and set access control lists on directories and files, and you also can take ownership of directories and files. Moreover, because you are working with PowerShell, it's just as easy to manipulate multiple directories and files matching specific parameters you specify as it is to work with individual directories and files.

Working with PowerShell Drives, Directories, and Files

You can use PowerShell to manage drives, directories, and files. The core set of features for performing related procedures were discussed previously in Chapter 8, "Using Providers," in *PowerShell: IT Pro Solutions*, and include the FileSystem provider, the cmdlets for working with data stores, and the cmdlets for working with provider drives.

Adding and Removing PowerShell Drives

Using the Get-PSDrive cmdlet, you can view the PowerShell drives that currently are available. As the following example and sample output shows, this includes actual drives and the resources PowerShell lets you work with as if they were drives:

```
get-psdrive
```

```
Name       Used (GB)     Free (GB)  Provider       Root
----       ---------     ---------  --------       ----
Alias                                Alias
C            87.75        149.53     FileSystem     C:\
Cert                                 Certificate    \
D              .04          7.90     FileSystem     D:\
E                                    FileSystem     E:\

Env                                  Environment
Function                             Function
HKCU                                 Registry       HKEY_CURRENT_USER
HKLM                                 Registry       HKEY_LOCAL_MACHINE
```

> **NOTE** To query multiple computers, use the Invoke-Command cmdlet as discussed in Chapter 11, "Executing Remote Commands," in *PowerShell: IT Pro Solutions*. Here is an example:
>
> invoke-command -computername Server43, Server27, Server82 -scriptblock { get-psdrive }

You can change the working location to any of these drives using Set-Location. Simply follow the cmdlet name with the desired drive or path relative to a drive, such as

```
set-location c:
```

or

```
set-location c:\logs
```

When you switch drives using only the drive designator, PowerShell remembers the working path, allowing you to return to the previous working path on a drive simply by referencing the drive designator.

You can use the New-PSDrive cmdlet to create a PowerShell drive that is mapped to a location in a data store, which can include a shared network folder, local directory, or registry key. The drive acts as a shortcut and is available only in the current PowerShell console. For example, if you frequently work with the C:\Data\Current\History\Files directory, you might want to create a new drive to quickly reference this location. When you create a drive, you specify the alias to the drive using the –Name parameter, the provider type using the –PSProvider parameter, and the root path using the –Root parameter, as shown in this example:

```
new-psdrive -name hfiles -psprovider filesystem -root
c:\data\current\history\files
```

Here, you create a drive called *hfiles* as a FileSystem type to act as a shortcut to C:\Data\Current\History\Files. You can switch to this drive by typing **set-location hfiles:**. As long as you have the appropriate permissions to create drives, the creation process should be successful. A common error you might see occurs when a like-named drive already exists.

Because the drive exists only in the current PowerShell session, the drive ceases to exist when you exit the PowerShell console. You also can remove a drive using Remove-PSDrive. Although you can remove drives you added to the console, you cannot delete Windows drives or mapped network drives created by using other methods.

> **NOTE** You can create a drive that maps to registry locations as well. If you do, the PSProvider type to reference is registry. Type **get-psprovider** to list all available provider types.

Creating and Managing Directories and Files

In PowerShell, you work with directories and files in much the same way. You view directories and files using Get-ChildItem as shown in many previous examples. To create directories and files, you use New-Item. The basic syntax is

```
new-item –type [Directory | File] –path Path
```

where you specify the type of item you are creating as either *Directory* or *File* and then use *Path* to specify where the directory or file should be created. When you create a directory or file, New-Item displays results that confirm the creation process. In the following example, you create a C:\Logs\Backup directory, and the resulting output confirms that the directory was successfully created:

```
new-item -type directory -path c:\logs\backup

    Directory: C:\logs
Mode            LastWriteTime      Length  Name
----            -------------      ------  ----
d----           7/18/2020   4:54 PM         backup
```

> **NOTE** To create directories and files on remote computers, use the Invoke-Command cmdlet as discussed in Chapter 11, "Executing Remote Commands," in *PowerShell: IT Pro Solutions*. Here is an example:
>
> invoke-command -computername Server43, Server27, Server82
>
> -scriptblock { new-item -type directory -path c:\logs\backup }

As long as you have the appropriate permissions to create a directory or file in the specified location, the creation process should be successful. The New-Item cmdlet even creates any required subdirectories for you automatically. In this example, if the C:\Logs directory doesn't exist, PowerShell creates this directory and then creates the Backup subdirectory. When you create a file, PowerShell creates an empty file with no contents.

Using similar procedures, you can copy, move, rename, and delete directories and files.

Copying Directories and Files

You can copy directories and files using Copy-Item. The basic syntax for directories and their contents is

```
copy-item SourcePath DestinationPath -recurse
```

where *SourcePath* is the path to the directory to copy, and *DestinationPath* is where you'd like to create a copy of the directory. In the following example, you copy the C:\Logs directory (and all its contents) to C:\Logs_Old:

```
copy-item c:\logs c:\logs_old -recurse
```

The command will create the Logs_Old directory if it does not already exist. The basic syntax for copying files is

```
copy-item PathToSourceFile DestinationPath
```

where *PathToSourceFile* is the path to the file or files to copy, and *DestinationPath* is where you'd like to create a copy of the file or files. In the following example, you copy all the .txt files in the C:\Logs directory to C:\Logs_Old:

```
copy-item c:\logs\*.txt c:\logs_old
```

As long as you have the appropriate permissions, you should be able to copy directories and files. You can use Copy-Item to copy resources across volumes as shown in the following example:

```
copy-item c:\logs d:\logs_old -recurse
```

Moving Directories and Files

You can move directories and files using Move-Item. The basic syntax is

```
move-item SourcePath DestinationPath
```

where *SourcePath* is the current path to the directory or file, and *DestinationPath* is the new path for the directory or file. When you move a directory or file, Move-Item displays an error that indicates failure but doesn't display any output to indicate success. In the following example, you move the C:\Logs directory (and all its contents) to C:\Backup\Logs:

```
move-item c:\logs c:\backup\logs
```

The following command moves all the .txt files in the C:\Logs directory to C:\Backup\Logs:

```
move-item c:\logs\*.txt c:\backup\logs
```

As long as you have the appropriate permissions, you should be able to move directories and files. However, some caveats apply. Because you cannot use Move-Item to move resources across volumes, the source and destination path must have identical roots. If files in a directory are in use, a file is in use, or a directory is shared, you won't be able to move the directory or file.

Renaming Directories and Files

To rename directories and files, you use the Rename-Item cmdlet. Rename-Item has the following syntax:

```
rename-item OriginalNamePath NewName
```

where *OriginalNamePath* is the full path to the directory or file, and *NewName* is the new name for the directory or file. In the following example, you rename Log1.txt in the C:\Logs directory as Log1_hist.txt:

```
rename-item c:\logs\log1.txt log1_hist.txt
```

As long as you have the appropriate permissions, you should be able to rename directories and files. However, if files in a directory are in use, a file is in use, or a directory is shared, you won't be able to rename the directory or file.

Deleting Directories and Files

You can delete directories and files using the Remove-Item cmdlet. Remove-Item has the following syntax:

```
remove-item NamePath [-force]
```

where *NamePath* is the full path to the directory or file that you want to remove, and *–Force* is an optional parameter to force the removal of a directory or file. In the following example, you delete the D:\Logs_Old directory (and all its contents):

```
remove-item d:\logs_old
```

As long as you have the appropriate permissions, you should be able to remove directories and files. However, if files in a directory are in use, a file is in use, or a directory is shared, you won't be able to remove the directory or file. Additionally, if a directory or file is marked Read-Only, Hidden, or System, use the –Force parameter to remove it.

Working with File Contents

Often when you are working with computers, you'll want to create your own configuration and inventory records or logs to record your activities. PowerShell makes this easy by providing a simple set of commands for reading the contents of files and writing new contents to files.

Commands for Managing File Contents

Commands that help you access file resources include the following:

- **Get-Content** Displays the contents of files in a specified location. Use –Force to force access to a hidden, system, or read-only file. Use –TotalCount to specify the number of lines in each matching file to display. Use –Include to limit the matches to files meeting specific criteria. Use –Exclude to omit specified files. Both –Include and –Exclude accept wildcard characters.

```
Get-Content [-LiteralPath | -Path] FilePath {AddtlParams}

AddtlParams=
[-Credential Credential] [-Delimiter String] [-Encoding
Encoding] [-Exclude FilesToExclude] [-Force] [-Include
FilesToInclude] [-TotalCount Count]
```

> **REAL WORLD** Many PowerShell cmdlets accept –Path and –LiteralPath
> parameters. Both parameters specify the path to an item. However, it's
> important to note that unlike –Path, the value of –LiteralPath is used exactly as
> it is typed. This means no characters are interpreted as wildcards. If a path
> includes actual escape characters, enclose them in single quotation marks
> because this tells PowerShell not to interpret any characters as escape
> sequences.

- **Set-Content**   Overwrites the contents of files in a specified location. Use –Force to force access to a hidden, system, or read-only file. Specify the content to write using the –Value parameter or by pipelining input from another command. Use –Include to limit the matches to files meeting specific criteria. Use –Exclude to omit specified files. Both –Include and –Exclude accept wildcard characters.

```
Set-Content [-LiteralPath | -Path] FilePath [-Value Content]
{AddtlParams}

AddtlParams=
[-Credential Credential] [-Encoding Encoding] [-Exclude
FilesToExclude] [-Force] [-Include FilesToInclude]
```

- **Add-Content**   Adds contents to files in a specified location. Use –Force to force access to a hidden, system, or read-only file. Specify the content to write using the –Value parameter or by pipelining input from another command.

```
Add-Content [-LiteralPath | -Path] FilePath [-Value NewContent]
{AddtlParams}

AddtlParams=
[-Credential Credential] [-Encoding Encoding] [-Exclude
FilesToExclude] [-Force] [-Include FilesToInclude]
```

- **Clear-Content** Clears the contents of files in a specified location. Use –Force to force access to a hidden, system, or read-only file. Use –Include to limit the matches to files meeting specific criteria.

```
Add-Content [-LiteralPath | -Path] FilePath {AddtlParams}

AddtlParams=
[-Credential Credential] [-Exclude FilesToExclude] [-Force]
[-Include FilesToInclude]
```

Reading and Writing File Content

By default, Get-Content searches the current directory for a file you specify by name or by partial name using wildcards and then displays its contents as text. This means you can quickly display the contents of any text-based file at the prompt simply by typing **Get-Content** followed by the name of a file in the current directory. The following example gets the log1.txt file in the current directory:

```
get-content log1.txt
```

To display the contents of a file in a specified path, type the full path to the file. The following example gets the log1.txt file in the C:\Logs directory:

```
get-content c:\logs\log1.txt
```

If you use wildcards, you can display the contents of any files that match the wildcard criteria. The following example displays the contents of any file in the C:\Logs directory that begins with "log":

```
get-content c:\logs\log*
```

To restrict wildcard matches to specific types of files, use the –Include parameter. To exclude specific files or types of files, use the –Exclude parameter. For example, to match only files with the .txt and .log extension, you can enter

```
get-content -include *.txt, *.log -path c:\logs\log*
```

Alternatively, to exclude .xml files and match all other files beginning with "log", you can enter

```
get-content -exclude *.xml -path c:\logs\log*
```

Additionally, if you want to see only the first few lines of matching files, use –
TotalCount to specify the number of lines in each matching file to display. The
following example displays the first 10 lines of each matching file:

```
get-content -totalcount 10 -path c:\logs\log*
```

Other cmdlets for working with the contents of files include Set-Content, Add-
Content, and Clear-Content. Set-Content overwrites the contents of one or more
files in a specified location with content you specify. Add-Content adds content you
specify to the end of one or more files in a specified location. Clear-Content removes
the contents of files in a specified location. Because Clear-Content does not delete
the files, this results in files with no contents (empty files).

Chapter 10. Configuring Security and Auditing

As an administrator, some of the most important tasks you perform have to do with configuring and maintaining file-system security. PowerShell makes this easy by providing a simple set of commands for viewing and configuring security descriptors. If you save a transcript of your work or use a script to perform the work, you can easily duplicate your efforts on one computer on other computers in the enterprise.

Commands for Working with Security Descriptors

Commands that help you access file resources include the following:

- **Get-Acl** Gets objects that represent the security descriptor of a file, registry key, or any other resource with a provider that supports the concept of security descriptors. Use –Audit to get the audit data for the security descriptor from the access control list.

```
Get-Acl [-Path] FilePaths {AddtlParams}

AddtlParams=
[-Audit] [-Exclude FilesToExclude] [-Include FilesToInclude]
[-AllCentralAccessPolicies]
```

- **Set-Acl** Changes the security descriptor of a file, registry key, or any other resource with a provider that supports the concept of security descriptors. Use –AclObject to set the desired security settings.

```
Set-Acl [-Path] FilePaths [-Aclobject] Security {AddtlParams}

AddtlParams=
[-Exclude FilesToExclude] [-Include FilesToInclude]
[[-CentralAccessPolicy] PolicyName]
[-ClearCentralAccessPolicy]
```

> **NOTE** On NTFS file system volumes, access permissions control access to files and directories. If you do not have appropriate access permissions, you will not be able to work with files and directories.

Getting and Setting Security Descriptors

Whenever you are working with system resources—such as directories, files, or registry keys—you might want to view or modify a resource's security descriptor. Use Get-Acl with the –Path parameter to specify the path to resources you want to work with. As with Get-Content, you can use wildcard characters in the path and also include or exclude files using the –Include and –Exclude parameters.

Get-Acl returns a separate object containing the security information for each matching file. By default, Get-Acl displays the path to the resource, the owner of the resource, and a list of the access control entries on the resource. The access control list is controlled by the resource owner. To get additional information—including the security group of the owner, a list of auditing entries, and the full security descriptor as an SDDL (Security Descriptor Definition Language) string—format the output as a list as shown in the following example and sample output:

```
get-acl c:\windows\system32\windowspowershell | format-list

Path: Microsoft.PowerShell.Core\FileSystem::
C:\windows\system32\windowspowershell
Owner   : NT AUTHORITY\SYSTEM
Group   : NT AUTHORITY\SYSTEM
Access  : NT SERVICE\TrustedInstaller Allow  FullControl
          NT SERVICE\TrustedInstaller Allow  268435456
          NT AUTHORITY\SYSTEM Allow  FullControl
          NT AUTHORITY\SYSTEM Allow  268435456
          BUILTIN\Administrators Allow  FullControl
          BUILTIN\Administrators Allow  268435456
          BUILTIN\Users Allow  ReadAndExecute, Synchronize
          BUILTIN\Users Allow  -1610612736
          CREATOR OWNER Allow  268435456
Audit   :
Sddl    : O:SYG:SYD:AI(A;ID;FA;;;S-1-5-80-956008885-3418522649-
1831038044-1853292631-2271478464)(A;CIIOID;GA;;;S-1-5-80-956008885-
3418522649-1831038044-1853292631-2271478464)(A;ID;FA;;;SY)
(A;OICIIOID;GA;;;SY)(A;ID;FA;;;BA)(A;OICIIOID;GA;;;BA)(A;ID;0x1200a9;
;;BU)(A;OICIIOID;GXGR;;;BU)(A;OICIIOID;GA;;;CO)
```

Here, Get-Acl returns a DirectorySecurity object representing the security descriptor of the C:\Windows\System32\WindowsPowerShell directory. The result is then sent to the Format-List cmdlet.

You can work with files in the same way. Here is an example:

```
get-acl -include *.txt, *.log -path c:\logs\log* | format-list
```

Here, Get-Acl returns FileSecurity objects representing the security descriptors of each matching file. The results are then sent to the Format-List cmdlet.

You can work with any properties of security objects separately, including:

- **Owner**   Shows the owner of the resource
- **Group**   Shows the primary group the owner is a member of
- **Access**   Shows the access control rules on the resource
- **Audit**   Shows the auditing rules on the resource
- **Sddl**   Shows the full security descriptor as an SDDL string

> **NOTE**   FileSecurity and DirectorySecurity objects have additional properties that aren't displayed as part of the standard output. To see these properties, send the output to Format-List *. You'll then see the following note and script properties: PSPath (the PowerShell path to the resource), PSParentPath (the PowerShell path to the parent resource), PSChildName (the name of the resource), PSDrive (the PowerShell drive on which the resource is located), AccessToString (an alternate representation of the access rules on the resource), and AuditToString (an alternate representation of the audit rules on the resource).

You can use the objects that Get-Acl returns to set the security descriptors on other system resources, including directories, files, and registry keys. To do this, you'll want to do the following:

1.   Open an administrator PowerShell prompt.
2.   Obtain a single security descriptor object for a resource that has the security settings you want to use.
3.   Use the security descriptor object to establish the desired security settings for another resource.

When you are setting security descriptors in PowerShell, it is a best practice either to specify exactly what you are including, what you are excluding, or both, or to specify only a single resource to modify. Previously, we were working with a log file named log1.txt in the C:\Logs directory. If this log file has a security descriptor that you want to apply to another file, you can do this as shown in the following example:

```
set-acl -path c:\logs\log2.txt -aclobject (get-acl c:\logs\log1.txt)
```

Here you use the security descriptor on log1.txt to set the security descriptor for log2.txt.

You can easily extend this technique. In this example, you use the security descriptor on log1.txt to set the security descriptor for all other .txt and .log files in the C:\Logs directory:

```
$secd = get-acl c:\logs\log1.txt
set-acl -include *.txt, *.log -path c:\logs\* -aclobject $secd
```

To include files in subdirectories, you need to use Get-ChildItem to obtain reference objects for all the files you want to work with. Here is an example:

```
$s = get-acl c:\logs\log1.txt

gci c:\logs -recurse -include *.txt, *.log -force |
set-acl -aclobject $s
```

Here, *gci* is an alias for Get-ChildItem. You obtain the security descriptor for log1.txt. Next you get a reference to all .txt and .log files in the C:\Logs directory and all subdirectories. Finally, you use the security descriptor on log1.txt to set the security descriptor for all these files.

If you want to work with directories rather than files, you need to limit the results returned by Get-ChildItem. For files and directories, each resource object returned by Get-ChildItem includes a Mode property as shown in the following example and sample output:

```
get-childitem c:\

    Directory: C:\
Mode                LastWriteTime         Length Name
----                -------------         ------ ----
d----         9/17/2020   2:10 PM                apps
da---         8/16/2020  10:58 AM                ClusterStorage
d----          6/1/2020   8:45 AM                data
```

```
d----            10/4/2020   11:50 AM             Drivers
d----             8/3/2020    4:26 PM             ExchangeSetupLogs
d----            4/26/2020    1:29 PM             inetpub
d----            10/4/2020   12:00 PM             Intel
d----            8/22/2016    8:22 AM             PerfLogs
d-r--            5/23/2016    9:26 AM             Program Files
d-r--            5/19/2020    2:57 PM             Program Files (x86)
d----            4/26/2020    2:56 PM             root
d-r--             6/1/2020    9:48 AM             Users
d----            5/19/2020    4:02 PM             Windows
```

The valid values for modes are the following:

- d (directory)
- a (archive)
- r (read-only)
- h (hidden)
- s (system)

Therefore, if you want to work only with directories, you can look for resources where the mode contains a *d* or is like *d**, for example,

```
where-object {$_.mode -like "d*"}
```

In addition, if you want to work only with files, you can use

```
where-object {$_.mode -notlike "d*"}
```

Knowing this, you can copy the security descriptor on C:\Data to C:\Logs and all its subdirectories as shown in this example:

```
gci c:\logs -recurse -force | where-object {$_.mode -like "d*"}
| set-acl -aclobject (get-acl c:\data)
```

Alternatively, you can copy the security descriptor on C:\Data\key.txt to all files in C:\Logs and all its subdirectories, as shown here:

```
gci c:\logs -recurse -force | where-object {$_.mode –notlike
"d*"} | set-acl -aclobject (get-acl c:\data\key.txt)
```

> **NOTE** For these examples to work, the directories and files must exist. If you want to try these examples on your computer, create the C:\Data and C:\Logs

directories and then add several .txt files to these directories, including a file called key.txt.

Working with Access Rules

As you can see, it is fairly easy and straightforward to copy security descriptors from one resource to another—and more importantly, the same techniques apply to any type of resource that has security descriptors, whether you are working with files, directories, registry keys, or whatever. If you want to create your own security descriptors, we'll have to dig deeper into the security object model. In this model, access control rules, such as security descriptors, are represented as objects. The Access property of security objects is defined as a collection of authorization rules. With directories and files, these rules have the following object type:

System.Security.AccessControl.FileSystemAccessRule

You can view the individual access control objects that apply to a resource in several ways. One way is to get a security descriptor object and then list the contents of its Access property as shown in the following example and sample output:

```
$s = get-acl c:\logs
$s.access

FileSystemRights   : FullControl
AccessControlType  : Allow
IdentityReference  : BUILTIN\Administrators
IsInherited        : True
InheritanceFlags   : None
PropagationFlags   : None

FileSystemRights   : ReadAndExecute, Synchronize
AccessControlType  : Allow
IdentityReference  : BUILTIN\Users
IsInherited        : True
InheritanceFlags   : ContainerInherit, ObjectInherit
PropagationFlags   : None

FileSystemRights   : Modify, Synchronize
AccessControlType  : Allow
IdentityReference  : NT AUTHORITY\Authenticated Users
IsInherited        : True
InheritanceFlags   : None
```

```
PropagationFlags    : None
```

Here you get the DirectorySecurity object for the C:\Logs directory and then display the contents of its Access property. Although each value listed is an access rule object, you cannot work with each access rule object separately. Note the following in the output:

- **FileSystemRights**   Shows the file system rights being applied
- **AccessControlType**   Shows the access control type as Allow or Deny
- **IdentityResource**   Shows the user or group to which the rule applies
- **IsInherited**   Specifies whether the access rule is inherited
- **InheritanceFlags**   Shows the way inheritance is being applied
- **PropagationFlags**   Specifies whether the access rule will be inherited

Another way to work with each access rule object separately is to use a ForEach loop as shown in this example:

```
$s = get-acl c:\logs

foreach($a in $s.access) {

 #work with each access control object

 if ($a.identityreference -like "*administrator*")
 {$a | format-list *}
}

FileSystemRights   : FullControl
AccessControlType  : Allow
IdentityReference  : BUILTIN\Administrators
IsInherited        : True
InheritanceFlags   : None
PropagationFlags   : None
```

Here, you examine each access rule object separately, which allows you to take action on specific access rules. In this example, you look for access rules that apply to administrators.

As an administrator, you'll often want to perform similar searches to find files and folders that aren't configured to allow access that might be required to perform backups or other administrative tasks. Previously, we discussed using Get-ChildItem to work with directories and files. For directories and files, each resource object returned by Get-ChildItem includes a Mode property that you can use to work with either directories or files. In the following example and sample output, you list every subdirectory and file under C:\logs that doesn't allow administrators full control:

```
$resc = gci c:\logs -recurse -force | where-object `
{$_.mode -notlike "*hs*"}

foreach($r in $resc) {
  $s = get-acl $r.FullName
  $found = $false

  foreach($a in $s.access) {
  if (($a.identityreference -like "*administrator*") -and `
    ($a.filesystemrights -eq "fullcontrol")) {
      if ($a.accesscontroltype -eq "allow") { $found = $true }
  }
  }

  if (-not $found) { write-host $r.FullName}
}
```

```
C:\logs\backup
C:\logs\backup2
C:\logs\logs
C:\logs\data.ps1
C:\logs\log1.txt
C:\logs\log2.txt
C:\logs\log3.txt
C:\logs\log4.txt
C:\logs\backup\backup
C:\logs\backup\backup\b2
```

Here, you should run the code using an administrator PowerShell prompt. The $resc variable stores a collection of objects that includes all files and directories under C:\logs, except for files and directories marked as Hidden or System. Using a ForEach loop, you then examine each related resource object. First, you get the access control list for the object by referencing the full name of the object. Then you initialize the $found variable to False so that you can use this variable to track whether a file has the access rights you are looking for.

In the second ForEach loop, you examine each access control object associated with a particular file or folder. If a resource allows administrators full control, you set

$found to True. Because you are checking the status of three properties, you use a logical AND to check two properties first. If those properties are both set as expected, you check the third property to see if it is True also. Finally, if $found is not True (meaning it's False), you write the full name of the file or folder to the output. The result is a list of all files and folders that are not configured so that all administrators have full control.

Configuring File and Directory Permissions

On NTFS volumes, you can assign two types of access permissions to files and directories: Basic and Special. These permissions grant or deny access to users and groups.

Setting Basic Permissions

The basic permissions you can assign to directories and files are shown in Table 10-1 and Table 10-2. These permissions are made up of multiple special permissions. Note the rule flag for each permission because this is the value you must reference when creating an access rule.

TABLE 10-1 Basic Folder Permissions

PERMISSION	DESCRIPTION	RULE FLAG
Full Control	This permission permits reading, writing, changing, and deleting files and subdirectories. If a user has Full Control over a folder, she can delete files in the folder regardless of the permission on the files.	FullControl
Modify	This permission permits reading and writing to files and subdirectories, and it allows deletion of the folder.	Modify
List Folder Contents	This permission permits viewing and listing files and subdirectories as well as executing files; it's inherited by directories only.	Synchronize

PERMISSION	DESCRIPTION	RULE FLAG
Read & Execute	This permission permits viewing and listing files and subdirectories as well as executing files; it's inherited by files and directories.	ReadAndExecute
Write	This permission permits adding files and subdirectories.	Write
Read	This permission permits viewing and listing files and subdirectories.	Read

TABLE 10-2 Basic File Permissions

PERMISSION	DESCRIPTION	RULE FLAG
Full Control	This permission permits reading, writing, changing, and deleting the file.	FullControl
Modify	This permission permits reading and writing of the file; it allows deletion of the file.	Modify
Read & Execute	This permission permits viewing and accessing the file's contents as well as executing the file.	ReadAndExecute
Write	This permission permits writing to a file. Giving a user permission to write to a file but not to delete it doesn't prevent the user from deleting the file's contents.	Write
Read	This permission permits viewing or accessing the file's contents. Read is the only permission needed to run scripts. Read access is required to access a shortcut and its target.	Read

When you are configuring basic permissions for users and groups, you can specify the access control type as either Allowed or Denied. If a user or group should be granted an access permission, you allow the permission. If a user or group should be denied an access permission, you deny the permission.

You configure basic permissions for resources using access rules. Access rules contain collections of arrays that define

- The user or group to which the rule applies.
- The access permission that applies.
- The allow or deny status.

This means regardless of whether you are adding or modifying rules, the basic syntax for an individual access rule is

```
"UserOrGroupName", "ApplicablePermission", "ControlType"
```

where *UserOrGroupName* is the name of the user or group to which the access rule applies, *ApplicablePermission* is the basic permission you are applying, and *ControlType* specifies the allow or deny status. User and group names are specified in COMPUTER\Name or DOMAIN\Name format. In the following example, you grant full control to BackupOpUser:

```
"BackupOpUser", "FullControl", "Allow"
```

When you are working with folders, you can use the basic syntax to configure permissions for folders. You also can use an expanded syntax to configure permissions for a folder and its contents. The expanded syntax for an access rule is

```
"UserOrGroupName", "ApplicablePermission", "InheritanceFlag",
"PropagationFlag","ControlType"
```

where *UserOrGroupName* is the name of the user or group to which the access rule applies, *ApplicablePermission* is the basic permission you are applying, *InheritanceFlag* controls inheritance, *PropagationFlag* controls propagation of inherited rules, and *ControlType* specifies the type of access control. In the following example, you grant full control to *DeploymentTesters* and apply inheritance to the folder and all its subfolders:

```
"BackupOpUser", "FullControl", "ContainerInherit", "None", "Allow"
```

With the inheritance flag, you can specify one of the following flag values:

- **None** The access rule is not inherited by child objects.

- **ContainerInherit**   The access rule is inherited by subfolders (child container objects).
- **ObjectInherit**   The access rule is inherited by files (child objects).
- **ContainerInherit, ObjectInherit**   The access rule is inherited by files and subfolders (child objects and child container objects).

With the propagation flag, you can specify the following flag values:

- **None**   The access rule is propagated without modification.
- **InheritOnly**   The access rule is propogated to immediate child and child container objects.
- **NoPropagateInherit**   The access rule applies to child objects and to child container objects but not to child objects of child container objects.
- **NoPropagateInherit, InheritOnly**   The access rule applies to child container objects.

You add access rules to a resource using either the SetAccessRule() method or the AddAccessRule() method of the access control object. You remove access rules from a resource using the RemoveAccessRule() method of the access control object. As discussed previously, access rules are defined as having the System.Security.AccessControl.FileSystemAccessRule type.

The easiest way to add and remove access rules is to

1. Get an access control object. This object can be the one that applies to the resource you want to work with or one that applies to a resource that has the closest access control permissions to those you want to use.

2. Create one or more instances of the System.Security.AccessControl.FileSystemAccessRule type, and store the desired permissions in these object instances.

3. Call AddAccessRule() or RemoveAccessRule() to add or remove access rules as necessary. These methods operate on the access control object you retrieved in the first step.

4. To apply the changes you've made to an actual resource, you must apply the access control object to a specified resource.

Consider the following example:

```
set-alias no new-object

$acl = get-acl c:\logs
$perm = "imaginedlands\dev","fullcontrol","allow"

$r = no system.security.accesscontrol.filesystemaccessrule $perm
$acl.addaccessrule($r)
$acl | set-acl c:\logs
```

Here, you get the access control object on C:\Logs. You store the values for an access rule in a variable called $perm and then create a new instance of the FileSystemAccessRule type for this access rule. The Dev group in the ImaginedLands domain must exist to create the access rule. To add the permission to the access control object you retrieved previously, you call its AddAccessRule() method. Although you could have created additional permissions and added or removed these, you didn't in this example. Finally, you applied the access control object to a specific resource using Set-Acl.

You can easily extend the previous examples to apply to multiple directories and files as shown in the following example:

```
set-alias no new-object

$acl = get-acl c:\logs
$perm = "room5\test","fullcontrol","allow"
$r = no system.security.accesscontrol.filesystemaccessrule $perm
$acl.addaccessrule($r)

$resc = gci c:\logs -recurse -force
foreach($f in $resc) {

  write-host $f.fullname
  $acl | set-acl $f.FullName
}

C:\logs\backup
C:\logs\backup2
C:\logs\logs
C:\logs\data.ps1
C:\logs\log1.txt
C:\logs\log2.txt
C:\logs\log3.txt
C:\logs\log4.txt
C:\logs\backup\backup
```

```
C:\logs\backup\backup\b2
```

Here, you apply an access control list with a modified permission set to every subdirectory of C:\Logs and every file in C:\Logs and its subdirectories. The Test group on the local computer (named Room5) must exist to create the access rule. In the output, you list the names of the directories and files you've modified. This helps you keep track of the changes.

Setting Special Permissions

The special permissions you can assign to directories and files are shown in Table 10-3. Because special permissions are combined to make the basic permissions, they are also referred to as *atomic permissions*. As with basic permissions, note the rule flag for each permission because this is the value you must reference when creating an access rule. When an item has two rule flags, you need to reference only one or the other to set the related special permission.

TABLE 10-3 Special Permissions

PERMISSION	DESCRIPTION	RULE FLAG
Traverse Folder/Execute File	Traverse Folder lets you directly access a folder even if you don't have explicit access to read the data it contains. Execute File lets you run an executable file.	Traverse, ExecuteFile
List Folder/Read Data	List Folder lets you view file and folder names. Read Data lets you view the contents of a file.	ListDirectory, ReadData
Read Attributes	Lets you read the basic attributes of a file or folder. These attributes include Read-Only, Hidden, System, and Archive.	ReadAttributes

PERMISSION	DESCRIPTION	RULE FLAG
Read Extended Attributes	Lets you view the extended attributes (named data streams) associated with a file. These include Summary fields, such as Title, Subject, and Author, as well as other types of data.	ReadExtendedAttributes
Create Files/Write Data	Create Files lets you put new files in a folder. Write Data allows you to overwrite existing data in a file (but not add new data to an existing file because this is covered by Append Data).	CreateFiles, WriteData
Create Folders/Append Data	Create Folders lets you create subfolders within folders. Append Data allows you to add data to the end of an existing file (but not to overwrite existing data because this is covered by Write Data).	CreateFolders, AppendData
Write Attributes	Lets you change the basic attributes of a file or folder. These attributes include Read-Only, Hidden, System, and Archive.	WriteAttributes
Write Extended Attributes	Lets you change the extended attributes (named data streams) associated with a file. These include Summary fields, such as Title, Subject, and Author, as well as other types of data.	WriteExtendedAttributes
Delete Subfolders and Files	Lets you delete the contents of a folder. If you have this permission, you can delete the subfolders and files in a folder even if you don't specifically have Delete permission on the subfolder or file.	DeleteSubdirectoriesAndFiles

PERMISSION	DESCRIPTION	RULE FLAG
Delete	Lets you delete a file or folder. If a folder isn't empty and you don't have Delete permission for one of its files or subfolders, you won't be able to delete it. You can do this only if you have the Delete Subfolders and Files permission.	Delete
Read Permissions	Lets you read all basic and special permissions assigned to a file or folder.	ReadPermissions
Change Permissions	Lets you change basic and special permissions assigned to a file or folder.	ChangePermissions
Take Ownership	Lets you take ownership of a file or folder. By default, administrators can always take ownership of a file or folder and can also grant this permission to others.	TakeOwnership

Tables 10-4 and 10-5 show how special permissions are combined to make the basic permissions for files and folders.

Table 10-4 Special Permissions for Folders

SPECIAL PERMISSIONS	FULL CONTROL	MODIFY	READ & EXECUTE	LIST FOLDER CONTENTS	READ	WRITE
Traverse Folder/Execute File	X	X	X	X		
List Folder/Read Data	X	X	X	X	X	
Read Attributes	X	X	X	X	X	

SPECIAL PERMISSIONS	FULL CONTROL	MODIFY	READ & EXECUTE	LIST FOLDER CONTENTS	READ	WRITE
Read Extended - Attributes	X	X	X	X	X	
Create Files/Write Data	X	X				X
Create Folders/Append Data	X	X				X
Write Attributes	X	X				X
Write Extended - Attributes	X	X				X
Delete Subfolders and Files	X					
Delete	X	X				
Read Permissions	X	X	X	X	X	X
Change Permissions	X					
Take Ownership	X					

Table 10-5 Special Permissions for Files

SPECIAL PERMISSIONS	FULL - CONTROL	MODIFY	READ & EXECUTE	READ	WRITE
Traverse Folder/Execute File	X	X	X		
List Folder/Read Data	X	X	X	X	
Read Attributes	X	X	X	X	
Read Extended Attributes	X	X	X	X	
Create Files/Write Data	X	X			X
Create Folders/Append Data	X	X			X
Write Attributes	X	X			X
Write Extended Attributes	X	X			X
Delete Subfolders and Files	X				
Delete	X	X			
Read Permissions	X	X	X	X	X
Change Permissions	X				
Take Ownership	X				

You configure special permissions for directories and files in the same way as basic permissions. You add access rules to a resource using either the SetAccessRule() method or the AddAccessRule() method of the access control object. You remove access rules from a resource using the RemoveAccessRule() method of the access control object.

Consider the following example:

```
set-alias no new-object

$acl = get-acl c:\logs
$p1 = "imaginedlands\dev","executefile","allow"
$r1 = no system.security.accesscontrol.filesystemaccessrule $p1
$acl.addaccessrule($r1)

$p2 = "imaginedlands\dev","listdirectory","allow"
$r2 = no system.security.accesscontrol.filesystemaccessrule $p2
$acl.addaccessrule($r2)

$acl | set-acl c:\logs
```

Here, you get the access control object on C:\Logs. After you define an access rule and store the related values in $p1, you create a new instance of the FileSystem-AccessRule type and add the permission to the access control object by calling the AddAccessRule() method. After you define a second access rule and store the related values in $p2, you create a new instance of the FileSystemAccessRule type and add the permission to the access control object by calling the AddAccessRule() method. Finally, you apply the access control object to a specific resource using Set-Acl. The Dev group in the ImaginedLands domain must exist to create the access rules.

Taking Ownership

In Windows, the file or directory owner isn't necessarily the file or directory's creator. Instead, the file or directory owner is the person who has direct control over the file or directory. File or directory owners can grant access permissions and give other users permission to take ownership of a file or directory.

The way ownership is assigned initially depends on where the file or directory is being created. By default, the user who created the file or directory is listed as the current owner. Ownership can be taken or transferred in several ways. Any administrator can take ownership. Any user or group with the Take Ownership permission can take ownership. Any user who has the Restore Files And Directories right, such as a member of the Backup Operators group, can take ownership as well. Any current owner can transfer ownership to another user as well.

You can take ownership using a file or directory using the SetOwner() method of the access control object. The easiest way to take ownership is to

1. Get an access control object for the resource you want to work with.
2. Get the IdentityReference for the user or group that will take ownership. This user or group must already have permission on the resource (as discussed previously).
3. Call SetOwner to specify that you want the user or group to be the owner.
4. Apply the changes you've made to the resource.

Consider the following example:

```
$acl = get-acl c:\logs
$found = $false
foreach($rule in $acl.access) {
 if ($rule.identityreference -like "*administrators*") {
   $global:ref = $rule.identityreference; $found = $true; break}
}

if ($found) {
 $acl.setowner($ref)
 $acl | set-acl c:\logs
}
```

Here, you get the access control object on C:\Logs. You then examine each access rule on this object, looking for the one that applies to the group you want to work with. If you find a match, you set $ref to the IdentityReference for this group, change $found to $true, and then break out of the ForEach loop. After you break out of the loop, you check to see if $found is True. If it is, you set the ownership permission on the access control object you retrieved previously and then apply the access control object to C:\Logs using Set-Acl.

Configuring File and Directory Auditing

You can use auditing to track what's happening on your computers. Auditing collects information related to resource usage, such as a file or directory audit. Any time an action occurs that you've configured for auditing, the action is written to the system's security log, where it's stored for your review. The security log is accessible from Event Viewer. For most auditing changes, you need to be logged on using an account that's a member of the Administrators group, or you need to be granted the Manage Auditing And Security Log right in Group Policy.

Auditing policies are essential to ensure the security and integrity of your systems. Just about every computer system on the network should be configured with some type of auditing. You can set auditing policies for directories and files using auditing rules.

Audit rules contain collections of arrays that define

- The user or group to which the rule applies.
- The permission usage that is audited.
- The type of auditing.

This means regardless of whether you are adding or modifying rules, the basic syntax for an individual audit rule is

```
"UserOrGroupName", "PermissionAudited", "AuditType"
```

where *UserOrGroupName* is the name of the user or group to which the audit rule applies, *PermissionAudited* is the basic or special permission you are tracking, and *AuditType* specifies the type of auditing. Use Success to track successful use of a specified permission. Use Failure to track failed use of a specified permission. Use None to turn off auditing of the specified permission. Use Both to track both failure and success.

As with security permissions, user and group names are specified in COMPUTER\Name or DOMAIN\Name format. In the following example, you track users in the ImaginedLands domain who are trying to access the resource but fail to do so because they don't have sufficient access permissions:

```
"IMAGINEDLANDS\USERS", "ReadData", "Failure"
```

When you are working with folders, you can use the basic syntax to configure auditing for folders. You also can use an expanded syntax to configure auditing for a folder and its contents. The expanded syntax for an access rule is

```
"UserOrGroupName", "PermissionAudited", "InheritanceFlag",
"PropagationFlag","AuditType"
```

where UserOrGroupName is the name of the user or group to which the access rule applies, PermissionAudited is the basic or special permission you are tracking, InheritanceFlag controls inheritance, PropagationFlag controls propagation of inherited rules, and AuditType specifies the type of auditing. In the following example, you apply an auditing rule to a resource as well as the files and subfolders it contains:

```
"IMAGINEDLANDS\USERS", "ReadData", "ContainerInherit", "None",
"Failure"
```

With the inheritance flag, you can specify one of the following flag values:

- **None**   The access rule is not inherited by child objects.
- **ContainerInherit**   The access rule is inherited by subfolders (child container objects).
- **ObjectInherit**   The access rule is inherited by files (child objects).
- **ContainerInherit, ObjectInherit**   The access rule is inherited by files and subfolders (child objects and child container objects).

With the propagation flag, you can specify the following flag values:

- **None**   The access rule is propagated without modification.
- **InheritOnly**   The access rule is propogated to immediate child and child container objects.
- **NoPropagateInherit**   The access rule applies to child objects and to child container objects but not to child objects of child container objects.
- **NoPropagateInherit, InheritOnly**   The access rule applies to child container objects.

You add audit rules to a resource using either the SetAuditRule() method or the AddAuditRule() method of the access control object. You remove audit rules from a resource using the RemoveAuditRule() method of the access control object. Audit rules are defined as having the System.Security.AuditControl.FileSystemAuditRule type.

The easiest way to add and remove audit rules is to do the following:

1. Get an access control object. This object can be the one that applies to the resource you want to work with or one that applies to a resource that has the closest audit control permissions to those you want to use.

2. Create one or more instances of the System.Security.AuditControl.FileSystemAuditRule type, and store the desired auditing settings in these object instances.

3. Call AddAuditRule() or RemoveAuditRule() to add or remove audit rules as necessary. These methods operate on the access control object you retrieved in the first step.

4. Apply the changes you've made to an actual resource.

Consider the following example:

```
set-alias no new-object

$acl = get-acl d:\data
$audit = "imaginedlands\users","readdata","failure"
$r = no system.security.accesscontrol.filesystemauditrule $audit
$acl.addauditrule($r)
$acl | set-acl d:\data
```

Here, you get the access control object on D:\Data. You store the values for an audit rule in a variable called $audit, and then you create a new instance of the FileSystemAuditRule type with this auditing rule. The Users group in the ImaginedLands domain must exist to create the auditing rule. To add the auditing setting to the access control object you retrieved previously, you call its AddAuditRule() method. Although you could have created additional auditing rules and added or removed these, you didn't in this example. Finally, you apply the access control object to a specific resource using Set-Acl.

You can easily extend the previous examples to apply to multiple directories and files as shown in the following example:

```
set-alias no new-object

$acl = get-acl d:\data
$audit = "imaginedlands\users","readdata","failure"
$r = no system.security.accesscontrol.filesystemauditrule $audit
$acl.addauditrule($r)

$resc = gci d:\data -recurse -force
foreach($f in $resc) {

  write-host $f.fullname
  $acl | set-acl $f.FullName
}

D:\data\backup
D:\data\backup\historydat.txt
D:\data\logs\datlog.log
D:\data\data.ps1
D:\data\transcript1.txt
D:\data\transcript2.txt
D:\data\backup\backup
```

Here, you apply an auditing rule to every subdirectory of D:\Data and every file in D:\Data and its subdirectories. In the output, you list the names of the directories and files you've modified. This helps you keep track of the changes. The Users group in the ImaginedLands domain must exist to create the auditing rule.

Chapter 11. Managing and Securing the Registry

The Windows registry stores configuration settings. Using the Registry provider built into PowerShell, you can view, add, delete, compare, and copy registry entries. Because the Windows registry is essential to the proper operation of the operating system, make changes to the registry only when you know how these changes will affect the system. As discussed in the final section of this chapter, you should perform all registry changes within the context of a transaction. With transactions, you:

1. Use Start-Transaction to start a transaction before you modify the registry.
2. Make changes and then verify your changes.
3. Use Stop-Transaction to finalize your changes or Undo-Transaction to roll back your changes.

After you finalize a transaction using Stop-Transaction, you can no longer undo your changes. Although helpful, transactions won't help you identify changes that will cause problems with a computer and its components. Therefore, before you edit the registry in any way, you should create a system restore point. This way, if you make a mistake, you can recover the registry and the system. See Chapter 13, "Enabling Recovery," for details on working with restore points.

> **CAUTION**   Improperly modifying the Windows registry can cause serious problems. If the registry becomes corrupted, you might have to reinstall the operating system. Double-check the commands you use. Make sure that they do exactly what you intend.

Understanding Registry Keys and Values

The Windows registry stores configuration settings for the operating system, applications, users, and hardware. Registry settings are stored as keys and values, which are placed under a specific root key controlling when and how the keys and values are used.

Table 11-1 lists the registry root keys you can work with in PowerShell as well as a description and the reference name you use to refer to the root key when working with the Registry provider. Under the root keys, you'll find the main keys that control system, user, application, and hardware settings. These keys are organized into a tree structure, with folders representing keys. Within these folders are the registry keys that store important service configuration settings and their subkeys.

TABLE 11-1 Keys in the Windows Registry

ROOT KEY	REFERENCE NAME	DESCRIPTION
HKEY_CURRENT_USER	HKCU	Stores configuration settings for the current user.
HKEY_LOCAL_MACHINE	HKLM	Stores system-level configuration settings.
HKEY_CLASSES_ROOT	HKCR	Stores configuration settings for applications and files. It also ensures that the correct application is opened when a file is accessed.
HKEY_USERS	HKU	Stores default-user and other-user settings by profile.
HKEY_CURRENT_CONFIG	HKCC	Stores information about the hardware profile being used.

Keys that you want to work with must be designated by their folder path. For example, under HKLM\SYSTEM\CurrentControlSet\Services, you'll find folders for all services installed on the system. Values associated with the DNS key in this folder path allow you to work with the Domain Name System (DNS) service and its configuration settings.

Key values are stored as a specific data type. Table 11-2 provides a summary of the main data types used with keys.

TABLE 11-2 Registry Key Values and Data Types

DATA TYPE	DESCRIPTION	REFERENCE NAME	EXAMPLE
REG_BINARY	Identifies a binary value. Binary values are stored using base2 (0 or 1 only) but are displayed and entered in hexadecimal (base16) format.	Binary	01 00 14 80 90 00 00 9C 00
REG_DWORD	Identifies a binary data type in which 32-bit integer values are stored as four byte-length values in hexadecimal.	Dword	0x00000002
REG_EXPAND_SZ	Identifies an expandable string value, which is usually used with directory paths.	Expandstring	%SystemRoot%\dns.exe
REG_MULTI_SZ	Identifies a multiple-string value.	Multistring	Tcpip Afd RpcSc
REG_NONE	Identifies data without a particular type. This data is written as binary values but is displayed and entered in hexadecimal (base16) format.	None	23 45 67 80
REG_QWORD	Identifies a binary data type in which 64-bit integer values are stored as eight byte-length values in hexadecimal.	Qword	0x0000EA3FC

REG_SZ	Identifies a string value containing a sequence of characters.	String	DNS Server

Navigating the Registry

The core set of features for performing related procedures was discussed previously in Chapter 8, "Using Providers," in *PowerShell: IT Pro Solutions*, and include the Registry provider, the cmdlets for working with data stores, and the cmdlets for working with provider drives. As long as you know the key path and understand the available key data types, you can use the Registry provider to view and manipulate keys in a variety of ways.

By default, only the HKLM and HKCU root keys are available in PowerShell. To make other root keys available, you can register them as new PowerShell drives. The following example shows how to register HKCR, HKU, and HKCC:

```
new-psdrive -name hkcr -psprovider registry -root hkey_classes_root

new-psdrive -name hku -psprovider registry -root hkey_users

new-psdrive -name hkcc -psprovider registry -root hkey_current_config
```

Now you can directly access these additional root keys. For example, if you want to access HKCC, you type

```
set-location hkcc:
```

You can access keys and values in any Registry location using Set-Location. For example, if you want to change the location to HKLM, you type

```
set-location hklm:
```

You can then work with registry keys and values in HKLM. Locations under HKLM (or any other root key) are navigated in the same way you navigate directory paths. If you are working with HKLM, for example, you can use Set-Location (or CD) to change to HKLM\SYSTEM\CurrentControlSet\Services by typing

```
set-location system\currentcontrolset\services
```

Alternatively, to access HKLM and start in this location in the first place, you can type

```
set-location hklm:\system\currentcontrolset\services
```

> **NOTE**   If you specify a nonexistent path, key, or value, an error message is displayed. Typically, it reads: **Cannot find _____ because it does not exist.**

When you are working with a Registry location and want to view the available keys, type **get-childitem** (or **dir**) as shown in the following example and sample output:

```
set-location hklm:\system\currentcontrolset\services
get-childitem


    Hive: HKEY_LOCAL_MACHINE\system\currentcontrolset\services

Name                 Property
----                 --------
.NET CLR Data
.NET CLR Networking
.NETFramework
1394ohci             ImagePath    :
                     \SystemRoot\System32\drivers\1394ohci.sys
                     Type         : 1
                     Start        : 3
                     ErrorControl : 1
                     DisplayName  :
                     @1394.inf,%PCI\CC_0C0010.DeviceDesc%;
                     1394 OHCI Compliant Host Controller
                     Owners       : {1394.inf}
                     Group        :
ACPI                 ImagePath    : System32\drivers\ACPI.sys
                     Type         : 1
                     Start        : 0
                     ErrorControl : 3
                     DisplayName  :
                     @acpi.inf,%ACPI.SvcDesc%;
                     Microsoft ACPI Driver
                     Owners       : {acpi.inf}
                     Tag          : 2
                     Group        : Core
```

The following information is provided in this output:

- SKC shows the subkey count under the named key.
- VC shows the value count, which is the number of values under the named key.
- Name shows the name of the subkey.
- Property lists the names of properties for the named key.

To learn more about navigating the registry, let's focus on the APCI key. In this example, you know ACPI has a number of named property values. You can list these property values by typing **get-itemproperty** as shown in the following example and sample output:

```
set-location hklm:\system\currentcontrolset\services\acpi
get-itemproperty .

ImagePath     : System32\drivers\ACPI.sys
Type          : 1
Start         : 0
ErrorControl  : 3
DisplayName   : @acpi.inf,%ACPI.SvcDesc%;Microsoft ACPI Driver
Owners        : {acpi.inf}
Tag           : 2
Group         : Core
PSPath        : Microsoft.PowerShell.Core\Registry:
:HKEY_LOCAL_MACHINE\system\currentcontrolset\services\acpi
PSParentPath  : Microsoft.PowerShell.Core\Registry:
:HKEY_LOCAL_MACHINE\system\currentcontrolset\services
PSChildName   : acpi
PSDrive       : HKLM
PSProvider    : Microsoft.PowerShell.Core\Registry
```

You don't have to access a location to view its properties. The value you provide to Get-Item Property is a path. In the previous example, the dot (.) refers to the current working location. If you were working with another drive or location, you could enter the full path to the key to get the same results, as shown in this example:

```
get-itemproperty hklm:\system\currentcontrolset\services\acpi
```

Continuing this example, you know there are two source keys and seven key values under ACPI. If you access ACPI, you can list the two source keys by typing **get-childitem** (or **dir**) as shown in this example and sample output:

```
set-location hklm:\system\currentcontrolset\services\acpi
get-childitem
```

```
Hive: HKEY_LOCAL_MACHINE\system\currentcontrolset\services\acpi
Name                            Property
----                            --------
Parameters                      WHEAOSCImplemented : {0, 0, 0, 0}
                                APEIOSCGranted     : {0, 0, 0, 0}
Enum                            0               : ACPI_HAL\PNP0C08\0
                                Count       : 1
                                NextInstance : 1
```

As with Get-ItemProperty, Get-ChildItem also accepts a path. This means you can use Get-ChildItem and enter the full path to the key to get the same results shown in the previous example:

```
get-childitem hklm:\system\currentcontrolset\services\acpi
```

If you access the enum key under ACPI, you'll find several properties, including Count and NextInstance. Although you can use Get-ChildItem to view the values of all related properties, you'll more typically want to view and work with individual property values. To do this, get the properties and store the results in a variable. This allows you to then view and work with properties individually as shown in the following example and sample output:

```
$p = get-itemproperty
hklm:\system\currentcontrolset\services\acpi\enum
$p.count


1
```

Alternatively, you can read registry values by referencing the full path and name of the property value that you want to examine. The basic syntax is

```
get-itemproperty [-path] KeyPath [-name] ValueName
```

where *KeyPath* is the path of the key you want to examine and *ValueName* is an optional parameter that specifies a specific key value. Here is an example with sample output:

```
get-itemproperty hklm:\system\currentcontrolset\services\acpi\enum
count

Count       : 1
```

```
PSPath        : Microsoft.PowerShell.Core\Registry:
:HKEY_LOCAL_MACHINE\system\currentcontrolset\services\acpi\enum
PSParentPath  : Microsoft.PowerShell.Core\Registry:
:HKEY_LOCAL_MACHINE\system\currentcontrolset\services\acpi
PSChildName   : enum
PSDrive       : HKLM
PSProvider    : Microsoft.PowerShell.Core\Registry
```

As you can see, the output includes path, drive, and provider values as well as the value of the property you are examining. You can filter the output so that you see only the property value using Format-List, as shown in the following example:

```
get-itemproperty hklm:\system\currentcontrolset\services\acpi\enum `
count | format-list -property count
```

```
Count         : 1
```

NOTE To work with the registry on remote computers, use the Invoke-Command cmdlet. Here is an example:

invoke-command -computername Server43, Server27, Server82 `

-scriptblock { get-itemproperty `

hklm:\system\currentcontrolset\services\acpi\enum }

Alternatively, you can establish remote sessions using the New-PSSession cmdlet and then run individual commands against each computer automatically. Here is an example:

$s = new-PSSession –computername Server43, Server27, Server82

invoke-command –session $s -scriptblock {get-itemproperty `

hklm:\system\currentcontrolset\services\acpi\enum}

Managing Registry Keys and Values

When you are working with the Registry provider, you have many Item and ItemProperty cmdlets available for managing registry keys and values. You'll use these cmdlets to create, copy, move, rename, and delete registry items.

Creating Registry Keys and Values

You can easily add subkeys and values to the Windows registry using PowerShell. To create keys, you use the New-Item cmdlet. To create key values, you use the New-ItemProperty cmdlet. The basic syntax for creating a key is

```
new-item [-type registrykey] [-path] Path
```

where you can optionally specify the type of item you are creating as Registrykey and then use *Path* to specify where the key should be created. When you create a registry key, New-Item displays results that confirm the creation process. In the following example, you create an HKCU:\Software\Test key, and the resulting output confirms that the key was successfully created:

```
new-item -type registrykey -path hkcu:\software\test

    Hive: HKEY_CURRENT_USER\software
Name                              Property
----                              --------
test
```

> **NOTE** To create keys and set key values on remote computers, use the Invoke-Command cmdlet. Here is an example:
>
> invoke-command -computername Server43, Server27, Server82 `
> -scriptblock { new-item hkcu:\software\test }

As long as you have the appropriate permissions to create the key in the specified location, the creation process should be successful. If the key already exists, however, you'll see an error stating the following: "A key at this path already exists."

The basic syntax for creating a key value is

```
new-itemproperty [-path] Path [-name] Name [-type Type]
[-value Value]
```

where *Path* is the path to an existing registry key, *Name* is the name of the value, *Type* is the value type, and *Value* is the value to assign. Permitted value types are listed by their reference name in Table 11-2. As the table shows, valid types include Binary, Dword, Expandstring, Multistring, None, and String.

When you create a key value, New-ItemProperty displays results that confirm the creation process. In the following example, you create a string value called Data under the HKCU:\Software\Test key, and the resulting output confirms that the key value was successfully created:

```
new-itemproperty -path hkcu:\software\test Data -type "string" `
-value "Current"
```

```
Data          : Current
PSPath        : Microsoft.PowerShell.Core\Registry:
:HKEY_CURRENT_USER\software\test
PSParentPath  : Microsoft.PowerShell.Core\Registry:
:HKEY_CURRENT_USER\software
PSChildName   : test
PSDrive       : HKCU
PSProvider    : Microsoft.PowerShell.Core\Registry
```

As long as you have the appropriate permissions to create the key in the specified location, the creation process should be successful. If the key value already exists, however, you'll see an error stating the following: "The property already exists."

Copying Registry Keys and Values

You can copy registry keys using Copy-Item. The basic syntax is

```
copy-item SourcePath DestinationPath
```

where *SourcePath* is the path to the registry key to copy and *DestinationPath* is where you'd like to create a copy of the registry. In the following example, you copy the HKCU:\Software\Test key (and all its contents) to HKLM:\Software\Dev:

```
copy-item hkcu:\software\test hklm:\software\dev
```

As long as you have the appropriate permissions, you should be able to copy registry keys. When you copy a key, Copy-ItemProperty displays an error that indicates failure but doesn't display any output to indicate success.

You can copy registry values using Copy-ItemProperty. The basic syntax is

```
copy-itemproperty [-path] SourcePath [-destination] DestinationPath
[-name] KeyValueToCopy
```

where *SourcePath* is the current path to the key value, *DestinationPath* is the new path for the copy of the key value, and *KeyValueToCopy* identifies the key value you want to copy. In the following example, you copy the Data value from the HKCU:\Software\Test key to the HKLM:\Software\Dev key:

```
copy-itemproperty -path hkcu:\software\test -destination `
hklm:\software\dev -name data
```

As long as you have the appropriate permissions and the source value exists, you should be able to copy the key value. You can use Copy-ItemProperty to copy multiple key values. Use comma-separated values or wildcard characters as appropriate.

Moving Registry Keys and Values

You can move keys and their associated values using Move-Item. The basic syntax is

```
move-item SourcePath DestinationPath
```

where *SourcePath* is the current path to the key and *DestinationPath* is the new path to the key. When you move a key, Move-Item displays an error that indicates failure but doesn't display any output to indicate success. In the following example, you move the HKCU:\Software\Test key (and all its contents) to the HKCU:\Software\Test2 key:

```
move-item hkcu:\software\test hkcu:\software\test2
```

As long as you have the appropriate permissions, you should be able to move keys. You can use Move-Item to move keys from one root to another. For example, you can move HKCU:\Software\Test to HKLM:\Software\Test.

You can move key values using Move-ItemProperty. The basic syntax is

```
move-itemproperty [-path] SourcePath [-destination] DestinationPath
[-name] KeyValueToMove
```

where *SourcePath* is the current path to the key value, *DestinationPath* is the new path to the key value, and *KeyValueToMove* identifies the key value you want to move. When you move a key value, Move-ItemProperty displays an error that indicates failure but doesn't display any output to indicate success. In the following example, you move the Data value from the HKCU:\Software\Test key to the HKLM:\Software\Test key:

```
move-itemproperty -path hkcu:\software\test -destination `
hklm:\software\test2 -name data
```

As long as you have the appropriate permissions and the source and destination keys exist, you should be able to move the key value. You can use Move-ItemProperty to move multiple key values. Use comma-separated values or wildcard characters as appropriate.

Renaming Registry Keys and Values

To rename keys, you use the Rename-Item cmdlet. Rename-Item has the following syntax

```
rename-item OriginalNamePath NewName
```

where *OriginalNamePath* is the full path to the key and *NewName* is the new name for the key. In the following example, you rename Test under HKCU:\Software as Test2:

```
rename-item hkcu:\software\test test2
```

As long as you have the appropriate permissions, you should be able to rename keys.

To rename key values, you use the Rename-ItemProperty cmdlet. Rename-ItemProperty has the following syntax

```
rename-item [-path] OriginalNamePath [-name] CurrentName [-newname]
NewName
```

where *OriginalNamePath* is the full path to the key value and *NewName* is the new name for the key value. In the following example, you rename Data under the HKCU:\Software\Test key as EntryType:

```
rename-itemproperty -path hkcu:\software\test2 -name data `
-newname entrytype
```

As long as you have the appropriate permissions, you should be able to rename keys.

Deleting Registry Keys and Values

You can delete registry keys using the Remove-Item cmdlet. Remove-Item has the following syntax

```
remove-item NamePath [-Force]
```

where *NamePath* is the full path to the registry key that you want to remove, and –Force is an optional parameter to force the removal of the key. In the following example, you delete the HKCU:\Software\Test2 key (and all its contents):

```
remove-item hkcu:\software\test2
```

As long as you have the appropriate permissions, you should be able to remove registry keys.

You can delete key values using the Remove-ItemProperty cmdlet. Remove-ItemProperty has the following syntax

```
remove-itemproperty [-Path] KeyPath [-Name] ValueName [-Force]
```

where *KeyPath* is the full path to the registry key that contains the value you want to remove, *ValueName* is the name of the value to remove, and –Force is an optional parameter to force the removal of the key value. In the following example, you delete the Data value for the HKCU:\Software\Test key:

```
remove-itemproperty -path hkcu:\software\test -name data
```

As long as you have the appropriate permissions, you should be able to remove key values.

Comparing Registry Keys

You can compare registry entries and values between and among computers or between two different keys on the same system. Performing registry comparisons is useful in the following situations:

- When you are trying to troubleshoot service and application configuration issues.

  At such times, it is useful to compare the registry configurations between two different systems. Ideally, these systems include one registry that appears to be configured properly and one that you suspect is misconfigured. You can then perform a comparison of the configuration areas that you suspect are causing problems.

- When you want to ensure that an application or service is configured the same way on multiple systems.

  Here you use one system as the basis for testing the other system configurations. Ideally, the basis system is configured exactly as expected before you start comparing its configuration with other systems.

To see how you can compare registry values across computers, consider the following example and sample output:

```
$c1 = "techpc18"
$c2 = "engpc25"

$p = invoke-command -computername $c1 -scriptblock {
get-itemproperty `
hklm:\system\currentcontrolset\services\acpi\enum }

$h = invoke-command -computername $c2 -scriptblock {
get-itemproperty `
hklm:\system\currentcontrolset\services\acpi\enum }

if ($p = $h) {write-host $True} else {
write-host "Computer: $c1"
write-host $p

write-host "Computer: $c2"
write-host $h}

True
```

When you run these commands at an administrator PowerShell prompt and the remote computers are configured for remoting, you get a comparison of the specified keys on both computers. If the keys have the same values, PowerShell writes True to the output as shown. Otherwise, PowerShell writes the values associated with each key on each computer, allowing you to see where there are differences.

You can easily extend this comparison technique so that you can compare the values on a computer you know is configured correctly with multiple computers in the enterprise that you want to check. An example and sample output follow:

```
$clist = "techpc18", "techpc25", "techpc36"
$src = "engpc25"

$ps = invoke-command -computername $clist -scriptblock {
get-itemproperty `
hklm:\system\currentcontrolset\services\acpi\enum }

$h = invoke-command -computername $src -scriptblock {
get-itemproperty `
hklm:\system\currentcontrolset\services\acpi\enum }

$index = 0

foreach ($p in $ps) {

if ($p = $h) {write-host $clist[$index] "same as $src" } else {
write-host "Computer:" $clist[$index]
write-host $p

write-host "Computer: $src"
write-host $h

$index++}
}

techpc18 same as engpc25
techpc25 same as engpc25
techpc36 same as engpc25
```

Here, you check the registry on multiple target computers and compare key values with a source computer. If a target computer has different values for the key compared, you list the target computer's values followed by the source computer's values. This allows you to see where there are differences.

Viewing and Managing Registry Security Settings

As an administrator, you'll sometimes need to view and manage security settings in the registry. In PowerShell, these tasks are accomplished using Get-Acl and Set-Acl. The syntax for these commands is as follows:

- **Get-Acl** Gets objects that represent the security descriptor of registry keys. Use –Audit to get the audit data for the security descriptor from the access control list.

```
Get-Acl [-Path] KeyPaths {AddtlParams}

AddtlParams=
[-Audit] [-Exclude KeysToExclude] [-Include KeysToInclude]
```

- **Set-Acl** Changes the security descriptor of registry keys. Use –Aclobject to specify the desired security settings.

```
Set-Acl [-Path] KeyPaths [-Aclobject] Security {AddtlParams}

AddtlParams=
[-Exclude KeysToExclude] [-Include KeysToInclude]
```

Whenever you are working with registry keys, you might want to view or modify the security descriptor. Use Get-Acl with the –Path parameter to specify the path to resources you want to work with. You can use wildcard characters in the path, and you can also include or exclude keys using the –Include and –Exclude parameters.

Getting and Setting Registry Security Descriptors

Get-Acl returns a separate object containing the security information for each matching key. By default, Get-Acl displays the path to the resource, the owner of the resource, and a list of the access control entries on the resource. The access control list is controlled by the resource owner. To get additional information, including the security group of the owner, a list of auditing entries, and the full security descriptor as an SDDL (Security Descriptor Definition Language) string, format the output as a list as shown in the following example and sample output:

```
get-acl hklm:\software\test | format-list

Path    : Microsoft.PowerShell.Core\Registry:
:HKEY_CURRENT_USER\software\test
Owner   : BUILTIN\Administrators
Group   : IMAGINEDLANDS\Domain Users
Access  : IMAGINEDLANDS\williams Allow  FullControl
          NT AUTHORITY\SYSTEM Allow  FullControl
          BUILTIN\Administrators Allow  FullControl
          NT AUTHORITY\RESTRICTED Allow  ReadKey
Audit   :
Sddl    : O:BAG:DUD:(A;OICIID;KA;;;S-1-5-21-3359847396-
3574526683-113705776-1107)(A;OICIID;KA;;;SY)
(A;OICIID;KA;;;BA)(A;OICIID;KR;;;RC)
```

> **NOTE** You can view and manage registry security on remote computers using any of the remoting techniques discussed in Chapter 12, "Establishing Remote Sessions," in *PowerShell: IT Pro Solutions*. Here is an example:
>
> invoke-command -computername Server16, Server12, Server18 `
>
> -scriptblock { get-acl hklm:\software\test | format-list }

Here, Get-Acl returns a RegistrySecurity object representing the security descriptor of the HKLM:\Software\Test key. The result is then sent to the Format-List cmdlet. You can work with any properties of security objects separately, including the following:

- **Owner** Shows the owner of the resource
- **Group** Shows the primary group the owner is a member of
- **Access** Shows the access control rules on the resource
- **Audit** Shows the auditing rules on the resource
- **Sddl** Shows the full security descriptor as an SDDL string

> **NOTE** RegistrySecurity objects have additional properties that aren't displayed as part of the standard output. To see these properties, send the output to Format-List *. You'll then see the following note and script properties: PSPath (the PowerShell path to the resource), PSParentPath (the PowerShell path to the parent resource), PSChildName (the name of the resource), PSDrive (the PowerShell drive on which the resource is located), AccessToString (an alternate representation of the access rules on the

resource), and AuditToString (an alternate representation of the audit rules on the resource).

You can use the objects that Get-Acl returns to set the security descriptors on registry keys. To do this, open an administrator PowerShell prompt, obtain a single security descriptor object for a registry key that has the security settings you want to use, and then use the security descriptor object to establish the desired security settings for another registry key. An example and sample output follow:

```
set-acl -path hkcu:\software\dev -aclobject (get-acl
hklm:\software\test)
```

Here you use the security descriptor on HKLM:\Software\Test to set the security descriptor for HKCU:\Software\Dev.

You can easily extend this technique. In this example, you use the security descriptor on HKLM:\Software\Test to set the security descriptor for subkeys directly under the HKCU:\Software\Dev key:

```
$secd = get-acl hklm:\software\test
set-acl -path hkcu:\software\dev\* -aclobject $secd
```

To include keys in subpaths, you need to use Get-ChildItem to obtain reference objects for all the keys you want to work with. Here is an example:

```
$s = get-acl hklm:\software\test
gci hkcu:\software\dev -recurse -force | set-acl -aclobject $s
```

Here, *gci* is an alias for Get-ChildItem. You obtain the security descriptor for HKLM:\Software\Test. Next you get a reference to all subpaths of HKCU:\Software\Dev. Finally, you use the security descriptor on HKLM:\Software\Test to set the security descriptor for these subkeys.

Working with Registry Access Rules

To create your own security descriptors, you need to work with access control rules. The Access property of security objects is defined as a collection of authorization rules. With registry keys, these rules have the following object type:

System.Security.AccessControl.RegistryAccessRule

One way to view the individual access control objects that apply to a registry key is shown in this example and sample output:

```
$s = get-acl hklm:\software\test
$s.access

RegistryRights     : FullControl
AccessControlType  : Allow
IdentityReference  : IMAGINEDLANDS\williams
IsInherited        : True
InheritanceFlags   : ContainerInherit, ObjectInherit
PropagationFlags   : None

RegistryRights     : FullControl
AccessControlType  : Allow
IdentityReference  : NT AUTHORITY\SYSTEM
IsInherited        : True
InheritanceFlags   : ContainerInherit, ObjectInherit
PropagationFlags   : None

RegistryRights     : FullControl
AccessControlType  : Allow
IdentityReference  : BUILTIN\Administrators
IsInherited        : True
InheritanceFlags   : ContainerInherit, ObjectInherit
PropagationFlags   : None

RegistryRights     : ReadKey
AccessControlType  : Allow
IdentityReference  : NT AUTHORITY\RESTRICTED
IsInherited        : True
InheritanceFlags   : ContainerInherit, ObjectInherit
PropagationFlags   : None
```

Here you get the RegistrySecurity object for the HKLM:\Software\Test key and then display the contents of its Access property. Although each value listed is an access rule object, you cannot work with each access rule object separately. Note the following in the output:

- **RegistryRights** Shows the registry rights being applied
- **AccessControlType** Shows the access control type as Allow or Deny
- **IdentityReference** Shows the user or group to which the rule applies

- **IsInherited**   Specifies whether the access rule is inherited
- **InheritanceFlags**   Shows the way inheritance is being applied
- **PropagationFlags**   Specifies whether the access rule will be inherited

Another way to work with each access rule object separately is to use a ForEach loop as shown in this example:

```
$s = get-acl hklm:\software\test

foreach($a in $s.access) {

 #work with each access control object

 if ($a.identityreference -like "*administrator*") {$a | format-list
*}
}
```

```
RegistryRights      : FullControl
AccessControlType : Allow
IdentityReference : BUILTIN\Administrators
IsInherited         : True
InheritanceFlags  : ContainerInherit, ObjectInherit
PropagationFlags  : None
```

Here, you examine each access rule object separately, which allows you to take action on specific access rules. In this example, you look for access rules that apply to administrators.

Configuring Registry Permissions

You can assign two types of access permissions to registry keys: basic and special. These permissions grant or deny access to users and groups.

The basic permissions you can assign to registry keys are shown in Table 11-3. The basic permissions are made up of multiple special permissions. Note the rule flag for each permission, because this is the value you must reference when creating an access rule.

TABLE 11-3 Basic Registry Permissions

PERMISSION	DESCRIPTION	RULE FLAG
Full Control	This permission permits reading, writing, changing, and deleting registry keys and values.	FullControl
Read	This permission permits reading registry keys and their values.	ReadKey, ExecuteKey
Write	This permission permits reading and writing registry keys and their values.	WriteKey

When you are configuring basic permissions for users and groups, you can specify the access control type as either Allowed or Denied. If a user or group should be granted an access permission, you allow the permission. If a user or group should be denied an access permission, you deny the permission.

You configure basic permissions for resources using access rules. Access rules contain collections of arrays that define:

- The user or group to which the rule applies.
- The access permission that applies.
- The Allow or Deny status.

This means regardless of whether you are adding or modifying rules, the basic syntax for an individual access rule is

```
"UserOrGroupName", "ApplicablePermission", "ControlType"
```

where *UserOrGroupName* is the name of the user or group to which the access rule applies, *ApplicablePermission* is the basic permission you are applying, and *ControlType* specifies the Allow or Deny status. User and group names are specified in COMPUTER\Name or DOMAIN\Name format. In the following example, you grant full control to DeploymentTesters:

```
"DeploymentTesters", "FullControl", "Allow"
```

The expanded syntax for an access rule is

```
"UserOrGroupName", "ApplicablePermission", "InheritanceFlag",
"PropagationFlag", "ControlType"
```

where *UserOrGroupName* is the name of the user or group to which the access rule applies, *ApplicablePermission* is the basic permission you are applying, *InheritanceFlag* controls inheritance, *PropagationFlag* controls propagation of inherited rules, and *ControlType* specifies the type of access control. In the following example, you grant full control to DeploymentTesters and apply inheritance to the key and all its subkeys:

```
"DeploymentTesters", "FullControl", "ContainerInherit", "None",
"Allow"
```

With the inheritance flag, you can specify one of the following flag values:

- **None**   The access rule is not inherited by subkeys of the current key.
- **ContainerInherit**   The access rule is inherited by child container objects.
- **ObjectInherit**   The access rule is inherited by child leaf objects.

Because all registry keys are containers, the only inheritance flag that is meaningful for registry keys is the ContainerInherit flag for InheritanceFlags. If this flag is not used, the propagation flags are ignored, and only the key you are working with is affected. If you use the ContainerInherit flag, the rule is propagated according to the propagation flags.

With the propagation flag, you can specify the following flag values:

- **None**   The access rule is propagated without modification. This means the rule applies to subkeys, subkeys with child keys, and subkeys of child keys.
- **InheritOnly**   The access rule is propagated to container and leaf child objects. This means the rule applies to subkeys with child keys and subkeys of child keys; the rule does not apply to subkeys of the key.
- **NoPropagateInherit**   The access rule applies to its child objects. This means the rule applies to subkeys of the key and subkeys with child keys but not to subkeys of child keys.
- **NoPropagateInherit, InheritOnly**   The access rule applies to containers. This means the rule applies to subkeys with child keys but not to subkeys of child keys or to subkeys of the key.

You add access rules to a resource using either the SetAccessRule() method or the AddAccessRule() method of the access control object. You remove access rules from a resource using the RemoveAccessRule() method of the access control object. As discussed previously, access rules are defined as having the System.Security.AccessControl.RegistryAccessRule type.

The easiest way to add and remove access rules is to follow these steps:

1. Get an access control object. This object can be the one that applies to the registry key you want to work with or one that applies to a registry key that has the closest access control permissions to those you want to use.

2. Create one or more instances of the System.Security.AccessControl.RegistryAccessRule type, and store the desired permissions in these object instances.

3. Call AddAccessRule() or RemoveAccessRule() to add or remove access rules as necessary. These methods operate on the access control object you retrieved in the first step.

4. To apply the changes you've made to an actual registry key, you must apply the access control object to a specified resource.

Consider the following example:

```
set-alias no new-object

$acl = get-acl hklm:\software\test
$perm = "imaginedlands\deploymenttesters","fullcontrol","allow"
$r = no system.security.accesscontrol.registryaccessrule $perm
$acl.addaccessrule($r)
$acl | set-acl hkcu:\software\dev
```

Here, you get the access control object on HKLM:\Software\Test. You store the values for an access rule in a variable called $perm and then create a new instance of the RegistryAccessRule type for this access rule. To add the permission to the access control object you retrieved previously, you call its AddAccessRule() method. Although you could have created additional permissions and added or removed these, you didn't in this example. Finally, you applied the access control object to a specific resource using Set-Acl.

You can easily extend the previous examples to apply to multiple registry keys as shown in the following example:

```
set-alias no new-object

$acl = get-acl hklm:\software\test
$perm = "imaginedlands\devtesters","fullcontrol","allow"
$r = no system.security.accesscontrol.registryaccessrule $perm
$acl.addaccessrule($r)

$resc = gci hkcu:\software\test -force
foreach($f in $resc) {

  write-host $f.pspath
  $acl | set-acl $f.pspath
}

Microsoft.PowerShell.Core\Registry:
:HKEY_CURRENT_USER\software\test\Dt\IO
Microsoft.PowerShell.Core\Registry:
:HKEY_CURRENT_USER\software\test\Queue
Microsoft.PowerShell.Core\Registry:
:HKEY_CURRENT_USER\software\test\Stats
```

Here, you apply an access control list with a modified permission set to every subkey of HKCU:\Software\Test. In the output, you list the names of the keys you've modified. This helps you keep track of the changes.

The special permissions you can assign to registry keys are shown in Table 11-4. As with basic permissions, note the rule flag for each permission, because this is the value you must reference when creating an access rule.

TABLE 11-4 Special Permissions

PERMISSION	DESCRIPTION	RULE FLAG
Query Values	Allows the user or group to read the values within a key.	QueryValues
Set Value	Allows the user or group to set the values within a key.	SetValue

PERMISSION	DESCRIPTION	RULE FLAG
Create Subkey	Allows the user or group to create subkeys under the selected key.	CreateSubKey
Enumerate Subkeys	Allows the user or group to list the subkeys under a key.	EnumerateSubKeys
Notify	Allows the user or group to get notifications for changes that occur in a key.	Notify
Create Link	Allows the user or group to create links from one key to another key.	CreateLink
Delete	Allows the user or group to delete the key, subkeys, and values associated with the key. Delete permission must apply on the key and on all the key's subkeys in order for a user or group to delete a registry key.	Delete
Write DAC	Allows the user or group to change the key's security permissions.	ChangePermissions
Take Ownership	Allows the user or group to modify ownership of a key.	TakeOwnership
Read Control	Allows the user or group to read the key's security permissions.	ReadPermissions

Table 11-5 shows how special permissions are combined to make the basic permissions for registry keys.

TABLE 11-5 Combining Special Permissions

PERMISSION	FULL CONTROL	READ	WRITE
Query Values	X	X	
Set Value	X		X
Create Subkey	X		X
Enumerate Subkeys	X	X	
Notify	X	X	
Create Link	X		
Delete	X		
Write DAC	X		
Write Owner	X		
Read Control	X	X	X

You configure special permissions for registry keys in the same way as basic permissions. You add access rules to a resource using either the SetAccessRule() method or the AddAccessRule() method of the access control object. You remove access rules from a resource using the RemoveAccessRule() method of the access control object.

Consider the following example:

```
set-alias no new-object

$acl = get-acl hklm:\software\test
$p1 = "imaginedlands\dev","queryvalues","allow"
$r1 = no system.security.accesscontrol.registryaccessrule $p1
```

```
$acl.addaccessrule($r1)

$p2 = "imaginedlands\dev","enumeratesubkeys","allow"
$r2 = no system.security.accesscontrol.registryaccessrule $p2
$acl.addaccessrule($r2)

$acl | set-acl hklm:\software\test
```

Here, you get the access control object on the HKLM:\Software\Test key. This key must exist for the example to work. After you define an access rule and store the related values in $p1, you create a new instance of the RegistryAccessRule type and add the permission to the access control object by calling the AddAccessRule() method. After you define a second access rule and store the related values in $p2, you create a new instance of the RegistryAccessRule type and add the permission to the access control object by calling the AddAccessRule() method. Finally, you apply the access control object to a specific resource.

Taking Ownership of Registry Keys

You can take ownership using a registry key using the SetOwner() method of the access control object. The easiest way to take ownership is to complete the following steps:

1. Get an access control object for the registry you want to work with.
2. Get the IdentityReference for the user or group that will take ownership. This user or group must already have permission on the registry key.
3. Call SetOwner to specify that you want the user or group to be the owner.
4. Apply the changes you've made to the registry key.

Consider the following example:

```
$acl = get-acl hklm:\software\test
$found = $false
foreach($rule in $acl.access) {
  if ($rule.identityreference -like "*administrators*") {
    $global:ref = $rule.identityreference; $found = $true; break}
}

if ($found) {
  $acl.setowner($ref)
```

```
$acl | set-acl hklm:\software\test
}
```

Here, you get the access control object on HKLM:\Software\Test. You then examine each access rule on this object, looking for the one that applies to the group you want to work with. If you find a match, you set $ref to the IdentityReference for this group, change $found to $true, and then break out of the ForEach loop. After you break out of the loop, you check to see if $found is True. If it is, you set the ownership permission on the access control object you retrieved previously and then apply the access control object to HKLM:\Software\Test using Set-Acl.

Auditing the Registry

Access to the registry can be audited, as can access to other areas of the operating system. Auditing allows you to track which users access the registry and what they're doing. All the permissions listed previously in Tables 11-1 and 11-2 can be audited. However, you usually limit what you audit to only the essentials to reduce the amount of data that is written to the security logs and to reduce the resources used to track registry usage.

Before you can enable auditing of the registry, you must enable the auditing function on the computer you are working with. You can do this either through the server's local policy or through the appropriate Group Policy object. The policy that controls auditing is Computer Configuration\Windows Settings\Security Settings\Local Policies\Audit Policy.

After auditing is enabled for a computer, you can configure how you want auditing to work for the registry. This means configuring auditing for each key you want to track. Thanks to inheritance, this doesn't mean you have to go through every key in the registry and enable auditing for it. Instead, you can select a root key or any subkey to designate the start of the branch for which you want to track access, and then ensure the auditing settings are inherited for all subkeys below it. (Inheritance is the default setting.)

You can set auditing policies for registry keys using auditing rules. Auditing rules contain collections of arrays that define the following:

- The user or group to which the rule applies
- The permission usage that is audited
- The inheritance flag specifying whether the audit rule applies to subkeys of the current key
- The propagation flag specifying how an inherited audit rule is propagated to subkeys of the current key
- The type of auditing

This means regardless of whether you are adding or modifying rules, the basic syntax for an individual audit rule is

```
"UserOrGroupName", "PermissionAudited", "InheritanceFlag",
"PropagationFlag", "AuditType"
```

where *UserOrGroupName* is the name of the user or group to which the audit rule applies, *PermissionAudited* is the basic or special permission you are tracking,

InheritanceFlag controls inheritance, *PropagationFlag* controls propagation of inherited rules, and *AuditType* specifies the type of auditing.

With the inheritance flag, you can specify one of the following flag values:

- **None**   The audit rule is not inherited by subkeys of the current key.
- **ContainerInherit**   The audit rule is inherited by child container objects.
- **ObjectInherit**   The audit rule is inherited by child leaf objects.

Because all registry keys are containers, the only inheritance flag that is meaningful for registry keys is the ContainerInherit flag for InheritanceFlags. If this flag is not used, the propagation flags are ignored, and only the key you are working with is affected. If you use the ContainerInherit flag, the rule is propagated according to the propagation flags.

With the propagation flag, you can specify the following flag values:

- **None**   The audit rule is propagated without modification. This means the rule applies to subkeys, subkeys with child keys, and subkeys of child keys.

- **InheritOnly**   The audit rule is propagated to container and leaf child objects. This means the rule applies to subkeys with child keys and subkeys of child keys; the rule does not apply to subkeys of the key.
- **NoPropagateInherit**   The audit rule applies to its child objects. This means the rule applies to subkeys of the key and subkeys with child keys but not to subkeys of child keys.
- **NoPropagateInherit, InheritOnly**   The audit rule applies to containers. This means the rule applies to subkeys with child keys but not to subkeys of child keys or to subkeys of the key.

With audit type, use Success to track successful use of a specified permission, Failure to track failed use of a specified permission, and None to turn off auditing of the specified permission. Use Both to track success and failure.

As with security permissions, user and group names are specified in COMPUTER

\Name or DOMAIN\Name format. In the following example, you track users in the IMAGINEDLANDS domain who are trying to query key values but fail to do so because they don't have sufficient access permissions:

```
"IMAGINEDLANDS\USERS", "QueryValues", "ContainerInherit", "None",
"Failure"
```

You add audit rules to a resource using either the SetAuditRule() method or the AddAuditRule() method of the access control object. You remove audit rules from a resource using the RemoveAuditRule() method of the access control object. Audit rules are defined as having the System.Security.AuditControl.RegistryAuditRule type.

The easiest way to add and remove audit rules is to complete these steps:

1. Get an access control object. This object can be the one that applies to the registry key you want to work with or one that applies to a registry key that has the closest audit control permissions to those you want to use.

2. Create instances of the System.Security.AuditControl.RegistryAuditRule type, and store the desired auditing settings in these object instances.

3. Call AddAuditRule() or RemoveAuditRule() to add or remove audit rules as necessary. These methods operate on the access control object you retrieved in the first step.

4. Apply the changes you've made to an actual resource.

Consider the following example:

```
set-alias no new-object

$acl = get-acl hklm:\software\test
$audit = "imaginedlands\users","queryvalues","containerinherit",
"none","failure"

$r = no system.security.accesscontrol.registryauditrule $audit

$acl.addauditrule($r)
$acl | set-acl hklm:\software\test
```

Here, you get the access control object on HKLM:\Software\Test. You store the values for an audit rule in a variable called $audit, and then you create a new instance of the RegistryAuditRule type with this auditing rule. To add the auditing setting to the access control object you retrieved previously, you call its AddAuditRule() method. Although you could have created additional auditing rules and added or removed these, you didn't in this example. Finally, you applied the access control object to a registry key using Set-Acl.

You can easily extend the previous examples to apply to multiple registry keys as shown in the following example:

```
set-alias no new-object

$acl = get-acl hklm:\software\test
$audit = "imaginedlands\users","queryvalues","containerinherit",
"none","failure"

$r = no system.security.accesscontrol.registryauditrule $audit
$acl.addauditrule($r)

$resc = gci hkcu:\software\test -recurse -force
foreach($f in $resc) {

  write-host $f.pspath
  $acl | set-acl $f.pspath
}

Microsoft.PowerShell.Core\Registry:
```

```
:HKEY_CURRENT_USER\software\test\Dt\IO
Microsoft.PowerShell.Core\Registry:
:HKEY_CURRENT_USER\software\test\Queue
Microsoft.PowerShell.Core\Registry:
:HKEY_CURRENT_USER\software\test\Stats
```

Here, you apply an auditing rule to every subkey of HKCU:\Software\Test. In the output, you list the names of the registry keys you've modified. This helps you keep track of the changes.

Creating Transactions

Whenever you work with the Registry, it's important to consider using transactions. A transaction is a block of commands that are managed as a unit where either all the commands are successful and completed, or all the commands are undone and rolled back because one or more commands failed. You can use transactions when you want to be sure that every command in a block of commands is successful and to avoid leaving the computer in a damaged or unpredictable state.

Understanding Transactions

Whether you are working with relational databases, distributed computing environments, or PowerShell, transactions are some of the most powerful commands you can work with. Why? Because transactions ensure that changes are applied only when appropriate, and when you encounter any problems, the changes are undone and the original working environment is restored.

To restore the working environment, transacted commands must keep track of changes that were made as well as the original content and values. Because of this, commands must be designed specifically to support transactions, and not all commands can or do support transactions. In PowerShell, support for transactions must be implemented at two levels:

- **Provider**   Providers that provide cmdlets must be designed to support transactions.
- **Cmdlet**   Individual cmdlets, implemented on compliant providers, must be designed to support transactions.

In the core PowerShell environment, the only component that supports transactions is the Registry provider. On this provider, the Item-related cmdlets support transactions, including New-Item, Set-Item, Clear-Item, Copy-Item, Move-Item, and Remove-Item. You can also use the System.Management.Automation.TransactedString class to include expressions in transactions on any version of Windows that supports PowerShell. Other providers can be updated to support transactions, and you can look for compliant providers by typing the following command:

```
get-psprovider | where {$_.Capabilities -like "*transactions*"}
```

At their most basic, transactions work like this:

1. You start a transaction.
2. You perform transacted commands.
3. You commit or undo transacted commands.

Transactions also can have subscribers. A subscriber is a sequence of transacted commands that is handled as a subunit within an existing transaction. For example, if you are using PowerShell to work with a database, you might want to start a transaction prior to changing data in the database. Then you might want to create subtransactions for each data set you are manipulating. Because the success or failure of each subtransaction determines the success or failure of the entire transaction, you must commit each subtransaction separately before you commit the primary transaction.

Cmdlets you can use with transactions include the following:

▪ **Get-Transaction**   Gets an object that represents the current active transaction in the session or the last transaction if there is no active transaction. This allows you to view the rollback preference, the subscriber count, and the status of the transaction.

```
Get-Transaction
```

▪ **Complete-Transaction**   Commits an active transaction, which finalizes the transaction and permanently applies any related changes. If the transaction includes multiple subscribers, you must type one Complete-Transaction command for every dependent subscriber to commit the transaction fully.

```
Complete-Transaction
```

- **Start-Transaction**   Starts a new independent transaction or joins an existing transaction as a dependent subscriber. The default rollback preference is Error. Although there is no default time-out for transactions started at the command line, the default timeout for transactions started in a script is 30 minutes.

```
Start-Transaction [-Independent] [-RollbackPreference {Error |
TerminatingError | Never}] [-Timeout Minutes]
```

- **Undo-Transaction**   Rolls back the active transaction, which undoes any related changes and restores the original working environment. If the transaction includes multiple subscribers, the Undo-Transaction command rolls back the entire transaction for all subscribers.

```
Undo-Transaction
```

- **Use-Transaction**   Adds a script block to the active transaction, enabling transacted scripting of compliant .NET Framework objects, such as instances of the System.Management.Automation.TransactedString class. You cannot use noncompliant objects in a transacted script block. To enter the active transaction, you must use the –UseTransaction parameter. Otherwise, the command is ineffective.

```
Use-Transaction [-TransactedScript] ScriptBlock
[-UseTransaction]
```

> **REAL WORLD**   Cmdlets that support transactions have a –UseTransaction parameter. As changes are made to PowerShell, you can find cmdlets that support transactions by using the following command: **get-help * - parameter UseTransaction**. If a cmdlet has this parameter, the cmdlet supports transactions. Note that default cmdlets, such as the Item cmdlets with the Registry provider, might not be listed in the help documents as having the –UseTransaction parameter.
>
> When you use transactions to modify a computer's configuration, keep in mind the data that is affected by the transaction is not changed until you commit the transaction. However, other commands that are not part of the transaction could make the same changes, and this could affect the working

environment. Although most transactional systems, such as relational databases, have a feature that locks data while you are working on it, PowerShell does not have a lock feature.

In each PowerShell session, only one independent transaction can be active at a time. If you start a new, independent transaction while a transaction is in progress, the new transaction becomes the active transaction, and you must complete the new transaction before making any changes to the original transaction. You complete transactions by committing or rolling back changes.

With a successful transaction, all the changes made by the commands are committed and applied to the working environment. With an unsuccessful transaction, all the changes made by the commands are undone, and the working environment is restored to its original state. By default, transactions are rolled back automatically if any command in the transaction generates an error.

Using Transactions

To start a new independent transaction or join an existing transaction as a dependent subscriber, you type start-transaction at the PowerShell prompt or in a script. By default, if you use Start-Transaction while a transaction is in progress, the existing transaction object is reused, and the subscriber count is incremented by one. You can think of this as joining the original transaction. To complete a transaction with multiple subscribers, you must type a Complete-Transaction command for each subscriber.

> **NOTE** PowerShell supports subscribers to transactions to accommodate environments when a script contains a transaction that calls another script that contains its own transaction. Because the transactions are related, they should be rolled back or committed as a unit.

With Start-Transaction, the –Independent parameter applies only when a transaction is already in progress in the session. If you use the –Independent parameter, a new transaction is created that can be completed or undone without affecting the original transaction. However, because only one transaction can be active at a time, you must complete or roll back the new transaction before resuming work with the original transaction.

In the following example and sample output, you start a transaction with automatic rollback set to Never and a timeout value of 30 minutes:

```
start-transaction -rollbackpreference "never" -timeout 30

Suggestion [1,Transactions]: Once a transaction is started, only
commands that get called with the -UseTransaction flag become part of
that transaction.
```

By adding the –RollbackPreference parameter, you can specify whether a transaction is automatically rolled back. Valid values are

- **Error**   Transactions are rolled back automatically if any command in the transaction generates a terminating or nonterminating error. This is the default.
- **TerminatingError**   Transactions are rolled back automatically if any command in the transaction generates a terminating error.
- **Never**   Transactions are never rolled back automatically.

You can use the –Timeout parameter to specify the maximum time, in minutes, that a transaction can be active. When the timeout expires, the transaction is automatically rolled back. By default, there is no timeout for transactions started at the command line. When transactions are started by a script, the default timeout is 30 minutes.

After you've started a transaction, you can perform transacted commands in two ways. You can

- Add script blocks to the active transaction with Use-Transaction.
- Add an individual command to the active transaction using the command's UseTransaction parameter.

PowerShell executes the script blocks and commands as you add them to the transaction, taking appropriate action if errors are encountered or if the timeout value is reached. You can obtain information about the transaction using Get-Transaction as shown in this example and sample output:

```
get-transaction
```

```
RollbackPreference    SubscriberCount    Status
-----------------     ---------------    ------
Never                 3                  Active
```

Here, Get-Transaction shows you the rollback preference is Never, the subscriber count is 3, and the status of the transaction is Active.

If PowerShell doesn't automatically roll back the transaction, because of errors or a timeout expiration, you can manually commit or roll back the transaction. To commit the transaction, you type complete-transaction once for each subscriber. To undo a transaction completely for all subscribers, you type undo-transaction.

Consider the following example:

```
start-transaction

cd hkcu:\Software
new-item MyKey -UseTransaction
new-itemproperty -path MyKey -Name Current `
-value "PowerShell" -UseTransaction

complete-transaction
```

Here, you start a transaction so that you can work safely with the registry. You access the HKCU\Software hive and create a new key called MyKey. Then you add a value to this key. As long as these operations did not generate an error, the transaction continues to be active, and you then apply the changes by completing the transaction.

Part IV: Tuning & Optimizing Performance

Chapter 12. Tracking System Issues

In Windows, an event is any significant occurrence in the operating system that requires users or administrators to be notified. Events are recorded in the Windows event logs and provide important historical information to help you monitor systems, maintain system security, solve problems, and perform diagnostics. It's not just important to sift regularly through the information collected in these logs, it is essential. Administrators should closely monitor the event logs of every business server and ensure that workstations are configured to track important system events. On servers, you want to ensure that systems are secure, that applications and services are operating normally, and that the server isn't experiencing errors that could hamper performance. On workstations, you want to ensure that the events you need to maintain systems and resolve problems are being logged and that the logs are accessible to you as necessary.

Working with Event Logs

The Windows service that manages event logging is called the Windows Event Log service. When this service is started, Windows logs important information. The logs available on a system depend on the system's role and the services installed. Two general types of log files are used:

- **Windows Logs** Logs that the operating system uses to record general system events related to applications, security, setup, and system components
- **Applications and Services Logs** Logs that specific applications and services use to record application-specific or service-specific events

Logs you might see include the following:

- **Application** This log records significant incidents associated with specific applications. For example, Microsoft Exchange Server logs events related to mail exchange, including events for the information store, mailboxes, and service states. By default, this log is stored in %SystemRoot%\System32\Winevt\Logs\Application.evtx.

- **DFS Replication** On domain controllers using DFS replication, this log records file replication activities on the system, including events for service status and control, scanning data in system volumes, and managing replication sets. By default, this log is stored in %SystemRoot%\System32\Winevt\Logs\DFS Replication.Evtx.

- **Directory Service** On domain controllers, this log records incidents from Active Directory Domain Services (AD DS), including events related to directory startup, global catalogs, and integrity checking. By default, this log is stored in %SystemRoot%\System32\Winevt\Logs\Directory Service.Evtx.

- **DNS Server** On Domain Name System (DNS) servers, this log records DNS queries, responses, and other DNS activities. By default, this log is stored in %SystemRoot%\System32\Winevt\Logs\DNS Server.Evtx.

- **Forwarded Events** When event forwarding is configured, this log records forwarded events from other servers. The default location is %SystemRoot%\System32\Winevt\Logs\FordwardedEvents.Evtx.

- **Hardware Events** When hardware subsystem event reporting is configured, this log records hardware events reported to the operating system. The default location is %SystemRoot%\System32\Winevt\Logs\HardwareEvent.Evtx.

- **Microsoft\Windows** A group of logs that track events related to specific Windows services and features. Logs are organized by component type and event category.

- **Security** This log records events related to security, such as logon/logoff, privilege use, and resource access. By default, this log is stored in %SystemRoot%\System32\Winevt\Logs\Security.Evtx.

> **TIP** To gain access to security logs, users must be granted the user right named Manage Auditing And Security Log. By default, members of the administrators group have this user right.

- **Setup** This log records events logged by the operating system or its components during setup and installation. The default location is %SystemRoot%\System32\Winevt\Logs\Setup.Evtx.

- **System** This log records events from the operating system or its components, such as the failure of a service to start, driver initialization, system-wide messages, and other messages that relate to the system. By default, this log is stored in %SystemRoot%\System32\Winevt\Logs\System.Evtx.

- **PowerShell** This log records activities related to the use of PowerShell. The default location is %SystemRoot%\System32\Winevt\Logs\PowerShell.Evtx.

Events range in severity from informational messages to general warnings to serious incidents such as critical errors and failures. The category of an event is indicated by its event level. Event levels include:

- **Information** Indicates an informational event has occurred, which is generally related to a successful action.
- **Warning** Indicates a general warning. Warnings are often useful in preventing future system problems.
- **Error** Indicates a critical error, such as a DHCPv6 address configuration problem.
- **Critical** Indicates a critical error, such as the computer rebooting after a power loss or crash.
- **Audit Success** Indicates the successful execution of an action that you are tracking through auditing, such as privilege use.
- **Audit Failure** Indicates the failed execution of an action that you are tracking through auditing, such as failure to log on.

TIP Of the many event types, the two you'll want to monitor closely are warnings and errors. Whenever these types of events occur and you're unsure of the reason, you should take a closer look to determine whether you need to take further action.

In addition to having a level, each event has the following common properties associated with it:

- **Computer** Identifies the computer that caused the event to occur.
- **Data** Any data or error code output by the event.
- **Date and Time** Specifies the date and time the event occurred.
- **Description** Provides a detailed description of the event and can include details about where to find more information with which to resolve or handle an issue. This field is available when you double-click a log entry in Event Viewer.
- **Event ID** Details the specific event that occurred with a numeric identifier. Event IDs are generated by the event source and used to uniquely identify the event.

- **Log Name**   Specifies the name of the log in which the event was entered.
- **Source**   Identifies the source of the event, such as an application, service, or system component. The event source is useful for pinpointing the cause of an event.
- **Task Category**   Specifies the category of the event, which is sometimes used to further describe the related action. Each event source has its own event categories. For example, with the security source, categories include logon/logoff, privilege use, policy change, and account management.
- **User**   Identifies the user account that caused the event to be generated. Users can include special identities, such as Local Service, Network Service, and Anonymous Logon, as well as actual user accounts. The user account can also be listed as N/A to indicate that a user account is not applicable in this particular situation.

The GUI tool you use to manage events is Event Viewer. You can start this tool by typing **eventvwr** at the PowerShell prompt for the local computer or **eventvwr ComputerName**, where *ComputerName* is the name of the remote computer whose events you want to examine. As with most GUI tools, Event Viewer is easy to use, and you might want to continue to use it for certain management tasks.

PowerShell provides several commands for working with the event logs, including the following:

- **Get-WinEvent**   Gets events from event logs and event tracing log files on the local computer or specified remote computers.

```
Get-WinEvent [-ListLog] LogNames {BasicParams}
Get-WinEvent [-ListProvider] ProviderNames {BasicParams}

Get-WinEvent [-Path] LogFilePath {BasicParams} {AddtlParams}
Get-WinEvent [-LogName] LogName {BasicParams} {AddtlParams}
Get-WinEvent [-ProviderName] Name {BasicParams} {AddtlParams}

Get-WinEvent -FilterHashTable Values {BasicParams} {AddtlParams}

{BasicParams}
[-ComputerName ComputerName] [-Credential CredentialObject]

{AddtlParams}
[-FilterXPath XPathQuery] [-Oldest] [-MaxEvents NumEvents]
```

- **Clear-EventLog** Deletes all entries from specified event logs on the local computer or specified remote computers. (Works with all standard Windows logs, but doesn't work with logs under Microsoft\Windows or other non-standard logs.)

```
Clear-EventLog [[-ComputerName] ComputerNames]
[-LogName] LogNames
```

- **Get-EventLog** Gets a list of the event logs or the events in a specified event log on local or remote computers. (Works with all standard Windows logs, but doesn't work with logs under Microsoft\Windows or other non-standard logs.)

```
Get-EventLog [-List] [-ComputerName ComputerNames]
[-AsString]

Get-EventLog [-ComputerName ComputerNames] [-LogName] LogName
[-AsBaseObject] [-After DateTime] [-Before DateTime]
[-EntryType EntryTypes] [-Index IndexValues]
[[-InstanceID] ID] [-Message Message] [-Newest NumEvents]
[-Source Sources] [-UserName UserNames]
```

- **Limit-EventLog** Configures limits on event log size and event retention for specified logs on specified computers. (Works with all standard Windows logs, but doesn't work with logs under Microsoft\Windows or other non-standard logs.)

```
Limit-EventLog [-ComputerName ComputerNames]
[-MaximumKiloBytes MaxSize] [-OverFlowAction {DoNotOverwrite
| OverwriteAsNeeded | OverwriteOlder] [-Retention MinDays]
[-LogName] LogNames
```

- **Show-EventLog** Displays the event logs of the local computer or a remote computer in Event Viewer. (Works with all standard Windows logs, but doesn't work with logs under Microsoft\Windows or other non-standard logs.)

```
Show-EventLog [[-ComputerName] ComputerName]
```

NOTE You can use Get-Event, Wait-Event, and Remove-Event to work with the PowerShell event log. When you are creating your own event logs, you can use New-EventLog, Register-ObjectEvent, Register-EngineEvent,

Unregister-Event, Get-EventSubscriber, and Register-WmiEvent. New-EventLog works with all standard Windows logs, but doesn't work with logs under Microsoft\Windows or other non-standard logs.

Monitoring system events isn't something you should do haphazardly. Rather, it is something you should do routinely and thoroughly. With servers, you will want to examine event logs at least once a day. With desktop computers, you will want to examine logs on specific computers as necessary, such as when a user reports a problem.

Viewing and Filtering Event Logs

You can obtain detailed information from the event logs using either Get-EventLog or Get-WinEvent. Get-EventLog is handy for its versatility and simplicity. Use Get-WinEvent when you want to apply complex filters, such as those based on XPath queries or hashtable strings. If you don't use complex filters, you really don't need Get-WinEvent.

The basic syntax for Get-EventLog is

```
get-eventlog "LogName" [-computername ComputerNames]
```

where *LogName* is the name of the log you want to work with—such as "Application," "System," or "Directory Service"—and *ComputerNames* are the names of remote computers you want to work with. In this example, you examine the Application log:

```
get-eventlog "Application" -computername fileserver87, dbserver23
```

NOTE Technically, the quotation marks are necessary only when the log name contains a space, as is the case with the DNS Server, Directory Service, etc.

The output of this query will look similar to the following:

```
Index   Time            EntryType    Source          InstanceID Message
-----   ----            ---------    ------          ---------- -------
22278   Feb 27 10:54 Information DQLWinService           0 The
description for Event ID '0' in Source 'DQL

22277   Feb 27 10:49  Information DQLWinService          0 The
description for Event ID '0' in Source 'DQL
```

As you can see, the output shows the Index, Time, EntryType, Source, InstanceID, and Message properties of events. The Index is the position of the event in the event log. The Time is the time the event was written. The EntryType shows the category of the event. The Source shows the source of the event. The InstanceID shows the specific event that occurred with a numeric identifier (and is the same as the EventID field in the event logs). The Message shows the description of the event.

Because the index is the position of the event in the log, this example lists events 22,277 and 22,278. By default, Get-EventLog returns every event in the specified event log from newest to oldest. In most cases, this is simply too much information, and you'll need to filter the events to get a usable amount of data. One way to filter the event logs is to specify that you want to see details about only the newest events. For example, you might want to see only the 50 newest events in a log.

Using the –Newest parameter, you can limit the return to the newest events. The following example lists the 50 newest events in the security log:

```
get-eventlog "security" -newest 50
```

One of the key reasons for using Get-EventLog is its ability to group and filter events in the result set. When you group events by type, you can more easily separate informational events from critical, warning, and error events. When you group by source, you can more easily track events from specific sources. When you group by event ID, you can more easily correlate the recurrence of specific events.

You can group events by Source, EventId, EntryType, and TimeGenerated using the following technique:

1. Get the events you want to work with, and store them in a variable, such as

```
$e = get-eventlog -newest 100 -logname "application"
```

2. Use the Group-Object cmdlet to group the event objects by a specified property. In this example, you group by EventType:

```
$e | group-object -property eventtype
```

Another way to work with events is to sort them according to a specific property. You can sort by Source, EventId, EntryType, or TimeGenerated using the following technique:

1. Get the events you want to work with, and store them in a variable, such as

```
$e = get-eventlog -newest 100 -logname "application"
```

2. Use the Sort-Object cmdlet to sort the event objects by a specified property. In this example, you sort by EntryType:

```
$e | sort-object -property entrytype
```

Typically, you won't want to see every event generated on a system. More often, you will want to see only warnings or critical errors, and that is precisely what filters are for. Using filters, you can include only events that match the criteria you specify. To do this, you search the EntryType property for occurrences of the word *error*. Here is an example:

1. Get the events you want to work with, and store them in a variable, such as

```
$e = get-eventlog -newest 500 -logname "application"
```

2. Use the Where-Object cmdlet to search for specific text in a named property of the event objects stored in $e. In this example, you match events with the Error entry type:

```
$e | where-object {$_.EntryType -match "error"}
```

With the –Match parameter, the Where-Object cmdlet uses a search algorithm that is not case-sensitive, meaning you can type **Error**, **error**, or **ERROR** to match error events. You can also search for warning, critical, and information events. Because Where-Object considers partial text matches to be valid, you don't want to enter the full entry type. You can also search for **warn**, **crit**, or **info**, such as

```
$e = get-eventlog -newest 100 -logname "application"
$e | where-object {$_.EntryType -match "warn"}
```

You can use Where-Object with other event object properties as well. The following example searches for event sources containing the text *User Profile Service*:

```
$e = get-eventlog -newest 500 -logname "application"
$e | where-object {$_.Source -match "User Profile Service"}
```

The following example searches for event ID *1530*:

```
$e = get-eventlog -newest 500 -logname "application"
$e | where-object {$_.EventID -match "1530"}
```

Sometimes, you'll want to find events that occurred before or after a specific date, and you can do this using the –Before and –After parameters. The –Before parameter gets only the events that occur before a specified date and time. The –After parameter gets only the events that occur after a specified date and time.

In the following example, you get all of the errors in the System log that occurred in July 2017:

```
$Jun30 = get-date 6/30/21
$Aug1 = get-date 8/01/21

get-eventlog -log "system" -entrytype Error –after
$jun30 -before $aug1
```

In the following example, you get all of the errors in the System log that occurred in the last seven days:

```
$startdate = (get-date).adddays(-7)
get-eventlog -log "system" -entrytype Error -after $startdate
```

You can automate the event querying process by creating a script that obtains the event information you want to see and then writes it to a text file. Consider the following example:

```
$e = get-eventlog -newest 100 -logname "system" $e |
where-object {$_.EntryType -match "error"} >
\\FileServer18\www\currentlog.txt

$e = get-eventlog -newest 100 -logname "application" $e |
where-object {$_.EntryType -match "error"} >>
\\FileServer18\www\currentlog.txt
```

```
$e = get-eventlog -newest 100 -logname "security" $e |
where-object {$_.EntryType -match "error"} >>
\\FileServer18\www\currentlog.txt
```

Here, you are examining the system, application, and security event logs and writing any resulting output to a network share on FileServer18. If any of the named logs have error events among the 100 most recent events in the logs, the errors are written to the CurrentLog.txt file. Because the first redirection is overwrite (>) and the remaining entries are append (>>), any existing Currentlog.txt file is overwritten each time the script runs. This ensures that only current events are listed. To take the automation process a step further, you could create a scheduled job that runs the script each day or at specific intervals during the day.

Setting Log Options

Log options allow you to control the size of the event logs as well as how logging is handled. By default, event logs are set with a maximum file size. Then, when a log reaches this limit, events are overwritten to prevent the log from exceeding the maximum file size.

You use Limit-EventLog to set log options. The basic syntax is

```
Limit-EventLog [-ComputerName ComputerNames] [-LogName] LogNames
Options
```

Here *ComputerNames* are the names of the computers you are configuring, *LogNames* sets the logs to modify, and *Options* includes one or more of the following:

- **–MaximumSize**   Sets the maximum size in bytes of a log file. The size must be in the range 64 KB to 4 GB, in increments of 64 KB. Make sure that the drive containing the operating system has enough free space for the maximum log size you select. Most log files are stored in the %SystemRoot%\System32\Winevt\Logs directory by default.
- **–OverFlowAction**   Sets the event log wrapping mode. The options are DoNotOverwrite, OverwriteAsNeeded, and OverwriteOlder. With DoNotOverwrite, the computer generates error messages telling you the event log is full when the

maximum file size is reached. With OverwriteAsNeeded, each new entry overwrites the oldest entry when the maximum file size is reached, and there are no limitations. With OverwriteOlder, new events overwrite only events older than the value specified by the Retention property when the maximum file size is reached. If there are no events older than the minimum retention value, the computer generates error messages telling you events cannot be overwritten.

- **–Retention**   Sets the minimum number of days that an event must remain in the event log.

In the following example, you configure the system log with a maximum size of 4096 KB, an overflow action of OverwriteOlder, and a minimum retention period of seven days:

```
limit-eventlog -maximumsize 4096kb -overflowaction
overwriteolder -retention 7 -logname system
```

If you are configuring multiple computers, you can use the –ComputerName property to specify the computer names. Or you can get the list of computer names from a text file as shown in the following example:

```
limit-eventlog -computername (get-content c:\data\clist.txt)
-maximumkilobytes 4096 -overflowaction overwriteolder
-retention 7 -logname system
```

Here, you get the list of remote computers to manage from a file called CList.txt in the C:\Data directory.

Archiving and Clearing Event Logs

On key systems such as domain controllers and application servers, you'll want to keep several months' worth of event logs. However, it usually isn't practical to set the maximum log size to accommodate this. Instead, you should allow Windows to periodically archive the event logs, or you should manually archive the event logs. Logs can be archived in four formats:

- Event files (.evtx) format, for access in Event Viewer

- Tab-delimited text (.txt) format, for access in text editors or word processors or for import into spreadsheets and databases
- Comma-delimited text (.csv) format, for import into spreadsheets or databases
- XML (.xml) format, for saving as a structured Extensible Markup Language (XML) file.

The best format to use for archiving is the .evtx format. Use this format if you plan to review old logs in the Event Viewer. However, if you plan to review logs in other applications, you might need to save the logs in a tab-delimited or comma-delimited format. With the tab-delimited or comma-delimited format, you sometimes need to edit the log file in a text editor for the log to be properly interpreted. If you have saved the log in the .evtx format, you can always save another copy in the tab-delimited or comma-delimited format later by doing another Save As after opening the archive in the Event Viewer.

Windows creates log archives automatically when you select the event log-wrapping mode Archive The Log When Full, Do Not Overwrite Events. This mode is set in Event Viewer.

You can create a log archive manually by following these steps:

1. In Event Viewer, you should see a list of event logs. Right-click the event log you want to archive, and select Save Events As from the shortcut menu.
2. In the Save As dialog box, select a directory and type a log file name.
3. In the Save As Type dialog box, Event Files (*.evtx) is the default file type. Select a log format as appropriate and then choose Save.
4. If the Display Information dialog box is displayed, choose the appropriate display options and then click OK.

If you plan to archive logs regularly, you might want to create an archive directory. This way you can easily locate the log archives. You should also name the log file so that you can easily determine the log file type and the period of the archive. For example, if you're archiving the system log file for January 2015, you might want to use the file name System Log January 2015.

When an event log is full and you want to clear it, you can do so using Clear-EventLog. The basic syntax is

```
Clear-EventLog [-ComputerName ComputerNames] [-LogName] LogNames
```

Here *ComputerNames* are the names of the computers you are configuring and *LogNames* sets the logs to clear, such as

```
clear-eventlog system
```

Writing Custom Events to the Event Logs

Whenever you work with automated scripts, scheduled jobs, or custom applications, you might want those scripts, tasks, or applications to write custom events to the event logs. For example, if a script runs normally, you might want to write an informational event in the application log that specifies this so that it is easier to determine that the script ran and completed normally. Similarly, if a script doesn't run normally and generates errors, you might want to log an error or warning event in the application log so that you'll know to examine the script and determine what happened.

PowerShell includes built-in logging features that log events to the PowerShell event log. You can view events in this log using Get-EventLog. You control logging using the following environment variables, which must be set in the appropriate profile or profiles to be applicable:

- **$LogCommandHealthEvent** Determines whether errors and exceptions in command initialization and processing are logged
- **$LogCommandLifecycleEvent** Determines whether PowerShell logs the starting and stopping of commands and command pipelines and security exceptions in command discovery
- **$LogEngineHealthEvent** Determines whether PowerShell logs errors and failures of sessions
- **$LogEngineLifecycleEvent** Determines whether PowerShell logs the opening and closing of sessions
- **$LogProviderHealthEvent** Determines whether PowerShell logs provider errors, such as read and write errors, lookup errors, and invocation errors
- **$LogProviderLifecycleEvent** Determines whether PowerShell logs adding and removing of PowerShell providers

If you set a logging variable to $True, the related events are logged in the PowerShell log. Use a value of $False to turn off logging.

You can create custom events using the Eventcreate utility. Custom events can be logged in any available log except the security log, and they can include the event source, ID, and description you want to use. The syntax for Eventcreate is as follows:

```
eventcreate /l LogName /so EventSource /t EventType /id EventID
/d EventDescr
```

- **LogName**   Sets the name of the log to which the event should be written. Use quotation marks if the log name contains spaces, as in "DNS Server."

> **TIP**   Although you cannot write custom events to the security log, you can write custom events to the other logs. Start by writing a dummy event using the event source you want to register for use with that log. The initial event for that source will be written to the application log. You can then use the source with the specified log and your custom events.

- **EventSource**   Specifies the source to use for the event, and can be any string of characters. If the string contains spaces, use quotation marks, as in "Event Tracker." In most cases, you'll want the event source to identify the application, task, or script that is generating the error.

> **REAL WORLD**   Carefully plan the event source you want to use before you write events to the logs using those sources. Each event source you use must be unique and cannot have the same name as an existing source used by an installed service or application. Further, you shouldn't use event source names used by Windows roles, role services, or features. For example, you shouldn't use DNS, W32Time, or Ntfrs as sources because these sources are used by Windows Server.
>
> Additionally, once you use an event source with a particular log, the event source is registered for use with that log on the specified system. For example, you cannot use "EventChecker" as a source in the application log and in the system log on FILESERVER82. If you try to write an event using "EventChecker" to the system log after writing a previous event with that source to the application log, you will see the following error message: "ERROR: Source already exists in 'Application' log. Source cannot be duplicated."

- **EventType** Sets the event type as Information, Warning, or Error. Audit Success and Audit Failure event types are not valid; these events are used with the security logs, and you cannot write custom events to the security logs.
- **EventID** Specifies the numeric ID for the event, and can be any value from 1 to 1,000. Before you assign event IDs haphazardly, you might want to create a list of the general events that can occur and then break these down into categories. You can then assign a range of event IDs to each category. For example, events in the 100s could be general events, events in the 200s could be status events, events in the 500s could be warning events, and events in the 900s could be error events.
- **EventDescr** Sets the description for the event, and can be any string of characters. Be sure to enclose the description in quotation marks.

Eventcreate runs by default on the local computer with the permissions of the user who is currently logged on. As necessary, you can also specify the remote computer whose tasks you want to query and the Run As permissions using **/S Computer /u [Domain\]User [/P Password]**, where *Computer* is the remote computer name or IP address, *Domain* is the optional domain name in which the user account is located, *User* is the name of the user account whose permissions you want to use, and *Password* is the optional password for the user account.

To see how you can use Eventcreate, consider the following examples:

Create an information event in the application log with the source Event Tracker and event ID 209:

```
eventcreate /l "application" /t information /so "Event Tracker"
/id 209 /d "evs.bat script ran without errors."
```

Create a warning event in the system log with the source CustApp and event ID 511:

```
eventcreate /l "system" /t warning /so "CustApp" /id 511
/d "sysck.exe didn't complete successfully."
```

Create an error event in the system log on FileServer18 with the source "SysMon" and event ID 918:

```
eventcreate /s FileServer18 /l "system" /t error /so "SysMon"
/id 918 /d "sysmon.exe was unable to verify write operation."
```

Creating and Using Saved Queries

Event Viewer supports XPath queries for creating custom views and filtering event logs. XPath is a non-XML language used to identify specific parts of XML documents. Event Viewer uses XPath expressions that match and select elements in a source log and copy them to a destination log to create a custom or filtered view.

When you are creating a custom or filtered view in Event Viewer, you can copy the XPath query and save it to an Event Viewer Custom View file. By running this query again, you can re-create the custom view or filter on any computer running Windows or Windows Server. For example, if you create a filtered view of the application log that helps you identify a problem with SQL Server, you can save the related XPath query to a Custom View file so that you can create the filtered view on other computers in your organization.

Event Viewer creates several filtered views of the event logs for you automatically. Filtered views are listed under the Custom Views node. When you select the Administrative Events node, you see a list of all errors and warnings for all logs. When you expand the Server Roles node and then select a role-specific view, you see a list of all events for the selected role.

You can create and save your own custom view by following these steps:

1. Start Event Viewer by clicking Event Viewer on the Tools menu in Server Manager.

2. Select the Custom Views node. In the Actions pane or on the Action menu, click Create Custom View.

3. In the Create Custom View dialog box, use the Logged list to select the included time frame for logged events. You can choose to include events from Anytime, Last Hour, Last 12 Hours, Last 24 Hours, Last 7 Days, or Last 30 Days. You also can specify a custom range.

4. Use the Event Level check boxes to specify the level of events to include. Select Verbose to get additional detail.

5. You can create a custom view for either a specific set of logs or a specific set of event sources:

- Use the Event Logs list to select event logs to include. You can select multiple event logs by selecting their related check boxes. If you select specific event logs, all other event logs are excluded.
- Use the Event Sources list to select event sources to include. You can select multiple event sources by selecting their related check boxes. If you select specific event sources, all other event sources are excluded.

6. Optionally, use the User and Computer(s) boxes to specify users and computers that should be included. If you do not specify the users and computers to be included, events generated by all users and computers are included.

7. Click the XML tab to display the related XPath query.

8. Click OK to close the Create Custom View dialog box. In the Save Filter To Custom View dialog box, type a name and description for the custom view.

9. Select where to save the custom view. By default, custom views are saved under the Custom View node. You can create a new node by clicking New Folder, typing the name of the new folder, and then clicking OK.

10. Click OK to close the Save Filter To Custom View dialog box. You should now see a filtered list of events.

11. Right-click the custom view and then select Export Custom View. Use the Save As dialog box to select a save location and enter a file name for the Event Viewer Custom View file.

The Custom View file contains the XPath query that was displayed on the XML tab previously. Members of the Event Log Readers group, administrators, and others with appropriate permissions can run the query to view events on remote computers using the following syntax:

```
eventvwr ComputerName /v: QueryFile
```

Here *ComputerName* is the name of the remote computer whose events you want to examine and *QueryFile* is the name or full path to the Custom View file containing the XPath query, such as

```
eventvwr fileserver18 /v: importantevents.xml
```

When Event Viewer starts, you'll find the custom view under the Custom Views node.

Chapter 13. Enabling Recovery

System Restore is only available with desktop versions of Windows. With System Restore enabled, a desktop computer makes periodic snapshots of the system configuration. These snapshots are called *restore points*. These restore points include Windows settings, lists of programs that have been installed, and so on. If the computer has problems starting or isn't working properly because of a system configuration change, you can use a restore point to restore the system configuration to the point at which the snapshot was made. For example, suppose your system is working fine and then you install a new service pack release for Microsoft Office. Afterward, the computer generates errors, and Office applications won't run. You try to uninstall the update, but that doesn't work, so you decide to run System Restore. Using System Restore, you can restore the system using a snapshot taken before the update.

System Restore automatically creates several types of restore points. These include the following:

- **Scheduled**   Checkpoints scheduled by the operating system and occurring at regular intervals
- **Windows Update**   Checkpoints created before applying Windows updates
- **Application Install**   Checkpoints created before installing applications
- **Application Uninstall**   Checkpoints created before uninstalling applications
- **Device Install**   Checkpoints created before installing devices
- **Device Uninstall**   Checkpoints created before uninstalling devices

You should create restore points manually before performing an operation that might cause problems on the system.

System Restore manages restore points on a per-drive basis. Each drive with critical applications and system files should be monitored for configuration changes. By default, System Restore is enabled only for the System drive. You can modify the System Restore configuration by turning on monitoring of other drives as needed. If a drive isn't configured for System Restore monitoring, configuration changes are not tracked, and the disk cannot be recovered if problems occur.

> **NOTE**   With Windows 8 and later, you create previous versions of personal files using File History backups.

Commands for Configuring System Restore

At an administrator PowerShell prompt, you can view and work with System Restore using the following commands:

- **Enable-ComputerRestore**   Turns on the System Restore feature on one or more fixed, internal drives. You cannot enable System Restore on external or network drives.

```
Enable-ComputerRestore [-Drive] DriveStrings
```

- **Disable-ComputerRestore**   Turns off the System Restore feature on one or more file system drives. As a result, attempts to restore the computer do not affect the specified drive.

```
Disable-ComputerRestore [-Drive] DriveStrings
```

- **Get-ComputerRestorePoint**   Gets one or more restore points on the local computer, or displays the status of the most recent attempt to restore the computer.

```
Get-ComputerRestorePoint [-RestorePoint] SequenceNumber
Get-ComputerRestorePoint -LastStatus
```

- **Checkpoint-Computer**   Creates a system restore point on the local computer. The –RestorePointType parameter optionally specifies the type of restore point.

```
Checkpoint-Computer [[-RestorePointType] Type] [-Description]
Description
```

- **Restore-Computer**   Restores the local computer to the specified system restore point. A restart of the computer is performed to complete the restore. The –RestorePoint parameter specifies the sequence number of the restore point.

```
Restore-Computer [-RestorePoint] SequenceNumber
```

The system process responsible for monitoring configuration and application changes is the System Restore service. This service is configured for automatic startup and runs under the Local System account. System Restore won't work properly if this service isn't running or configured appropriately.

System Restore saves system checkpoint information for all monitored drives and requires at least 300 MB of disk space on the System volume to save restore points. System Restore reserves additional space for restore points as necessary, up to 10 percent of the total disk capacity, but this additional space is always available for user and application storage. System Restore frees up additional space for you as necessary. If System Restore runs out of available space, the operating system overwrites previously created restore points.

Enabling and Disabling System Restore

You can enable System Restore for a volume using Enable-ComputerRestore. The basic syntax is

```
Enable-ComputerRestore [-Drive] DriveStrings
```

With the −Drive parameter, specify one or more drive letters, each followed by a colon and a backslash and enclosed in quotation marks, as shown in the following example:

```
enable-computerrestore -drive "C:\", "D:\"
```

To enable System Restore on any drive, it must be enabled on the system drive, either first or concurrently. When you enable System Restore, restore points are created automatically as discussed previously.

You can disable System Restore for a volume using Disable-ComputerRestore. The basic syntax is

```
Disable-ComputerRestore [-Drive] DriveStrings
```

With the −Drive parameter, specify one or more file system drive letters, each followed by a colon and a backslash and enclosed in quotation marks, as shown in the following example:

```
disable-computerrestore -drive "C:\", "D:\"
```

You cannot disable System Restore on the System volume without disabling System Restore on all other volumes.

Although these commands don't support the –ComputerName parameter, you can use the remoting techniques discussed in Chapters 10 – 12 of *PowerShell: IT Pro Solutions*, to invoke System Restore–related commands on remote computers. Here is an example:

```
invoke-command -computername techpc24 -scriptblock
{ enable-computerrestore -drive "C:\", "D:\" }
```

Here, you enable System Restore on the C and D drives of TechPC25.

Creating and Using Checkpoints

You can manually create a restore point by typing **checkpoint-computer** followed by a description of the checkpoint. Consider the following example:

```
checkpoint-computer "Modify PowerShell"
```

Here, you create a "Modify PowerShell" checkpoint. PowerShell displays a progress bar while the restore point is being created. Optionally, you can specify the type of restore point using the –RestorePointType parameter. The default is APPLICATION_INSTALL. Valid values are as follows:

- APPLICATION_INSTALL, for when you are planning to install an application
- APPLICATION_UNINSTALL, for when you are planning to uninstall an application
- DEVICE_DRIVER_INSTALL, for when you are planning to modify device drivers
- MODIFY_SETTINGS, for when you are planning to modify configuration settings

You can use Get-ComputerRestorePoint to list all available restore points or a specific restore point by its sequence number. The sequence number is simply an incremented value that makes it possible to track a specific instance of a restore point.

To list all available restore points, type **get-computerrestorepoint**, as shown in the following example and sample output:

```
get-computerrestorepoint
```

```
CreationTime            Description   SequenceNumber EventType
RestorePointType
-----------             -----------   -------------- ---------      -------------
---
11/19/2020 2:53:46 PM   Windows Update    48         BEGIN_SYSTEM_C... 18
12/1/2020 8:58:08 AM    Windows Update    49         BEGIN_SYSTEM_C... 18
12/8/2020 9:22:51 AM    Scheduled Checkpoint  50     BEGIN_SYSTEM_C... 7
```

From the output, you can see restore points are listed by creation time, description, sequence number, event type, and restore point type. Once you identify a restore point that you want to work with, note its sequence number. Using the – RestorePoint parameter, you can get that specific restore point. In this example, you get restore point 289:

```
get-computerrestorepoint 289
```

As each value returned for a restore point is set in a like-named property, you can filter the output of Get-ComputerRestorePoint using Where-Object. In the following example, you get all restore points created in the last three days:

```
$date = (get-date).adddays(-3)
get-computerrestorepoint | where-object {$_.creationtime -gt $date}
```

In the following example, you get restore points with a specific description:

```
get-computerrestorepoint | where-object {$_.description -eq
"Modify PowerShell"}
```

To get restore points by description, you need to know the numeric value that denotes a specific type. These values include the following:

- 0 for application install checkpoints, which include Windows Update check points
- 1 for application uninstall checkpoints
- 7 for scheduled checkpoints
- 10 for device driver install checkpoints
- 12 for modify settings checkpoints

In the following example, you get all restore points for application installs:

```
get-computerrestorepoint | where-object {$_.restorepointtype -eq 0}
```

Recovering from Restore Points

To recover a computer from a restore point, type **restore-computer** followed by the sequence number of the restore point to restore. Use Get-ComputerRestorePoint to display a list of available restore points by their sequence number if necessary. In the following example, you initiate a restore of the computer using restore point 353:

```
restore-computer 353
```

Here, you initiate a restore of EngPC85 to restore point 276:

```
invoke-command -computername engpc85 -scriptblock
{ restore-computer 276 }
```

During the restoration, System Restore shuts down the computer. After the restore is complete, the computer is restarted using the settings from the date and time of the snapshot. After the computer restarts, you can type **get-computerrestorepoint -laststatus** to check the status of the restore operation. Read the message provided to confirm the restore was successful. If the restore was unsuccessful, this is stated explicitly, such as

```
The last restore was interrupted.
```

If Windows isn't working properly after a restore, you can apply a different restore point or reverse the restore operation by repeating this procedure and selecting the restore point that was created automatically before applying the current system state.

Chapter 14. Optimizing System Performance

An important part of every administrator's job is to monitor network systems and ensure that everything is running smoothly—or as smoothly as can be expected, anyway. As you learned in the previous chapter, watching the event logs closely can help you detect and track problems with applications, security, and essential services. Often when you detect or suspect a problem, you'll need to dig deeper to search out the cause of the problem and correct it. If you're fortunate, by pinpointing the cause of a problem, you can prevent it from happening again.

Whenever the operating system or a user starts a service, runs an application, or executes a command, Windows starts one or more processes to handle the related program. Several commands are available to help you manage and monitor programs. These commands include the following:

- **Debug-Process** Debugs one or more processes running on the local computer.

```
Debug-Process [-Id] ProcessIDs | -InputObject Objects |
-Name Names
```

- **Get-Process** Lists all running processes by name and process ID. The list includes information on memory usage.

```
Get-Process -Id ProcessIDs | -InputObject Objects |
[[-Name] Names] [-ComputerName ComputerNames]
[-FileVersionInfo] [-Module]
```

- **Start-Process** Starts one or more processes on the local computer. To specify the program that runs in the process, enter the path to an executable file or script file. Alternatively, you can specify a file that can be opened in a program, such as a Microsoft Office Word document or Office Excel worksheet. If you specify a nonexecutable file, Start-Process starts the program that is associated with the file by using the default action. Typically, the default action is Open. You can set the action to take using the –Verb parameter.

```
Start-Process [-Verb {Edit|Open|Print|...}]
[-WorkingDirectory DirectoryPath] [[-ArgumentList] Args]
[-FilePath] PathToExeOrDoc [-Credential CredentialObject]
[-LoadUserProfile {$True|$False}] [-NoNewWindow] [-PassThru]
```

```
[-RedirectStandardError FilePath] [-RedirectStandardInput
FilePath] [-RedirectStandardOutput FilePath]
[-UseNewEnvironment] [-Wait] [-WindowStyle
{Normal|Hidden|Minimized|Maximized}]
```

- **Stop-Process** Stops running processes by name or process ID. Using filters, you can also halt processes by process status, session number, CPU time, memory usage, and more.

```
Stop-Process [-Id] ProcessIDs | -InputObject Objects |
-Name Names [-Force] [-PassThru]
```

- **Wait-Process** Waits for a specified process to be stopped before accepting more input.

```
Wait-Process -Id ProcessIDs | -InputObject Objects |
[-Name] Names [[-TimeOut] WaitTime]
```

In the sections that follow, you'll find detailed discussions on how these commands are used. First, however, let's look at the ways processes are run and the common problems you might encounter when working with them.

Understanding System and User Processes

When you want to examine processes that are running on a local or remote system, you can use Get-Process and other commands. With Get-Process, you can obtain the process ID, status, and other important information about processes running on a system. You also can use filters to include or exclude processes from Get-Process queries. To dig deeper, you can use the Win32_Process and Win32_Service classes.

Generally, processes that the operating system starts are referred to as system processes; processes that users start are referred to as user processes. Most user processes are run in interactive mode. That is, a user starts a process interactively with the keyboard or mouse. If the application or program is active and selected, the related interactive process has control over the keyboard and mouse until you switch control by terminating the program or selecting a different one. When a process has control, it's said to be running "in the foreground."

Processes can also run in the background, independently of user logon sessions. Background processes do not have control over the keyboard, mouse, or other input devices and are usually run by the operating system. Using the Task Scheduler, users can run processes in the background as well, however, and these processes can operate regardless of whether the user is logged on. For example, if Task Scheduler starts a scheduled job while the user is logged on, the process can continue even when the user logs off.

Windows tracks every process running on a system by image name, process ID, priority, and other parameters that record resource usage. The image name is the name of the executable that started the process, such as Msdtc.exe or Svchost.exe. The process ID is a numeric identifier for the process, such as 1160. The base priority is an indicator of how much of the system's resources the process should get relative to other running processes. With priority processing, a process with a higher-priority gets preference over processes with lower priority, and the higher-priority process might not have to wait to get processing time, access memory, or work with the file system. A process with lower priority, on the other hand, usually must wait for a higher-priority process to complete its current task before gaining access to the CPU, memory, or the file system.

In a perfect world, processes would run perfectly and would never have problems. The reality is, however, that problems occur and they often appear when you least want them to. Common problems include the following:

- Processes become nonresponsive, such as when an application stops processing requests. When this happens, users might tell you that they can't access a particular application, that their requests aren't being handled, or that they were kicked out of the application.
- Processes fail to release the CPU, such as when you have a runaway process that is using up CPU time. When this happens, the system might appear to be slow or nonresponsive because the runaway process is hogging processor time and is not allowing other processes to complete their tasks.
- Processes use more memory than they should, such as when an application has a memory leak. When this happens, processes aren't properly releasing memory that they're using. As a result, the system's available memory might gradually decrease over time and, as the available memory gets low, the system might be slow to respond to requests or it might become nonresponsive. Memory leaks can also make other programs running on the same system behave erratically.

In most cases, when you detect these or other problems with system processes, you'll want to stop the process and start it again. You'll also want to examine the event logs to see whether you can determine the cause of the problem. In the case of memory leaks, you'll want to report the memory leak to the developers and see whether an update that resolves the problem is available.

A periodic restart of an application with a known memory leak is often useful. Restarting the application should allow the operating system to recover any lost memory.

Examining Running Processes

To get a list of all processes running on a system, type **get-process** at the command prompt as shown in the following example and sample output:

```
get-process -computername fileserver86
```

Handles	NPM(K)	PM(K)	WS(K)	VM(M)	CPU(s)	Id	ProcessName
56	7	2088	5868	59	0.09	3680	conhost
387	11	2148	1924	44	0.42	436	csrss
92	22	1804	528	39	0.22	496	csrss
217	12	1828	13480	55	3.31	2928	csrss
169	14	7000	5324	122	0.41	896	dwm
192	19	22220	36228	188	4.78	3040	dwm
1389	82	47260	51548	579	10.39	1540	explorer
0	0	0	4	0		0	Idle
357	28	26752	27464	302	0.39	812	LogonUI
915	26	4940	8084	38	1.92	588	lsass
523	54	110704	58340	299	139.34	1456	MsMpEng
255	11	5328	1996	50	6.39	2136	NisSrv
387	26	117412	123608	615	1.20	3700	powershell
218	10	2212	4792	81	0.73	1736	rdpclip
1005	52	22424	10576	320	1.25	1692	
SearchIndexer							
218	11	4248	4068	30	0.95	580	services
47	2	284	452	4	0.05	320	smss
458	62	41324	12420	324	2.02	3548	Snagit32
522	86	29832	22424	263	9.59	3864	
SnagitEditor							
81	9	1256	36	52	0.00	3732	SnagPriv
201	11	2620	1260	75	0.00	3992	splwow64

```
904        23      6092        7704    71      0.67    1068 spoolsv
602        19      6116        6692    47      0.81     660 svchost
```

Because the –ComputerName parameter accepts multiple name values, you can check the status of processes on multiple computers simply by typing the names of the computers to check in a comma-separate list as shown in the following example:

```
get-process –computername fileserver86, dcserver22, printserver31
```

Rather than type computer names each time, you can type computer names on separate lines in a text file and then get the list of computer names from the text file as shown in the following example:

```
get-process -computername (get-content c:\data\clist.txt)
```

Here, you get the list of remote computers to check from a file called Clist.txt in the C:\Data directory.

When you are looking for a specific process, you can reference the process by its process name or process ID. To match partial names, you can use wildcard characters as shown in the following example and sample output:

```
get-process win* –computername fileserver86
```

Handles	NPM(K)	PM(K)	WS(K)	VM(M)	CPU(s)	Id	ProcessName
77	8	868	764	40	0.06	480	wininit
121	7	1336	912	52	0.02	540	winlogon
146	7	1248	10036	57	0.13	2956	winlogon
485	26	45992	69220	441	83.34	5200	WINWORD

Here, you look for all processes where the process name begins with *win*.

Get-Process returns objects representing each process matching the criteria you specify. As you can see from previous examples and sample output, the standard output includes:

- **CPU** An alias for TotalProcessorTime.TotalSeconds. This item shows the number of seconds of CPU time the process has used.
- **Handles** An alias for the HandleCount property. This item shows the number of file handles maintained by the process.

- **NPM**   An alias for the NonpagedSystemMemorySize property. This item shows the amount of virtual memory for a process that cannot be written to disk.
- **PM**   An alias for the PagedMemorySize property. This item shows the amount of committed virtual memory for a process that can be written to disk.
- **VM**   An alias for the VirtualMemorySize property. This item shows the amount of virtual memory allocated to and reserved for a process.
- **WS**   An alias for the WorkingSet property. This item shows the amount of memory the process is currently using, including both the private working set and the nonprivate working set.
- **Id**   The process identification number.
- **ProcessName**   The name of the process or executable running the process.

As you examine processes, keep in mind that a single application might start multiple processes. Generally, these processes are dependent on the central application process, and from this main process a process tree containing dependent processes is formed. When you terminate processes, you'll usually want to target the main application process or the application itself rather than dependent processes. This approach ensures that the application is stopped cleanly.

To view all of the available properties, you need to format the output as a list, as shown in the following example and partial output:

```
get-process winword -computername server12 | format-list *

Name                    : WINWORD
Id                      : 8692
PriorityClass           : Normal
FileVersion             : 16.0.7766.2060
HandleCount             : 2238
WorkingSet              : 365899776
PagedMemorySize         : 356823040
PrivateMemorySize       : 356823040
VirtualMemorySize       : 1101127680
TotalProcessorTime      : 02:02:01.6875000
SI                      : 1
Handles                 : 2238
VM                      : 1101127680
WS                      : 365899776
PM                      : 356823040
NPM                     : 111824
```

```
Path                          : C:\Program Files (x86)\Microsoft
Office\root\Office16\WINWORD.EXE
Company                       : Microsoft Corporation
CPU                           : 7321.6875
ProductVersion                : 16.0.7766.2060
Description                   : Microsoft Word
Product                       : Microsoft Office 2016
__NounName                    : Process
BasePriority                  : 8
ExitCode                      :
HasExited                     : False
ExitTime                      :
Handle                        : 2624
SafeHandle                    :
Microsoft.Win32.SafeHandles.SafeProcessHandle
MachineName                   : .
MainWindowHandle              : 722104
MainWindowTitle               : PowerShell PT for Admin - Final
Ebook.docx - Word
MainModule                    : System.Diagnostics.ProcessModule
(WINWORD.EXE)
MaxWorkingSet                 : 1413120
MinWorkingSet                 : 204800
Modules                       : {System.Diagnostics.ProcessModule
(WINWORD.EXE), System.Diagnostics.ProcessModule
                                (ntdll.dll),
System.Diagnostics.ProcessModule (wow64.dll),
                                System.Diagnostics.ProcessModule
(wow64win.dll)...}
NonpagedSystemMemorySize      : 111824
NonpagedSystemMemorySize64    : 111824
PagedMemorySize64             : 356823040
PagedSystemMemorySize         : 1442704
PagedSystemMemorySize64       : 1442704
PeakPagedMemorySize           : 446967808
PeakPagedMemorySize64         : 446967808
PeakWorkingSet                : 458342400
PeakWorkingSet64              : 458342400
PeakVirtualMemorySize         : 1298112512
PeakVirtualMemorySize64       : 1298112512
PriorityBoostEnabled          : True
PrivateMemorySize64           : 356823040
PrivilegedProcessorTime       : 00:06:46.7812500
ProcessName                   : WINWORD
ProcessorAffinity             : 255
Responding                    : True
SessionId                     : 1
```

```
StartInfo                  : System.Diagnostics.ProcessStartInfo
StartTime                  : 3/27/2020 3:23:34 PM
SynchronizingObject        :
Threads                    : {8696, 8800, 8812, 8824...}
UserProcessorTime          : 01:55:14.9062500
VirtualMemorySize64        : 1101127680
EnableRaisingEvents        : False
StandardInput              :
StandardOutput             :
StandardError              :
WorkingSet64               : 365899776
Site                       :
Container                  :
```

The output shows the exact configuration of the process. The properties you will work with the most are summarized in Table 14-1.

> **NOTE** By default, many properties that measure memory usage are defined as 32-bit values. When working with Get-Process on 64-bit systems, you'll find that these properties have both a 32-bit and a 64-bit version. On 64-bit systems, you'll need to use the 64-bit versions to ensure you get accurate values.

TABLE 14-1 Properties of Get-Process and How They Are Used

PROPERTY NAME	PROPERTY DESCRIPTION
BasePriority	Shows the priority of the process. Priority determines how much of the system resources are allocated to a process. The standard priorities are Low (4), Below Normal (6), Normal (8), Above Normal (10), High (13), and Real-Time (24). Most processes have a Normal priority by default, and the highest priority is given to real-time processes.
CPU	Shows TotalProcessorTime in seconds.
Description	Shows a description of the process.
FileVersion	Shows the file version of the process's executable.

PROPERTY NAME	PROPERTY DESCRIPTION
HandleCount	Shows the number of file handles maintained by the process. The number of handles used is an indicator of how dependent the process is on the file system. Some processes have thousands of open file handles. Each file handle requires system memory to maintain.
Id	Shows the run-time identification number of the process.
MinWorkingSet	Shows the minimum amount of working set memory used by the process.
Modules	Shows the executables and dynamically linked libraries used by the process.
NonpagedSystemMemorySize/ NonpagedSystemMemorySize64	Shows the amount of virtual memory for a process that cannot be written to disk. The nonpaged pool is an area of RAM for objects that can't be written to disk. You should note processes that require a high amount of nonpaged pool memory. If the server doesn't have enough free memory, these processes might be the reason for a high level of page faults.
PagedSystemMemorySize/ PagedSystemMemorySize64	Shows the amount of committed virtual memory for a process that can be written to disk. The paged pool is an area of RAM for objects that can be written to disk when they aren't used. As process activity increases, so does the amount of pool memory the process uses. Most processes have more paged pool than nonpaged pool requirements.
Path	Shows the full path to the executable for the process.
PeakPagedMemorySize/ PeakPagedMemorySize64	Shows the peak amount of paged memory used by the process.
PeakVirtualMemorySize/	Shows the peak amount of virtual memory used by the process.

PROPERTY NAME	PROPERTY DESCRIPTION
PeakVirtualMemorySize64	
PeakWorkingSet/ PeakWorkingSet64	Shows the maximum amount of memory the process used, including both the private working set and the nonprivate working set. If peak memory is exceptionally large, this can be an indicator of a memory leak.
PriorityBoostEnabled	Shows a Boolean value that indicates whether the process has the PriorityBoost feature enabled.
PriorityClass	Shows the priority class of the process.
PrivilegedProcessorTime	Shows the amount of kernel-mode usage time for the process.
ProcessName	Shows the name of the process.
ProcessorAffinity	Shows the processor affinity setting for the process.
Responding	Shows a Boolean value that indicates whether the process responded when tested.
SessionId	Shows the identification number user (session) within which the process is running. This corresponds to the ID value listed on the Users tab in Task Manager.
StartTime	Shows the date and time the process was started.
Threads	Shows the number of threads that the process is using. Most server applications are multithreaded, which allows concurrent execution of process requests. Some applications can dynamically control the number of concurrently executing threads to improve application performance. Too many threads, however, can actually reduce performance, because the operating system has to switch thread contexts too frequently.

PROPERTY NAME	PROPERTY DESCRIPTION
TotalProcessorTime	Shows the total amount of CPU time used by the process since it was started. If a process is using a lot of CPU time, the related application might have a configuration problem. This can also indicate a runaway or nonresponsive process that is unnecessarily tying up the CPU.
UserProcessorTime	Shows the amount of user-mode usage time for the process.
VirtualMemorySize/ VirtualMemorySize64	Shows the amount of virtual memory allocated to and reserved for a process. Virtual memory is memory on disk and is slower to access than pooled memory. By configuring an application to use more physical RAM, you might be able to increase performance. To do this, however, the system must have available RAM. If it doesn't, other processes running on the system might slow down.
WorkingSet/WorkingSet64	Shows the amount of memory the process is currently using, including both the private working set and the nonprivate working set. The private working set is memory the process is using that cannot be shared with other processes. The nonprivate working set is memory the process is using that can be shared with other processes. If memory usage for a process slowly grows over time and doesn't go back to the baseline value, this can be an indicator of a memory leak.

Filtering Process Output

By redirecting the output to Where-Object, you can filter Get-Process using any of the properties available. This means you can specify that you want to see only processes that aren't responding or only processes that use a large amount of CPU time.

You designate how a filter should be applied using filter operators. The available filter operators include:

- **–Eq** Equals. If the property contains the specified value, the process is included in the output.
- **–Ne** Not equals. If the property contains the specified value, the process is excluded from the output.
- **–Gt** Greater than. If the property contains a numeric value and that value is greater than the value specified, the process is included in the output.
- **–Lt** Less than. If the property contains a numeric value and that value is less than the value specified, the process is included in the output.
- **–Ge** Greater than or equal to. If the property contains a numeric value and that value is greater than or equal to the value specified, the process is included in the output.
- **–Le** Less than or equal to. If the property contains a numeric value and that value is less than or equal to the value specified, the process is included in the output.
- **–Match** Pattern match. If the property contains a match for this string, the process is included in the output.

As Table 14-2 shows, the values that you can use with filter operators depend on the Get-Process property you use. Remember that all properties are available even if they aren't normally displayed with the parameters you've specified.

TABLE 14-2 Filter Operators and Valid Values for Get-Process

PROPERTY NAME	OPERATORS TO USE	VALID VALUES
BasePriority	–eq, –ne, –gt, –lt, –ge, –le	Any value from 0 to 24
HandleCount	–eq, –ne, –gt, –lt, –ge, –le	Any valid positive integer
MachineName	–eq, –ne	Any valid string of characters
Modules	–eq, –ne, –match	Dynamic-link library (DLL) name

PROPERTY NAME	OPERATORS TO USE	VALID VALUES
PrivilegedProcessorTime	–eq, –ne, –gt, –lt, –ge, –le	Any valid time in the format hh:mm:ss
ProcessID	–eq, –ne, –gt, –lt, –ge, –le	Any valid positive integer
ProcessName	–eq, –ne	Any valid string of characters
Responding	–eq, –ne	$True, $False
SessionID	–eq, –ne, –gt, –lt, –ge, –le	Any valid session number
Username	–eq, –ne	Any valid user name, with user name only or in domain\user format
UserProcessorTime	–eq, –ne, –gt, –lt, –ge, –le	Any valid time in the format hh:mm:ss
WorkingSet	–eq, –ne, –gt, –lt, –ge, –le	Any valid integer, expressed in kilobytes (KB)

By default, Get-Process looks at all processes regardless of their status. With the Responding property, you can find processes that either are or aren't responding. This property is set to a Boolean value. Consider the following examples:

```
get-process | where-object {$_.responding -eq $False}
get-process | where-object {$_.responding -eq $True}
```

In the first example, you list all processes that aren't responding. In the second example, you list all processes that are responding.

Because high-priority processes use more processor time than other processes, you might want to review the high-priority processes running on a computer when you are evaluating performance. Most processes have a normal priority and a priority value of 8. You can find processes with a priority higher than 8 as shown in the following example and sample output:

```
get-process | where-object {$_.basepriority -gt 8}
```

Handles	NPM(K)	PM(K)	WS(K)	VM(M)	CPU(s)	Id	ProcessName
209	12	1712	3712	48	0.16	400	csrss
87	11	1280	3452	43	0.42	464	csrss
162	14	1876	34108	197	0.67	1636	csrss
177	15	21800	33568	102	0.09	896	dwm
198	21	14320	62948	157	1.39	2852	dwm
322	22	16952	29480	240	0.28	888	LogonUI
1749	306	55964	62696	1421	10.70	604	lsass
279	11	4832	8656	34	2.59	596	services
55	2	272	1052	4	0.03	296	smss
84	8	812	3704	42	0.08	472	wininit
125	7	1396	5716	56	0.05	500	winlogon
153	7	1252	5276	51	0.11	2328	winlogon

You also might want to find processes that are using a lot of CPU time. In the following example and sample output, you check for processes that are using more than 30 minutes of privileged processor time:

```
get-process | where-object {$_.privilegedprocessortime -gt
"00:30:00"}
```

Handles	NPM(K)	PM(K)	WS(K)	VM(M)	CPU(s)	Id	ProcessName
553	32	52924	80096	487	3026.42	5200	W3SVC

Viewing the Relationship Between Running Processes and Services

When you use Win32_Service with Get-Process, you can examine the relationship between services configured on a computer and running processes. The ID of the process under which a service is running is shown as part of the standard output when you work with Win32_Service. Here is an example and sample output for the DFS service:

```
get-wmiobject -class win32_service -filter "name='dfs'"
```

```
ExitCode  : 0
Name      : Dfs
ProcessId : 1772
StartMode : Auto
State     : Running
Status    : OK
```

Using the ProcessId property of the Win32_Service object, you can view detailed information about the process under which a service is running, as shown in the following example:

```
$s = get-wmiobject -class win32_service -filter "name='dfs'"
get-process -id $s.processid
```

```
Handles  NPM(K)    PM(K)      WS(K) VM(M)    CPU(s)       Id ProcessName
-------  ------    -----      ----- -----    ------       -- -----------
    127      11     1888       5312    33      0.03     1772 dfssvc
```

Alternatively, you can get the same result using the following code:

```
get-wmiobject -class win32_service -filter "name='dfs'" |
foreach ($a) {get-process -id $_.processid}
```

By default, the output of Get-Process is formatted as a table, but you can also format the output as a list. Beyond formatting, the important thing to note here is that Get-Process lists services by the base name of the executable that starts the service.

You can use the correlation between processes and services to help you manage systems. For example, if you think you are having problems with the World Wide Web Publishing Service (W3svc), one step in your troubleshooting process is to begin monitoring the service's related process or processes. You would want to track the following:

- Process status, such as whether the process is responding or not responding
- Memory usage, including the working set, paged system memory, and virtual memory
- CPU time, including privileged processor time and user processor time

By tracking these statistics over time, you can watch for changes that can indicate the process has stopped responding, the process is a runaway process hogging CPU time, or there is a memory leak.

Viewing Lists of DLLs Being Used by Processes

When you use Get-Process, you can examine the relationship between running processes and DLLs configured on the system. In the output, the names of DLLs that the process uses are stored in the Modules property. However, the standard output might not show you the complete list. Consider the following example and sample output:

```
get-process dwm | format-list modules

Modules : {System.Diagnostics.ProcessModule (dwm.exe),
System.Diagnostics.ProcessModule (ntdll.dll),
System.Diagnostics.ProcessModule (KERNEL32.DLL),
System.Diagnostics.ProcessModule (KERNELBASE.dll)...}

Modules : {System.Diagnostics.ProcessModule (dwm.exe),
System.Diagnostics.ProcessModule (ntdll.dll),
System.Diagnostics.ProcessModule (KERNEL32.DLL),
System.Diagnostics.ProcessModule (KERNELBASE.dll)...}
```

> **TIP** The preference variable $FormatEnumerationLimit controls how many enumerated items are included in a grouped display. The default value is 4, and this is why only four DLLs are shown here. If you increment this variable, you'll be able to see more values by default. In this example, you would have needed to set this variable to 30 or more to see all the DLLs.

Here, per the default configuration of PowerShell, you see only four values for the Modules property, and the rest of the values are truncated. To see all the DLLs, store the Process object in a variable and then list the value of the Modules property as shown in the following example and sample output:

```
$p = get-process dwm
$p.modules

Size(K) ModuleName               FileName
------- ----------               --------
    140 dwm.exe                  C:\Windows\system32\dwm.exe
   1712 ntdll.dll                C:\Windows\SYSTEM32\ntdll.dll
   1272 KERNEL32.DLL             C:\Windows\system32\KERNEL32.DLL
   1108 KERNELBASE.dll           C:\Windows\system32\KERNELBASE.dll
    568 apphelp.dll              C:\Windows\system32\apphelp.dll
    680 msvcrt.dll               C:\Windows\system32\msvcrt.dll
   1500 USER32.dll               C:\Windows\system32\USER32.dll
```

```
 1348 GDI32.dll                C:\Windows\system32\GDI32.dll
  216 IMM32.dll                C:\Windows\system32\IMM32.dll
. . .
  280 powrprof.dll             C:\Windows\SYSTEM32\powrprof.dll
```

Alternatively, you can get the same result using the following code:

```
get-process dwm | foreach ($a) {$_.modules}
```

Knowing which DLL modules a process has loaded can further help you pinpoint what might be causing a process to become nonresponsive, to fail to release the CPU, or to use more memory than it should. In some cases, you might want to check DLL versions to ensure that they are the correct DLLs that the system should be running. To do this, you need to consult the Microsoft Knowledge Base or manufacturer documentation to verify DLL versions and other information.

If you are looking for processes using a specified DLL, you can also specify the name of the DLL you are looking for. For example, if you suspect that the printer spooler driver Winspool.drv is causing processes to hang up, you can search for processes that use Winspool.drv instead of Winspool32.drv and check their status and resource usage.

The syntax that you use to specify the DLL to find is

```
get-process | where-object {$_.modules -match "DLLName"}
```

where *DLLName* is the name of the DLL to search for. Get-Process matches the DLL name without regard to the letter case, and you can enter the DLL name in any letter case. In the following example, you are looking for processes using Winspool.drv, and the output shows the processes using the DLL, along with their basic process information:

```
get-process | where-object {$_.modules -match "winspool.drv"}
```

Handles	NPM(K)	PM(K)	WS(K)	VM(M)	CPU(s)	Id	ProcessName
1063	55	29152	77720	439	2.28	3228	explorer
217	10	1804	7208	85	0.20	3116	rdpclip
467	23	4724	11840	91	0.33	1372	spoolsv
367	28	9236	13056	860	11.23	2320	svchost

Stopping Processes

When you want to stop processes that are running on a local or remote system, you can use Stop-Process. With Stop-Process, you can stop processes by process ID using the –Id parameter or by name using the –Name parameter. Although you cannot use wildcards with the –Id parameter, you can use wildcards with the –Name parameter.

By default, Stop-Process prompts for confirmation before stopping any process that is not owned by the current user. If you have appropriate permissions to stop a process and don't want to be prompted, use the –Force parameter to disable prompting.

If you want to stop multiple processes by process ID or name, you can enter multiple IDs or names as well. With process names, however, watch out, because Stop-Process stops all processes that have that process name. Thus, if three instances of Svchost are running, all three processes are stopped if you use Stop-Process with that image name.

> **REAL WORLD**   As you examine processes, keep in mind that a single application might start multiple processes. Generally, you will want to stop the parent process, which should stop the entire process tree, starting with the parent application process and including any dependent processes.

Consider the following examples to see how you can use Stop-Process:

Stop process ID 1106:
```
stop-process 1106
```

Stop all processes with the name W3Svc:
```
stop-process -name w3svc
```

Stop processes 1106, 1241, and 1546:
```
stop-process 1106, 1241, 1546
```

Force process 891 to stop:
```
stop-process -force -id 891
```

To ensure that only processes matching specific criteria are stopped, you can use Get-Process and Stop-Process together. For example, you might want to use Get-

Process to get only instances of Winword that are not responding and should be stopped, rather than all instances of Winword (which is the default when you use the −Name parameter). Or you might want to get and stop all processes using a specific DLL.

When you are stopping processes, you want to be careful not to accidentally stop critical system processes, such as Lsass, Wininit, or Winlogon. Typically, system processes have a process ID with a value less than 1000. One safeguard you can use when stopping processes is to ensure the process ID is greater than 999.

Consider the following examples to see how you can use Get-Process with Stop-Process:

Stop instances of Winword that are not responding:
```
get-process −name winword | where-object {$_.responding
-eq $False} | stop-process
```

Stop all processes with a process ID greater than 999 if they aren't responding:
```
get-process | where-object {$_.id -gt 999} | where-object
{$_.responding -eq $False} | stop-process
```

Stop all processes using the Winspool.drv DLL:
```
get-process | where-object {$_.modules -match "winspool.drv"} |
stop-process
```

Although Stop-Process doesn't support the −ComputerName parameter, you can use the following technique to manage the processes on remote computers:

```
get-process w3svc -computername engpc18 | stop-process

invoke-command -computername engpc18 -scriptblock { get-process w3svc
| stop-process }
```

Here, you use Get-Process to get a Process object on a remote computer, and then you stop the process by using Stop-Process. Note that this command reports only failure. It won't confirm that a process was stopped, but it will tell you that the process was not found or could not be stopped.

Digging Deeper into Processes

In addition to using Get-Process to get information about running processes, you can use Get-WmiObject and the Win32_Process class. If you type **get-wmiobject - class win32_process**, you'll see detailed information on every process running on the computer. To examine a specific process, you can filter by image name. As shown in the following example and sample output, the image name is the name of the executable for the process:

```
get-wmiobject -class win32_process -filter "name='msdtc.exe'"
```

```
Caption                      : msdtc.exe
CommandLine                  :
CreationClassName            : Win32_Process
CreationDate                 : 20211227160132.839493-420
CSCreationClassName          : Win32_ComputerSystem
CSName                       : DESKTOP-SH4ETFD
Description                  : msdtc.exe
ExecutablePath               :
ExecutionState               :
Handle                       : 3960
HandleCount                  : 187
InstallDate                  :
KernelModeTime               : 625000
MaximumWorkingSetSize        :
MinimumWorkingSetSize        :
Name                         : msdtc.exe
OSCreationClassName          : Win32_OperatingSystem
OSName                       : Microsoft Windows 10
Pro|C:\WINDOWS|\Device\Harddisk0\Partition3
OtherOperationCount          : 343
OtherTransferCount           : 2370
PageFaults                   : 6176
PageFileUsage                : 2764
ParentProcessId              : 904
PeakPageFileUsage            : 3980
PeakVirtualSize              : 2199076859904
PeakWorkingSetSize           : 11188
Priority                     : 8
PrivatePageCount             : 2830336
ProcessId                    : 3960
QuotaNonPagedPoolUsage       : 13
QuotaPagedPoolUsage          : 84
QuotaPeakNonPagedPoolUsage   : 14
```

```
QuotaPeakPagedPoolUsage    : 85
ReadOperationCount         : 2
ReadTransferCount          : 232
SessionId                  : 0
Status                     :
TerminationDate            :
ThreadCount                : 10
UserModeTime               : 156250
VirtualSize                : 2199074181120
WindowsVersion             : 10.0.19041
WorkingSetSize             : 2883584
WriteOperationCount        : 6
WriteTransferCount         : 1978688
PSComputerName             : DESKTOP-85
ProcessName                : msdtc.exe
Handles                    : 187
VM                         : 2199074181120
WS                         : 2883584
Path                       :
```

Win32_Process objects provide some information that Process objects don't, including details on read and write operations. The rest of the information is the same as that provided by Get-Process, albeit in some cases the information is presented in a different way.

Process objects have a StartTime property, and Win32_Process objects have a CreationDate property. Whereas the StartTime property is presented in datetime format, the CreationDate property is presented as a datetime string. Using the StartTime property, you can search for all processes that have been running for longer than a specified period of time. In the following example, you look for processes that have been running longer than one day:

```
$yesterday = (get-date).adddays(-1)
get-process | where-object {$_.starttime -gt $yesterday}
```

Alternatively, you can get the same result using the following code:

```
get-process | where-object {$_.starttime -gt
(get-date).adddays(-1)}
```

With the CreationDate property, you can perform the same search. Here is an example:

```
$yesterday = (get-date).adddays(-1)

get-wmiobject -class win32_process | where-object
{$_.creationdate -gt $yesterday}
```

Win32_Process objects have a property called *threadcount*, which is a count of threads associated with a process. You can list the thread count as shown in the following example:

```
get-wmiobject -class win32_process -filter "name='msdtc.exe'" |
format-list name, threadcount

name        : msdtc.exe
threadcount : 9
```

Process objects have a Threads property that contains all the threads associated with a process. You can count the threads as shown in the following example:

```
$p = get-process -name msdtc
write-host "Number of threads: " ($p.threads).count

Number of threads: 9
```

You can view and work with each individual Thread object as well. As shown in the following example and sample output, you can list the information associated with each Thread object:

```
$p = get-process -name msdtc
$p.threads

BasePriority             : 8
CurrentPriority          : 8
Id                       : 14532
IdealProcessor           :
PriorityBoostEnabled     :
PriorityLevel            :
PrivilegedProcessorTime  :
StartAddress             : 140720301043888
StartTime                :
ThreadState              : Wait
TotalProcessorTime       :
UserProcessorTime        :
WaitReason               : UserRequest
ProcessorAffinity        :
```

```
Site                    :
Container               :

BasePriority            :  8
CurrentPriority         :  8
.  .  .
```

Or you can view details for a specific thread by referencing its index position in the Threads object array. For example, if you want to view the first Thread object, you can reference $p.threads[0].

Each thread has a base priority, a current priority, an ID, a start address, and a thread state. If the thread is waiting for another process or thread, the wait reason is also listed. Wait reasons include Executive (when the thread is waiting on the operating system kernel components) and UserRequest (when the thread is waiting on user-mode components).

When you are working with Win32_Process objects, you can use several methods to work with processes. These methods include the following:

- **GetOwner()**   Gets the user account under which the process is running
- **GetOwnerSid()**   Gets the security identifier of the user account under which the process is running
- **Terminate()**   Stops a process that is running on a local or remote system

The basic syntaxes for getting the process owner and the owner's security identifier are

```
$processObject.GetOwner()
```

and

```
$processObject.GetOwnerSid()
```

where *$processObject* is a reference to a Win32_Process object. Here is an example and partial output:

```
$p = get-wmiobject -class win32_process -filter "name='notepad.exe'"
$p.getowner()

Domain              : IMAGINEDLANDS
```

```
ReturnValue      : 0
User             : WILLIAMS
```

Here, you examine a running instance of Notepad and get the owner of the Notepad process. In the return value, note the Domain and User properties, which show the domain and user account of the process owner, respectively. As shown in the following example and partial output, you can display the security identifier of the process owner by typing

```
$p.getownersid()
```

```
Sid              : S-1-5-21-4857584848-3848484848-8484884848-1111
```

In the return value, the Sid property contains the owner's security identifier.

As shown in the following example and partial output, you can stop the process by typing the following:

```
$p.terminate()
```

```
ReturnValue      : 0
```

The return value in the output is what you want to focus on. A return value of 0 indicates success. Any other return value indicates an error. Typically, errors occur because you aren't the process owner and don't have appropriate permissions to terminate the process. You can resolve this problem by providing credentials or by using an administrator PowerShell prompt.

You can use the techniques discussed previously to work with processes when Get-WmiObject returns a single matching Win32_Process object. However, these techniques won't work as expected when Get-WmiObject returns multiple Win32_Process objects. The reason for this is that the objects are stored in an array and you must specify the instance within the array to work with. One technique for doing so is shown in the following example and partial output:

```
$procs = get-wmiobject -class win32_process -filter
"name='notepad.exe'"
foreach ($p in $procs) { $p.getowner() }
```

```
Domain           : IMAGINEDLANDS
ReturnValue      : 0
```

```
User               : WILLIAMS

Domain             : IMAGINEDLANDS
ReturnValue        : 0
User               : WILLIAMS
```

Here, two instances of Notepad are running, and you list the owner of each process. This technique works when there is only one instance of Notepad running as well.

Chapter 15. Detecting and Resolving Performance Issues

Previously, I discussed techniques for monitoring and optimizing Windows systems. Monitoring is the process by which systems are regularly checked for problems. Optimization is the process of fine-tuning system performance to maintain or achieve its optimal capacity. Now that you know the essentials for monitoring and optimization, let's dig deeper and look at techniques that you can use to detect and resolve performance issues.

Understanding Performance Monitoring Commands

Performance monitoring helps you watch for adverse conditions and take appropriate action to resolve them. PowerShell has several commands for this purpose, and in this section, we'll look at the ones you'll use the most.

Commands you can use to monitor performance include:

- **Get-Counter** Gets objects representing real-time performance counter data directly from the performance monitoring instrumentation in Windows. You can list the performance counter sets and the counters that they contain, set the sample size and interval, and specify the credentials of users with permission to collect performance data.

```
Get-Counter [-MaxSamples NumSamples] [-Counter] CounterPaths
[-SampleInterval Interval] {AddtlParams}

Get-Counter -ListSet SetNames {AddtlParams}

{AddtlParams}
[-Credential CredentialObject] [-ComputerName ComputerNames]
```

- **Export-Counter** Exports performance counter data to log files in BLG (binary performance log, the default), CSV (comma-separated), or TSV (tab-separated) format. This cmdlet is designed to export data that is returned by the Get-Counter and Import-Counter cmdlets.

```
Export-Counter [-FileFormat Format] [-Path] SavePath
-InputObject PerformanceCounterSampleSets {AddtlParams}
```

```
{AddtlParams}
[-Force {$True | $False}] [-Circular {$True | $False}]
[-MaxSize MaxSizeInBytes]
```

- **Import-Counter**   Imports performance counter data from performance counter log files and creates objects for each counter sample in the file. The objects created are identical to those that Get-Counter returns when it collects performance counter data. You can import data from BLG, CSV, and TSV formatted log files. When you are using BLG, you can import up to 32 files in each command. To get a subset of data from a file, use the parameters of Import-Counter to filter the data that you import.

```
Import-Counter [-Path] FilePaths {AddlParams}
Import-Counter -ListSet SetNames [-Path] FilePaths
Import-Counter [-Summary {$True | $False}]
```

```
{AddtlParams}
[-Counter CountersToInclude] [-MaxSamples NumSamples]
[-StartTime DateTime] [-EndTime DateTime]
```

Get-Counter is designed to track and display performance information in real time. It gathers information on any performance parameters you've configured for monitoring and presents it as output. Each performance item you want to monitor is defined by the following three components:

- **Performance object**   Represents any system component that has a set of measurable properties. A performance object can be a physical part of the operating system, such as the memory, the processor, or the paging file; a logical component, such as a logical disk or print queue; or a software element, such as a process or a thread.
- **Performance object instance**   Represents single occurrences of performance objects. If a particular object has multiple instances, such as when a computer has multiple processors or multiple disk drives, you can use an object instance to track a specific occurrence of that object. You can also elect to track all instances of an object, such as whether you want to monitor all processors on a system.
- **Performance counter**   Represents measurable properties of performance objects. For example, with a paging file, you can measure the percentage utilization using the %Usage counter.

In a standard installation of Windows, many performance objects are available for monitoring. As you add services, applications, and components, additional performance objects can become available. For example, when you install the Domain Name System (DNS) on a server, the DNS object becomes available for monitoring on that computer.

Tracking Performance Data

Using Get-Counter, you can write performance data to the output or to a log file. The key to using Get-Counter is to identify the path names of the performance counters you want to track. The performance counter path has the following syntax:

```
\\ComputerName\ObjectName\ObjectCounter
```

where *ComputerName* is the computer name or IP address of the local or remote computer you want to work with, *ObjectName* is the name of a counter object, and *ObjectCounter* is the name of the object counter to use. For example, if you want to track the available memory on Dbserver79, you type the following, and the output would be similar to that shown:

```
get-counter "\\dbs79\memory\available mbytes"

Timestamp               CounterSamples
---------               --------------
12/27/2020 4:26:54 PM   \\dbs79\memory\available mbytes : 16375
12/27/2020 4:26:55 PM   \\dbs79\memory\available mbytes : 16072
```

> **NOTE** Enclosing the counter path in double quotation marks is required in this example because the counter path includes spaces. Although double quotation marks aren't always required, it is good form to always use them.

Specifying the computer name as part of the counter path is optional. If you don't specify the computer name in the counter path, Get-Counter uses the values you specify in the –ComputerName parameter to set the full path for you. If you don't specify computer names, the local computer name is used. Although this allows you to easily work with multiple computers, you should familiarize yourself with the full path format because this is what is recorded in performance traces and performance logs. Without the computer name in the path, the abbreviated path becomes

```
\ObjectName\ObjectCounter
```

In the following example, you check the available memory on multiple computers by using the –ComputerName parameter:

```
get-counter –computername fileserver12, dbserver18, dcserver21
"\memory\available mbytes"
```

When you are working with a remote computer, you might need to provide alternative credentials. You can do this as shown in the following example:

```
$cred = get-credential
get-counter –computername fileserver12, dbserver18, dcserver21
"\memory\available mbytes" –credential $cred
```

When you use Get-Credential, PowerShell prompts you for a user name and password and then stores the credentials provided in the $cred variable. These credentials are then passed to the remote computers for authentication.

You can easily track all counters for an object by using an asterisk (*) as the counter name, such as in the following example:

```
get-counter "\\dbserver79\Memory\*"
```

Here, you track all counters for the Memory object.

When objects have multiple instances, such as with the Processor or LogicalDisk object, you must specify the object instance you want to work with. The full syntax for this is as follows:

```
\\ComputerName\ObjectName(ObjectInstance)\ObjectCounter
```

Here, you follow the object name with the object instance in parentheses. When an object has multiple instances, you can work with all instances of that object using _Total as the instance name. You can work with a specific instance of an object by using its instance identifier. For example, if you want to examine the Processor\% Processor Time counter, you can use this command to work with all processor instances:

```
get-counter "\\dbserver79\Processor(_Total)\% Processor Time"
```

Or you use this command to work with a specific processor instance:

```
get-counter "\\dbserver79\Processor(0)\% Processor Time"
```

Here, Processor(0) identifies the first processor on the system.

Get-Counter has several parameters. –MaxSamples sets the number of samples to collect. –SampleInterval sets the time between samples where the default is 1 second. –ListSet lists installed counters for the specified objects.

Get-Counter writes its output to the prompt by default. You can redirect the output to a performance log by sending the output to Export-Counter. By default, Export-Counter exports performance counter data to log files in binary performance log format. Using the –FileFormat parameter, you can set the format as CSV for a comma-delimited text file, TSV for a tab-delimited text file, or BLG for a binary file. Consider the following example:

```
get-counter "\\dbserver79\Memory\*" | export-counter –fileformat
tsv –path .\dbserver79.txt
```

Here, you track all counters for the Memory object and write the output to a tab-delimited text file called Dbserver79.txt in the current working directory. When you want to work with this data later, you use Import-Counter. Type **import-counter -path** followed by the path to the performance log to view the performance data. Type **import-counter -summary -path** followed by the path to the performance log to get a summary view of the data. Type **import-counter -listset * -path** followed by the path to the performance log to see what counters were tracked. Optionally, use –StartTime and –EndTime to specify a datetime range to review. Consider the following example:

```
$startdate = (get-date).adddays(-1)
$enddate = (get-date)
import-counter –path .\data.txt -starttime $startdate –endtime
$enddate
```

Here, you examine the performance data in a file in the current directory, called Data.txt. You review the performance details from yesterday at the current time to today at the current time.

If you need help determining how an object can be used and what its counters are, type **get-counter -listset** followed by the object name for which you want to view counters. The following example and sample output show how this can be used to get all the Memory-related counters:

```
get-counter -listset Memory

Counter: {\Memory\Page Faults/sec, \Memory\Available Bytes,
\Memory\Committed Bytes, \Memory\Commit Limit...}
CounterSetName      : Memory
MachineName         : EngPC85
CounterSetType      : SingleInstance
Description         : The Memory performance object  consists of
counters that describe the behavior of physical and virtual memory on
the computer.  Physical memory is the amount of random access memory
on the computer.  Virtual memory consists of the space in physical
memory and on disk.  Many of the memory counters monitor paging,
which is the movement of pages of code and data between disk and
physical memory.  Excessive paging, a symptom of a memory shortage,
can cause delays which interfere with all system processes.
Paths: {\Memory\Page Faults/sec, \Memory\Available Bytes,
\Memory\Committed Bytes, \Memory\Commit Limit...}
PathsWithInstances : {}
```

As with all results returned in PowerShell, the output is returned as an object that you can manipulate. To get a complete list of counter paths, you can reference the Paths property as shown in the following example and partial output:

```
$c = get-counter -listset Memory
$c.paths

\Memory\Page Faults/sec
\Memory\Available Bytes
\Memory\Committed Bytes
\Memory\Commit Limit
```

Alternatively, you can get the same result using the following code:

```
get-counter -listset memory | foreach ($a) {$_.paths}
```

If an object has multiple instances, you can list the installed counters with instances by using the PathsWithInstances property. An example and partial output follow:

```
$d = get-counter -listset PhysicalDisk
```

```
$d.pathswithinstances
```

```
\PhysicalDisk(0 E: C:)\Current Disk Queue Length
\PhysicalDisk(1 W:)\Current Disk Queue Length
\PhysicalDisk(2 D:)\Current Disk Queue Length
\PhysicalDisk(3 I:)\Current Disk Queue Length
\PhysicalDisk(4 J:)\Current Disk Queue Length
\PhysicalDisk(5 K:)\Current Disk Queue Length
\PhysicalDisk(6 L:)\Current Disk Queue Length
\PhysicalDisk(7 N:)\Current Disk Queue Length
\PhysicalDisk(8 O:)\Current Disk Queue Length
\PhysicalDisk(9 P:)\Current Disk Queue Length
\PhysicalDisk(10 Q:)\Current Disk Queue Length
\PhysicalDisk(_Total)\Current Disk Queue Length
```

Alternatively, you can get the same result using the following code:

```
get-counter -listset PhysicalDisk | foreach ($a)
{$_.pathswithinstances}
```

Either way, the output is a long list of available counters arranged according to their object instances. You can write the output to a text file, such as in the following example:

```
get-counter -listset PhysicalDisk > disk-counters.txt
```

Then edit the text file so that only the counters you want to track are included. You can then use the file to determine which performance counters are tracked, as shown in the following example:

```
get-counter (get-content .\disk-counters.txt) | export-counter
-path c:\perflogs\disk-check.blg
```

Here, Get-Counter reads the list of counters to track from Disk-Counters.txt, and then it writes the performance data in binary format to the Disk-Check.blg file in the C:\Perflogs directory.

By default, Get-Counter samples data once every second until you tell it to stop by pressing Ctrl+C. This might be okay when you are working at the PowerShell prompt and actively monitoring the output. However, it doesn't work so well when you have other things to do and can't actively monitor the output—which is probably most of the time. Therefore, you'll usually want to control the sampling interval and duration.

To control the sampling interval and set how long to sample, you can use the –SampleInterval and –MaxSamples parameters, respectively. For example, if you want Get-Counter to sample every 120 seconds and stop logging after 100 samples, you can enter the following command:

```
get-counter (get-content .\disk-counters.txt) –sampleinterval
120 –maxsamples 100 | export-counter –path
c:\perflogs\disk-check.blg
```

Monitoring System Resource Usage and Processes

Get-Process and Get-Counter provide everything you need for detecting and resolving most performance issues. However, you'll often need to dig deep to determine whether a problem exists and, if so, what is causing the problem.

When you are working with processes, you'll often want to get a snapshot of system resource usage, which will show you exactly how memory is being used. One way to get a snapshot is to use the Get-Counter command to display current values for key counters of the memory object. As discussed previously, the Memory object is one of many performance objects available, and you can list its related performance counters by typing the following command at the PowerShell prompt:

```
get-counter -listset memory | foreach ($a) {$_.paths}
```

The Memory object has many counters you can work with. Most counters of the Memory object display the last observed value or the current percentage value rather than an average.

Sample 15-1 provides an example of how you can use Get-Counter to get a snapshot of memory usage. In this example, you use a counter file called Perf.txt to specify the counters you want to track. You collect five samples with an interval of 30 seconds between samples and save the output in a file called SaveMemData.txt. If you import the data into a spreadsheet or convert it to a table in a Word document, you can make better sense of the output and gain a better understanding of how the computer is using the page file and paging to disk.

I chose to track these counters because they give you a good overall snapshot of memory usage. If you save the command line as a script, you can run the script as a scheduled job to get a snapshot of memory usage at various times of the day.

SAMPLE 15-1 Getting a Snapshot of Memory Usage

Commands

```
get-counter (get-content .\perf.txt) -maxsamples 5
-sampleinterval 30 > SaveMemData.txt
```

Source for Perf.txt

```
\memory\% Committed Bytes In Use
\memory\Available MBytes
\memory\Cache Bytes
\memory\Cache Bytes Peak
\memory\Committed Bytes
\memory\Commit Limit
\memory\Page Faults/sec
\memory\Pool Nonpaged Bytes
\memory\Pool Paged Bytes
```

Sample output

```
Timestamp                    CounterSamples
---------                    --------------
12/28/2020 11:04:37 PM  \\techpc22\memory\% committed bytes in use:
                             22.9519764760423
                             \\techpc22\memory\available mbytes :
                             1734
                             \\techpc22\memory\cache bytes :
                             390168576
                             \\techpc22\memory\cache bytes peak :
                             390688768
                             \\techpc22\memory\committed bytes :
                             1650675712
                             \\techpc22\memory\commit limit :
                             7191867392
                             \\techpc22\memory\page faults/sec :
                             3932.45999649944
                            \\techpc22\memory\pool nonpaged bytes :
                             70017024
                             \\techpc22\memory\pool paged bytes :
                             154710016

12/28/2020 11:05:07 PM  \\techpc22\memory\% committed bytes in use:
                             23.2283134955779
                             \\techpc22\memory\available mbytes :
```

```
1714
\\techpc22\memory\cache bytes :
389664768
\\techpc22\memory\cache bytes peak :
390701056
\\techpc22\memory\committed bytes :
1670549504
\\techpc22\memory\commit limit :
7191867392
\\techpc22\memory\page faults/sec :
617.601067565369
\\techpc22\memory\pool nonpaged bytes :
70008832
\\techpc22\memory\pool paged bytes :
154791936
```

If you suspect there is a problem with memory usage, you can obtain detailed information about running processes by using Get-Process. At a PowerShell prompt, you can view important statistics for all processes by typing the following command:

```
get-process | format-table -property ProcessName,
BasePriority, HandleCount, Id, NonpagedSystemMemorySize,
PagedSystemMemorySize, PeakPagedMemorySize,
PeakVirtualMemorySize, PeakWorkingSet, SessionId, Threads,
TotalProcessorTime, VirtualMemorySize, WorkingSet, CPU, Path
```

The order of the properties in the comma-separated list determines the display order. If you want to change the display order, simply move a property to a different position in the list. If desired, you can redirect the output to a file as shown in the following example:

```
get-process | format-table -property ProcessName,
BasePriority, HandleCount, Id, NonpagedSystemMemorySize,
PagedSystemMemorySize, PeakPagedMemorySize,
PeakVirtualMemorySize, PeakWorkingSet, SessionId, Threads,
TotalProcessorTime, VirtualMemorySize, WorkingSet, CPU, Path >
savedata.txt
```

Whether you write output to the prompt or to a file, modify the properties of the PowerShell prompt and set the width to at least 180 characters. This ensures you can read the output.

Monitoring Memory Paging and Paging to Disk

Often, you'll want to get detailed information on hard and soft page faults that are occurring. A page fault occurs when a process requests a page in memory and the system can't find it at the requested location. If the requested page is elsewhere in memory, the fault is called a soft page fault. If the requested page must be retrieved from disk, the fault is called a hard page fault.

To see page faults that are occurring in real time, type the following at the command line:

```
get-counter "\memory\Page Faults/sec" -sampleinterval 5

Timestamp                  CounterSamples
---------                  --------------
12/18/2020 6:00:01 PM       \\techpc22\memory\page faults/sec :
                           172.023153991804
12/18/2020 6:00:06 PM       \\techpc22\memory\page faults/sec :
                           708.944308818821
12/18/2020 6:00:11 PM       \\techpc22\memory\page faults/sec :
                           14.5375722784541
```

Here, you check memory page faults every 5 seconds. To stop Get-Counter, press Ctrl+C. Page faults are shown according to the number of hard and soft faults occurring per second. Other counters of the Memory object that you can use for tracking page faults include the following:

- Cache Faults/sec
- Demand Zero Faults/sec
- Page Reads/sec
- Page Writes/sec
- Write Copies/sec
- Transition Faults/sec
- Transition Pages RePurposed/sec

Pay particular attention to the Page Reads/sec and Page Writes/sec, which provide information on hard faults. Although developers will be interested in the source of page faults, administrators are more interested in how many page faults are occurring. Most processors can handle large numbers of soft faults. A soft fault simply means the system had to look elsewhere in memory for the requested memory page. With a hard fault, on the other hand, the requested memory page must be retrieved from disk, which can cause significant delays. If you are seeing a lot of hard faults, you might need to increase the amount of memory or reduce the amount of memory being cached by the system and applications.

In addition to counters of the Memory object discussed previously, you can use other objects and counters to check for disk paging issues. If a particular object has multiple instances, such as when a computer has multiple physical disks or multiple paging files, you can use an object instance to track a specific occurrence of that object. You can also elect to track all instances of an object, such as whether you want to monitor all physical disks on a system. Specify _Total to work with all counter instances, or specify individual counter instances to monitor.

Sample 15-2 provides an example of how you can use Get-Counter to get a snapshot of disk paging. In this example, you use a counter file called PagePerf.txt to specify the counters you want to track. You collect five samples with an interval of 30 seconds between samples and save the output in a file called SavePageData.txt. If you import the data into a spreadsheet or convert it to a table in a Word document, you can make better sense of the output and gain a better understanding of how the computer is using the page file and paging to disk.

SAMPLE 15-2 Checking Disk Paging

Commands
```
get-counter (get-content .\pageperf.txt) -maxsamples 5
-sampleinterval 30 > SavePageData.txt
```

Source for PagePerf.txt
```
\memory\Pages/Sec
\Paging File(_Total)\% Usage
\Paging File(_Total)\% Usage Peak
\PhysicalDisk(_Total)\% Disk Time
\PhysicalDisk(_Total)\Avg. Disk Queue Length
```

Monitoring Memory Usage and the Working Memory Set for Individual Processes

You can use Get-Process to get basic memory usage for a process. The syntax you can use is

```
get-process -id ProcessID
```

where *ProcessID* is the ID number of the process you want to work with. The output from Get-Process shows you how much memory the process is currently using. For example, if you were tracking process ID 1072, your output might look like the following:

```
Handles  NPM(K)  PM(K)      WS(K) VM(M)  CPU(s)     Id ProcessName
-------  ------  -----      ----- -----  ------     -- -----------
    493      13  15520      13452    77            1072 svchost
```

In this example, the process is using 13,452 KB of memory. By watching the memory usage over time, you can determine whether the memory usage is increasing. If memory usage is increasing compared to a typical baseline, the process might have a memory-related problem.

Sample 15-3 provides the source for a PowerShell script that checks the memory usage of a process over a timed interval. The script expects the process ID you want to work with to be passed as the first parameter. If you do not supply a process ID, error text is written to the output.

SAMPLE 15-3 Viewing Memory Usage at the PowerShell Prompt

MemUsage.ps1
```
$p = read-host "Enter process id to track"
$n = read-host "Enter number of minutes to track"

for ($c=1; $c -le $n; $c++) {get-process -id $p;
start-sleep -seconds 60}
```

Sample output

```
Enter process id to track: 1072
Enter number of minutes to track: 1
```

Handles	NPM(K)	PM(K)	WS(K)	VM(M)	CPU(s)	Id	ProcessName
497	13	15548	13464	77		1072	svchost
494	13	15520	13452	77		1072	svchost
495	13	15520	13452	77		1072	svchost
493	13	15520	13452	77		1072	svchost
495	13	15548	13464	77		1072	svchost
495	13	15520	13452	77		1072	svchost

In Sample 15-3, the process's memory usage shows small variances over time, but there isn't a trend of increasing memory usage over time. Because of this, it is unlikely the process has a memory leak, but to be sure you'd need to sample over a longer period.

You can use Get-Process to track detailed memory usage for individual processes as well. The syntax you can use is

```
get-process ProcessName | format-table –property
NonpagedSystemMemorySize, PagedSystemMemorySize,
VirtualMemorySize, PeakVirtualMemorySize, MinWorkingSet,
WorkingSet, PeakWorkingSet
```

where *ProcessName* is the name of the process without the .exe or .dll. In a PowerShell script, such as the one shown as Sample 15-4, you can combine Get-Process and Start-Sleep to view the memory usage for a process at timed intervals.

SAMPLE 15-4 Viewing Detailed Memory Usage

DetMemUsage.ps1

```
$p = read-host "Enter process name to track"
$n = read-host "Enter number of minutes to track"

for ($c=1; $c -le $n; $c++) { get-process $p | format-table
–property NonpagedSystemMemorySize, PagedSystemMemorySize,
VirtualMemorySize, PeakVirtualMemorySize, MinWorkingSet,
WorkingSet, PeakWorkingSet

start-sleep -seconds 60}
```

Sample output

Nonpaged System MemorySize	Paged System MemorySize	Virtual MemorySize	Peak Virtual MemorySize	Min WorkingSet	Working Set	Peak WorkingSet
4776	96368	52891648	161480704		6946816	7282688
8424	137056	61505536	161480704		8986624	9039872
13768	121136	137351168	161480704		38670336	73658368
13792	128904	82386944	161480704		13889536	73658368
14320	167912	187904000	258859008		74432512	138919936
44312	235704	221302784	429953024		65249280	278482944
25288	156520	91754496	429953024		15536128	278482944
30112	159376	123875328	429953024		23248896	278482944
25296	118424	86568960	429953024		20758528	278482944
2248	48088	24174592	429953024		2924544	278482944
7112	105160	55832576	429953024		6393856	278482944
5368	110960	63991808	429953024		7655424	278482944
1472	30400	15618048	429953024		2330624	278482944

The Get-Counter properties examined in Sample 15-4 provide the following information:

- **NonPagedSystemMemorySize**   Shows the amount of allocated memory that can't be written to disk
- **PagedSystemMemorySize**   Shows the amount of allocated memory that is allowed to be paged to the hard disk
- **VirtualMemorySize**   Shows the amount of virtual memory allocated to and reserved for a process
- **PeakVirtualMemorySize**   Shows the peak amount of paged memory used by the process
- **WorkingSet**   Shows the amount of memory allocated to the process by the operating system
- **PeakWorkingSet**   Shows the peak amount of memory used by the process

When you focus on these properties, you are zeroing in on the memory usage of a specific process. The key aspect to monitor is the working memory set. The working set of memory shows how much memory is allocated to the process by the operating system. If the working set increases over time and doesn't eventually go back to baseline usage, the process might have a memory leak. With a memory leak, the process isn't properly releasing memory that it's using, which can lead to reduced performance of the entire system.

In Sample 15-4, the process's memory usage changes substantially over the sampled interval. Although it is most likely the process is simply actively being used by users or the computer itself, the process should eventually return to a baseline memory usage. If this doesn't happen, the process might have a memory-related problem.

Because memory is usually the primary performance bottleneck on both workstations and servers, I've discussed many techniques previously in this chapter that you can use to help identify problems with memory. Memory is the resource you should examine first to try to determine why a system isn't performing as expected. However, memory isn't the only bottleneck. Processors, hard disks, and networking components can also cause bottlenecks.

Index

F

G

S

Find William on Twitter at http://www.twitter.com/WilliamStanek and on Facebook at http://www.facebook.com/William.Stanek.Author.

Connect with Will by visiting him on LinkedIn @ linkedin.com/in/will-stanek/.

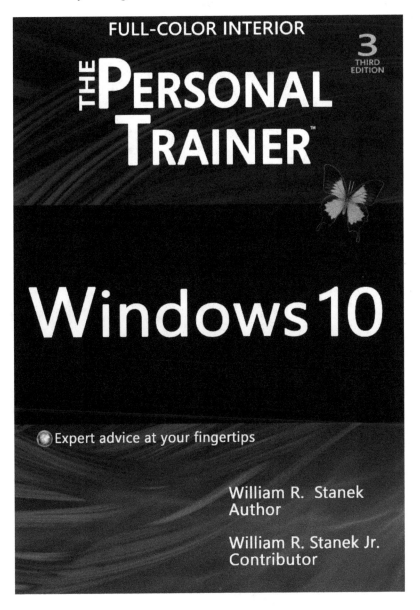

Thank you for purchasing this book. If you found this book to be useful, helpful or informative, raise your voice and support this work by sharing online.

Unsure how to share? Here are some tips:

- Blog about the book
- Write a review at your favorite online store
- Post about the book on Facebook or elsewhere
- Tweet about the book

Stay in touch!

www.ingramcontent.com/pod-product-compliance
Lightning Source LLC
Chambersburg PA
CBHW060521060326
40690CB00017B/3341